Children's Play in Diverse Cultures

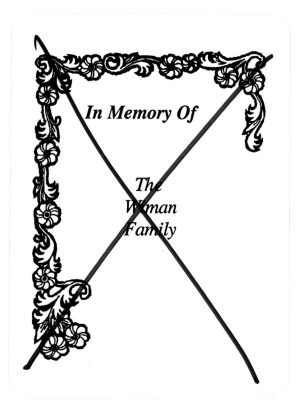

SUNY Series, Children's Play in Society
Anthony D. Pellegrini, Editor

Children's Play in Diverse Cultures

Jaipaul L. Roopnarine,
James E. Johnson, and
Frank H. Hooper,
Editors

STATE UNIVERSITY OF NEW YORK PRESS

Published by
State University of New York Press, Albany

© 1994 State University of New York

For information, address State University of New York
Press, State University Plaza, Albany, N.Y., 12246

Production by E. Moore
Marketing by Bernadette La Manna

Library of Congress Cataloging-in-Publication Data

Children's play in diverse cultures / [edited by] Jaipaul L.
  Roopnarine, James E. Johnson, Frank H. Hooper.
      p.   cm. — (SUNY series, children's play in society)
    Includes index.
    ISBN 0-7914-1753-0 (alk. paper). — ISBN 0-7914-1754-9 (pbk. :
  alk. paper)
    1. Play—Cross-cultural studies. 2. Child development—Cross
  -cultural studies. I. Roopnarine, Jaipaul L. II. Johnson, James
  E. (James Ewald), 1947-   . III. Hooper, Frank H. IV. Series.
  HQ782.C44 1994
  155.4′18—dc20   93-12177
                                                          CIP

10 9 8 7 6 5 4 3 2 1

Contents

JAIPAUL L. ROOPNARINE
JAMES E. JOHNSON

1

The Need to Look at Play in Diverse Cultural Settings

Educational reformers have long recognized the value of learning that is culturally contextualized. They have often argued that the recognition of the unique contributions of diverse cultural groups and multicultural activities in general could only serve to foster respect for individual differences while simultaneously enhancing cultural pride and children's self-esteem. It was not until quite recently, however, that issues pertaining to intracultural and intercultural variations in young children's cognitive and social development eased their way to the forefront of American society.

Over the last two decades we have witnessed the emergence of societies such as the Association for the Study of Play. Its journal, *Play and Culture*, explores the content of play itself and its cultural and developmental underpinnings (Chick & Sutton-Smith 1988), cross-national comparisons of children's achievement and parental values (Stevenson 1988), and an emphasis on antibias curriculum (Derman-Sparks & Ramsey 1993). We have also seen the push to adopt multicultural approaches to educating young children in the United States and Canada (Ogbu 1981; Ramsey 1987; Saracho & Spodek 1990), and newer conceptual frameworks within education and developmental psychology that consider the cultural ecology of child development (Bloch & Pellegrini 1989; Lamb, Sternberg, Hwang, & Broberg 1992; Roopnarine & Carter 1992).

In this volume we have attempted to extend our cultural realm of understanding on a key aspect of young children's development, namely, play. Adult-child play and peer play have been linked to the acquisition and refinement or extension of a wide range of cognitive and social skills (Johnson, Christie, & Yawkey 1987). Several issues motivated us to compile this volume: (a) the changing demography in countries such as the United States, the population movement to urban centers in developing countries, and the diverse social-structural familial organizational patterns that are evident in preschool-age children and their families in the United States and abroad; (b) the increased emphasis on early childhood stimulation through play for young children prior to kindergarten and the establishment of national preschool/day-care programs in a number of countries in the world; (c) the need to broaden our theoretical understanding of the cultural context and developmental dynamic in young children; and (d) the need to expose and educate early childhood professionals so that they become sensitive to cultural issues both in and out of the classroom. Let us examine these issues more closely.

THE CHANGING ECOLOGY OF CHILDHOOD

In most Western industrialized societies a large number of mothers are employed full- or part-time outside of the home. Similarly, in the developing nations of the world women have begun to challenge patriarchy and in growing numbers are joining the ranks of their male counterparts in the labor market. At the same time, familial structural organizations have been changing in some developing nations where couples are now marrying for companionship, as opposed to institutional practice, and are choosing to live in nuclear units. The influx of women into the paid labor force worldwide, women working double shifts, and the decrease in extended family units and network support for child care especially in urban areas of developing countries have created a demand for alternative child care arrangements for very young children (Lamb et al 1992; O'Connor 1988; Roopnarine & Carter 1992). In industrialized nations some form of day care or home-based care exists in which there may be a formalized curriculum. By and large, these caregiving arrangements have play objects and equipment and children are encouraged to play. By contrast, in developing nations day care or crèches are still rare and parents rely on relatives or friends to provide supplemental care. In most accounts of developing societies, play occurs in children's groups but is rarely encouraged (Bloch 1989; Roopnarine, Ahmeduzzaman, Hossain, & Riegraf 1992; Whiting & Edwards 1988).

The changes in the structural organization of families in wide-ranging societies and the emphasis on early childhood education prior to formal schooling have placed children in contact with peers very early in their lives (e.g., infant day care; group-rearing situations such as the kibbutz in Israel). This may suggest that the peer group and peer play interaction would assume a burgeoning role in children's social and cognitive development. Indeed, researchers have demonstrated the contributions of peers and peer interactions in different dimensions of play to cognitive and social development (Johnson, Christie, & Yawkey 1987). However, despite the fact that the societies discussed in this volume are, in some cases, introducing changes in their approaches to educating young children by introducing bilingual education and native ideas, their approaches to doing so vary quite a bit. While we should not lose sight of this, we believe that, regardless of the nature of early caregiving patterns, play is an integral part of parent-child and peer relations in diverse societies and as societies move to implement massive preschool and kindergarten programs, play can assume a pivotal role in this endeavor. The challenge may be in being culturally sensitive to issues relevant to the needs of specific societies, native themes and practices, and shared cultural knowledge regarding schooling and childrearing practices. For instance, in the United States educators are struggling to develop and provide culturally appropriate practices for Native Americans, mainland Puerto Ricans, African Americans, Latinos, and Asian Americans. In India and other developing nations educators grapple with the notion of how to modify Western conceptions of early childhood education to fit prevailing cultural beliefs about children and their educational needs.

THE NEED TO BROADEN CONCEPTUAL
FRAMEWORKS ON PLAY

Play is biologically based and is sustained as an evolutionary contribution to human development. Taxonomies of play forms and discussions of the significance of play have typically been based on studies of Western children and have assumed a global orientation. Obviously, in order to achieve a more comprehensive, coherent, and integrated account of play, it is necessary to incorporate sociocultural factors in theory construction. Steps in this direction have been taken and this volume builds upon contributions that have been made within the cultural-ecological framework (Bronfenbrenner 1979; Jipson 1991; Ogbu 1981; Tobin, Wu, & Davidson 1989; Whiting 1980).

Cultural-ecological models of behavior and development stress the importance of three interacting layers of environmental influence on play: (1) physical and social aspects of children's immediate settings; (2) historical influences that affect the way adults (and children) conceptualize play; and (3) cultural and ideological beliefs relative to the meaning of play for subgroups of children. Hence, the overall environment of influences is defined widely and includes social and economic realities that have an impact on families as mediators of children's experiences. Children's immediate settings are determined, in other words, by larger forces that include societal norms, class, caste, and gender ideologies, geography, climatic characteristics, and a culture's history. Developing children not only experience the family's tradition or cultural mores, but are also exposed to extrafamilial agents (e.g., peers, media, marketing forces) who acquaint them with cultural variations that teach children about cultural meaning of majority and minority status and the like. Children's play, then, is an outcome of being a participant within a particular cultural or subcultural milieu. Cultural-ecological frameworks subscribe to the notion that the kinds of immediate contexts that children experience is also constrained and moderated by broad cultural forces and available toys and other play items within the culture.

Cultural-ecological and developmental contextual models explicitly recognize the bidirectional influence of children and the environment. These directional relations are seen as a set of feedback systems forming a closed loop suggesting dynamic processes within the system. In other words, play behaviors and cultural products in general are formed from individual traits and processes that are in turn influenced by overall societal structures. Play, a dominant activity of children in all cultures, is viewed to be both a cause and an effect of culture. Play is an expression of a particular culture; play is an important context or vehicle for cultural learning/transmission, as well as an indicator and reflection of child development (Schwartzman 1978). Structure-function relations are reciprocal and are culturally contextually bound in play as in other important human behaviors or experiences.

This volume is predicated on the belief that contemporary theorizing, stemming primarily but not exclusively from the cultural-ecological framework, is needed to extend our conceptual outlook on children's play in the modern and postmodern world. Both inter-individual or intergroup comparative work and intra-individual and intragroup analysis are required to illuminate the internal meaning of play within and across cultural settings. Our goal is to further an understanding of the relationship between play and the larger cultural and social ecology (cf. Jipson 1991; Roopnarine et al 1992; Schwartzman 1978).

TEACHING AND PLAY IN A DIVERSE WORLD

This volume intends to shed light on play as a universal and culture-specific activity on the theoretical side, but also to draw attention to the applications of the topic for parent education, teacher preparation, and in-service training. The chapters of this volume, with the exception of the accounts of the play of Puerto Rican and Yup'ik children in the United States, focus upon play behavior in *culturally continuous* contexts, which for some individuals means that the child's family has lived in its current broad ecological context for at least two generations (Slaughter & Dombrowski 1989). Of increasing concern will be the need for information about the behavior of children in *culturally discontinuous* contexts (i.e., play of immigrant, refugee, foreign student family, or migrant children). Moreover, many children live in families disenfranchised from the mainstream dominant majority society and hence may perhaps best be described as residing and participating in "continuous but unassimilated" cultural or subcultural contexts (i.e., the underclass, the homeless, oppressed minorities, learning new language, etc.). Of course to become culturally assimilated into the dominant culture is not an option or a goal of some ethnic/cultural groups. The present volume intends to sensitize us to diversity and variation as it now exists in the play of children from select regions around the world in the hope that it will prepare us to deal more effectively and humanistically with important differences that confront us daily on our own shores as well as abroad.

That the challenge to address these issues is gaining import, witness the urgency with which educational critics are calling for curricular reform to include greater attention to issues of equity and cultural diversity, sensitivity, and responsivity (see recent volumes by Lamb, et al. 1992; Gibson & Ogbu 1991; Swadener & Kessler 1991). In the field of early childhood education, for example, revisionists seek a better understanding of different countries and cultures as a way to enlightenment regarding one's own situation and greater insight into alternative possible conceptions of theory and practice, including potentials for achieving common goals (Saracho & Spodek 1990; Tobin, Wu & Davidson 1989).

To conclude, then, the present volume hopefully will add to the vision and mission of education that is multicultural by expanding the knowledge base of researchers, teachers, educators, and parents. The scope and limits of our information about children's play, adult roles, culture, and educational practice is in a dynamic state, as the chapters of this volume attest.

REFERENCES

Apple, M. W. (1979). *Ideology and curriculum.* London: Routledge, Kegan Paul.

Bloch, M. (1989). Young boys' and girls' play at home and in the community: A cultural-ecological framework. In M. N. Bloch & A. D. Pellegrini (Eds.), *The ecological context of children's play.* Norwood, NJ: Ablex.

Bronfenbrenner, U. (1979). *The ecology of human development.* Cambridge, MA: Harvard University Press.

Chick, G. & Sutton-Smith, B. (1988). Editorial comment. *Play and Culture, 1,* 1-2.

Derman-Sparks, L. & Ramsey, P. (1993). Early childhood multicultural, anti-bias education in the 1990s: Toward the 21st century. In J. L. Roopnarine & J. J. Johnson (Eds.), *Approaches to early childhood education* (2nd ed.). Columbus, OH: Macmillan.

Gibson, M. & Ogbu, J. (Eds.) (1991). *Minority status and schooling: A comparative study of immigrant and involuntary minorities.* New York: Garland.

Jipson, J. (1991). Developmentally appropriate practice: Culture, curriculum, connections. *Early Education and Development, 2,* 120-136.

Johnson, J. E., Christie, J., & Yawkey, T. D. (1987). *Play and early childhood development.* Evanston, IL: Scott Foresman.

Lamb, M. E., Sternberg, K., Hwang, C., & Broberg, A. (Eds.) (1992). *Child care in context.* Hillsdale, NJ: Erlbaum.

O'Connor, S. M. (1988). Women's labor force participation and preschool enrollment: A cross-national perspective, 1965-80. *Sociology of Education, 61,* 15-28.

Ogbu, J. (1981). Origins of human competence: A cultural-ecological perspective. *Child Development, 52,* 413-429.

Ramsey, P. G. (1987). *Teaching and learning in a diverse world: Multicultural education for young children.* New York: Teachers College Press.

Roopnarine, J. L. & Carter, B. (Eds.) (1992). *Parent-child socialization in diverse cultures.* Norwood, NJ: Ablex.

Roopnarine, J. L., Ahmeduzzaman, M., Hossain, Z., & Riegraf, N. B. (1992). Parent-infant rough play: Its cultural specificity. *Early Education and Development, 4,* 298-311.

Saracho, O. N. & Spodek, B. (1990). Early childhood teacher preparation in cross-cultural perspective. In B. Spodek & O. Saracho (Eds.), *Early childhood teacher preparation.* New York: Teachers College Press.

Schwartzman, H. (1978). *Transformations: The anthropology of children's play.* New York: Plenum.

Slaughter, D. & Dombrowski, J. (1989). Cultural continuities and discontinuities: Impact on social and pretend play. In M. N. Block & A. D. Pellegrini (Eds.), *The ecological content of children's play.* Norwood, NJ: Ablex.

Stevenson, H. W. (1988). Culture and schooling: Influences on cognitive development. In E. M. Hetherington, R. M. Lerner, & M. Perlmutter (Eds.), *Child development in life-span perspective.* Hillsdale, NJ: Erlbaum.

Swadener, B., & Kessler, S. (Eds.) (1991). Reconceptualizing early childhood education. *Early Education and Development, 2*, 81-176.

Tobin, J. J., Wu, D. Y., & Davidson, D. H. (1989). *Preschool in three cultures: Japan, China, and the United States.* New Haven, CT: Yale University Press.

Whiting, B. B. (1980). Culture and social behavior. *Ethos, 2*, 95-116.

Whiting, B. B. & Edwards, C. P. (1988). *The company they keep: The effect of age, gender, and culture on social behavior of children aged two to ten.* Cambridge, MA: Harvard University Press.

JAIPAUL L. ROOPNARINE
ZIARAT HOSSAIN
PREETI GILL
HOLLY BROPHY

2

Play in the
East Indian Context

Without engaging in an elaborate excursion into the play lit-erature. it can safely be said that most of the studies on young children's play are based on observations and assessments con-ducted on North American and European children. Compara-tively less has been written on children's play in other cultures around the world. This state of affairs is rather surprising for sev-eral reasons: (a) by virtue of sheer numbers, most children in the world live in the developing nations and a play literature based on North American and European children would be incomplete and biased and may have limited relevance to early childhood education in nonindustrialized nations; (b) cultures vary in terms of techno-economic demands, motivations, instrumental com-petencies, and linguistic and social texture, which makes it dif-ficult to implement nonnative cultural ideals in wide-ranging societies; (c) in order to develop more valid general theories of play, we need data from children in other cultures as well (Ogbu

1981); and (d) Euro-American mainstream ideas about play and early childhood education do not thoroughly consider the cultural imperatives and social agendas in the discussion of the implications of play in early childhood education in other societies.

With these points in mind, we sought to examine play in an old and complex civilization, India. India is vast and varied in language, social customs, educational attainment, religious belief structures, and social-structural organization. Before we turn to a discussion of play we provide a brief description of some defining features of life in India (Kakar 1978; Mandelbaum 1970; Roopnarine & Hossain 1992). In addition, we have attempted to interweave more directly the contextual factors that influence adult-child and child-child play.

The structural ideal for the socialization of children in Indian families is the joint family system that is deeply embodied in patriarchy. Despite movement toward nuclear lifestyles in larger cities (Sarma 1969; Strauss & Winkelmann 1969), the extended family system has remained stable for centuries. Moreover, even when individuals move to the city, concerted attempts are made to maintain strong ties to familial members. Extended families vary in kinship composition, however, Some may include brothers and their wives and children without parents, while others may include the stem family that is made up of parents and one of their married children and his wife and children. Thus, as Kakar (1978) notes, "most Indians spend the formative years of early childhood in an extended family setting" (p. 115). Not surprisingly, then, grandparents, aunts, uncles, and cousins are viable agents of socialization for young infants. Within the Indian context, the transmission of socio-cultural values is governed by metaphysical belief systems, family solidarity, and caste.

Family solidarity is based on the hierarchical principle. According to Kakar (1978) "the ordering principles of this hierarchical system are age and sex. Elders have more formal authority than younger persons—even a year's difference in age is sufficient to establish the fact of formal superiority—and men have greater authority than women. . . . Regardless of personal talents or achievements, or changes in his own or others' lives, an Indian's relative position in the hierarchy of the extended family, his obligations to those 'above' him and his expectations of those 'below' him are immutable, lifelong" (p.117). A woman's status and authority are largely dependent on her husband's position within the family and a wife relinquishes control over domestic affairs in deference to her mother-in-law. Besides the father, the eldest son commands the most respect and obedience and assumes a central role in guiding the family's fate, both economically and socially (Kakar 1978). Daughters generally receive more protection and care (Mandelbaum 1970). No doubt, the structural and social ideal of the Hindu family varies considerably depending on caste distinctions, economics, and educational level. For example, as Kakar (1978) pointed out, the differential *pativarata*, complete loyalty to husband, may be "a masculine wish fulfillment rather than an accurate description" of the life of Indian women. While older women may defer to their husbands in the presence of others, they may and indeed do wield a good deal of power on a number of domestic issues and expenditures.

An inescapable and prominent aspect of Indian life is the social phenomenon of caste. We see caste in the sense that Kakar (1978) and others (Mandelbaum 1970) have discussed it—*jati*. "Jati is caste in all the immediacy of daily social relations and occupational specializations. Essentially, it is a social group to which an individual belongs at birth. Usually, a jati member participates in one of the jati's several traditional occupations, and his marriage partner will almost certainly belong to his jati" (Kakar 1978, p. 122). Jati defines and dictates the confines of Indian childhood While it tugs at the nerves of some educated members of Indian society, it continues to play a central role in the everyday social fabric of Indian life. Obviously, a child from a specific jati begins to learn very early about the social ideals, not only of his/her own jati, but of others as well.

Intertwined with the notions of family organization and the caste system is the Hindu traditional world view. The rituals and myths inherent in the Hindu world view are integrated very early in an individual's life. The rituals, myths, and religious practices vary depending on the region and socio-cultural group. We will attempt to provide some common concepts and Hindu ideals that are expressed in Indian society. (For a detailed account of the Hindu world view, see Bharati 1982; Kakar 1978.) These practices and belief structures provide the Hindu with a sense of semblance of his own existence, an understanding of his immediate environment and the interpersonal relationships within it, and are the basis for connecting aspects of experiences within the immediate environment and the larger world.

For Hindus, *Moksha*—"self-realization, transcendence, salvation, a release from worldly involvement"—is a key tenet of their existence (Kakar 1978, p. 16). Being in the state of Moksha,the 'self' immersed in the 'greater self' and a complete understanding of others, allows the individual to move away from ignorance or false consciousness and to move toward a reality of the liberated person" (Kakar 1978, p. 17). Few Hindus actually achieve this ideal in a single lifetime. However, many Hindus may choose other options such as *Bhakti*, serious devotion, Karma Yoga, or the way of Jnana, the development of intellectual capabilities that enable one to differentiate between the real and the apparent (Kakar 1978).

The concepts of Dharma and Karma also govern the Hindu way of life. In simplistic terms, *Dharma* refers to the interdependent and complementary nature of roles and responsibilities, while *Karma* directs the cycles of birth and death in which a person regresses or progresses depending on past deeds (Kakar 1978). Members of Hindu society may be judged in these terms and relationships molded or shunned on the basis of these ideologies; they generate either tolerance or rejection of individual differences.

In the main, then, the search for inner sanctity and the personification of certain epics, such as the Ramayan, guide the ego ideals of men and women who bear and raise children, influence the treatment of boys and girls, and lay the foundation for the development of family solidarity. At the same time, role and caste distinctions ensure that rigid boundaries are maintained in familial relationships and during social commerce within the society at large.

In this chapter, our discussion centers around the following issues:

(a) cultural, social, and cognitive messages conveyed during adult-child play;
(b) child-child play in formal and informal settings;
(c) play training studies as a mechanism to provide cognitive and social enrichment for young children;
(d) the role of objects and materials in the play of Indian children; and
(e) culturally relevant practices in early childhood education.

Before proceeding into a discussion of these issues, a few words of caution are in order. There is a dearth of information based on formal studies of adult-child and child-child play in India. Thus, we relied on anecdotal accounts, personal observations conducted during the time three of us worked and lived in South Asia for different durations, anthropological studies that are usually more qualitatively than quantitatively based, and a handful of studies conducted by Indian and Western scholars. Of course, our discussions cannot possibly cover the multitude of ethnic groups in India. We, therefore, are cautious in drawing general conclusions about all Indian children. Nevertheless, there are certain issues regarding play and cognitive and social development that may pertain to all children despite the fact that there are different mechanisms whereby a society socializes its children to adapt to the challenges in the immediate environment. In other words, there is shared cultural knowledge regarding the attainment of social and cognitive goals among children pursuant with environmental demands.

ADULT-CHILD PLAY

Adult-child play has been linked to the development of attachment relationships (Lamb 1985; Stern 1974) as involving visual, tactile, and auditory stimulation (Stern 1974; 1977), containing the structural elements of language (Ratner & Bruner 1978), and the turn-taking rules of social conversation (Rubin, Fein, & Vandenburg 1983). Moreover, adult-child games have been implicated in the development of rules, the learning of social roles, and the development of representational thinking and use of reconstructive memory (Sigel 1982). Thus, adult-child play allows children to gain a sense of control over social stimuli and assists in the development of close parent-child relationships. Further, the early parent-child relationship may set the stage for the development of meaningful and successful peer group participation (Easterbrooks & Lamb 1979; Roopnarine, Church, & Levy 1990).

With these functions of adult-child play in mind, we examine early adult-child play patterns and games in India. Our recent work on adult-child play in India has focused on the activities mothers and fathers engage in with infants (Roopnarine, Talukder, Jain, Joshi, & Srivastav 1990; Roopnarine & Hossain 1992) and on early mother-child play and performance on infant development scales. The observations conducted on mother-child and father-child play have been couched within the context of attachment theory (Ainsworth 1969; Lamb 1985). While most agree that the formation of attachment to the mother develops as a result of close involvement with the baby on a daily basis, the development of attachment to the father may occur through physically stimulating bouts of interaction through play (Lamb 1985). These formulations are based on data collected on Euro-American families and, therefore, may not be culturally valid for other groups of people. Indeed, assessments conducted in Malaysia (Lu 1987; Roopnarine, Lu, & Ahmeduzzaman 1989) and among the Aka (Hewlett 1987) suggest that mothers and fathers rarely engage in rough, stimulating activities with their young children. Similarly, among middle-income Indian mothers and fathers residing in New Delhi, rough play rarely occurred in the context of adult-child play in the home (see Table 2.1). These findings may suggest that in a culture that values physical closeness, affective bonds to fathers may develop through holding and the display of affection (Roopnarine, Hooper, Ahmeduzzaman, & Pollack 1993). In fact, commonly held beliefs suggest that children should not be awakened suddenly during sleep, and should not be snatched or thrown in the air. A premium is placed on the baby's happiness and future psychological well-being (Kakar 1979).

TABLE 2.1
Parent-Infant Play in Single- and Dual-Earner Indian Families

| | Single Earner (N = 54) | | Dual Earner (N = 34) | |
	Mother	Father	Mother	Father
Minor Physical	0.26	0.40	0.03	0.20
Rough Physical	0.00	0.30	0.23	0.67
Peek-a-boo	0.25	0.00	0.29	0.11
Object Mediated	2.38	2.14	2.05	1.32

In the above-mentioned studies, both mothers and fathers were observed to engage in object-mediated play, peek-a-boo, and hide-and-seek with their one-year-olds. These generally occurred at low frequencies and one may be tempted to conclude that Indian parents engage in very little play with young children. This could not be further from what actually happens.

Parents engage their children in a wide variety of games and physically close play. These occur during massage, during informal sessions when the mother is resting with the baby, or when the mother is engaged in routine caregiving. Although the games vary from region to region and across age groups, there are common elements mirrored in them: physical closeness, their high tactile nature, social messages about the culture, and their rich linguistic content.

During infancy, adults have been observed to engage in a range of popular games with babies in different regions of India (Muralidharan, Khosla, Mian, & Kaur 1981). A number of infant games involve rocking, holding, and face-to-face interaction. Other games are played during periods when the baby receives a massage. Regardless of the context, parents often sing to their children during the games. In the thirty-one infant games we analyzed, twenty-seven (87%) contained elaborate tactile stimulation in the absence of objects, where the baby was held close to the body or was massaged; in twenty-one (68%) of the same games, the mother sang to the baby; and 52% involved face-to-face interactions (figure 2.1). For example, in a Bengali game, *Kan Dol Dol*, the mother and child sit facing each other with each holding the other's ears while the mother rocks the baby and sings:

> Kan dol, dol, du luo ni,
> Ran ga ma thae chiruni,
> Bar ash be ek hu ni
> Ni ye ju be ta knu mi.

> (The bride is decked and waiting.
> The bridegroom will come just now
> and take her away).
> (From Muralidharan et al. 1981)

In a game in Maharasttra the mother demonstrates to the infant, through a song, the content of a game in the palm of the hand:

> Eithe, Eithe, nach re mora,
> Bal ghattia chara,
> Chara ka pani pee,
> Bhalkan uddon ja.

(Here, here, dance. Oh peacock!
The Baby gives you grass,
Eat grass, drink water,
Quickly fly away.)
(From Muralidharan, Khosla,
Mian, & Kaur 1981)

In yet other games, mothers may encourage children to walk (e.g., *Chal Chal Mate*), count the fingers and toes (e.g., *Habba Bonthu Anthanthe*) and point out familial relationships by naming kinship members (e.g., *Aa Gay Koni*). Lest you think that early infant-parent Indian games are primarily tactile, these games contain labeling, substitution (twenty-nine percent of the infant games we examined emphasized numbers and labeled objects), and convey social messages of family relationships. This latter issue is closely tied to the Indian conception of family solidarity and loyalty that extends beyond immediate kinship members.

The tactile nature of infant games mirrors the childrearing beliefs of Indian parents. In most households, babies are constantly held, cuddled, crooned, and attended to; they are massaged daily and are carried on the mother's hip or close to the body. The close physical contact manifested in the games facilitates the development of attachment relationships and the "massage improves tissue metabolism and blood formation, intensifies blood circulation and improves tissue nutrition" (Sharma, Shrinawas, Anandalakshmy, & Capilia 1989, p. 4). The massage enables the caregiver to become relaxed too. Given these alleged benefits, it is not surprising that the experience of close physical contact manifested during infant games is highly valued in the Indian context.

When we move beyond infancy, there is little, if any, information on parent-child play during the preschool and early school years. Anecdotal accounts suggest that mothers continue to be close and indulgent, while fathers appear more distant. Fathers are strict and authoritarian. This being the case, mothers may be more involved in playing with preschoolers than are fathers. Of course in nonindustrialized societies with oral traditions, children may imitate their parents' behaviors and actions and play is often embedded in work. However, this is conjecture and we must await observations of adult-child play during the preschool years.

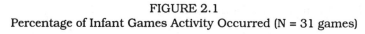

FIGURE 2.1
Percentage of Infant Games Activity Occurred (N = 31 games)

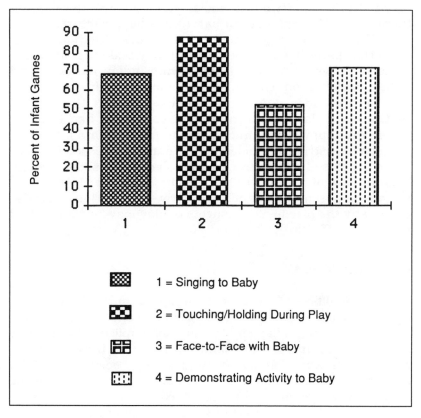

Beliefs about Early Parent-Child Play

It is well established that parental beliefs about socialization are intimately interwoven into childrearing practices (Laosa & Sigel 1982). Without doubt, beliefs about the value of play will most certainly influence the nature and degree of parent-child play. In India, close physical contact in parent-child interaction does not guarantee that parents will necessarily play with their children. A few researchers (e.g., Sharma et al. 1989) have noted that among low socioeconomic-status families, mothers may hold their babies for lengthy periods but rarely play or interact with them.

In a country where childrearing practices are molded by

tradition and not by information generated from child development research, how cognizant are parents of the value of play in early cognitive and social development? Here again, there is little information on parental belief structures about play. That parents engage in elaborate games with infants suggests that parents enjoy the bouts of play and must attribute some social value to play. In surveying Indian mothers' and fathers' beliefs about early play, Roopnarine and his associates (Roopnarine, Hooper, Ahmeduzzaman, & Pollack 1993) noted that parents played with infants for enjoyment and to make the infant happy. Thus, in contrast to mothers and fathers in western industrialized societies, few parents stressed the cognitive benefits of play or the acquisition of social skills through play. In view of parents' tendencies to follow the child's inclinations in parental guidance and early socialization, it is easy to see why the pleasurable aspects of play may be emphasized in India.

CHILD-CHILD PLAY

Because of illiteracy, low school enrollment in rural areas, and economic factors associated with schooling and social status, a sizable number of Indian children are not enrolled in formal peer groups in structured educational settings. For these children, contact with peers and opportunities for play occur around the home with siblings and neighbors' children. In contrast, for those children who are enrolled in formal educational settings, play may not be an integral part of their early childhood curricula. Parents and educators stress a more formal curriculum that emphasizes traditional academic subjects. In this section of the chapter, we discuss preschoolers' play activities in formal and informal settings. In our treatment of play in school settings, we highlight a model early childhood program at Lady Irwin College of the University of Delhi.

Children in Nonschool Settings

For nonschool-going children, joint family life eases children into play with siblings and cousins. Moreover, the joint family structure itself provides opportunities for completing chores, working alongside parents, and the daily life within the joint family is an educational process for much of India's rural population (cf. Baig 1979). Whereas in towns and cities children have greater opportunities to buy a wide range of toys, to view films, and to engage in a variety of extracurricular sport activities, rural children may engage in craftwork and children in general are quite ingenious in constructing toys from available materials. As Baig (1979, p. 203) has noted, children who live in the slums can be quite resourceful: "Who has not seen three or four youngsters in slum or crowded city streets, dragging a rickety wooden crate with uneven wheels made out of old tins, in which one small boy or girl is gleefully having a ride. Any flat piece of wood becomes a slide down a sand heap at a construction site or salvaged bits of rope, a swing on which children scramble and compete, as a tree bough almost breaks under their weight."

Most nonschool-going children face extreme poverty, are malnourished, and are incorporated into work early in their lives. Others are expected to fend for themselves. Poverty itself can have dire consequences on children's functioning and the responsibilities placed on very young children are often burdensome. Thus, whatever play activities and games they engage in may hardly be adequate for optimal intellectual and social development. Nonetheless, nonschool-going children engage in a wide variety of games that are also common in the play of school-going children. In Bengal, children use cooking sets built from mud and leaves in pretending to prepare food, and use empty cigarette boxes as currency to engage in commerce with peers. Rural children in particular have been observed to sing about harvesting crops and engage in pretend marriages. Marble games, hide-and-seek, tag games (e.g., *Kana Machi Bho Bho*), and "police and thief" are commonly witnessed in the play of rural and urban children. In addition, they sometimes engage in the more structured play activities of children in school yards.

The benefits nonschool-going youngsters derive from these modes of activities have not been formally assessed. It is our guess that because of their content, the activities' adaptive value for later adult roles and the cooperation they engender must assist children to integrate conceptions of social responsibility and modes of appropriate behavior into their psyche. The harsh reality is that most of India's children struggle with nutritional, health, and housing problems so that play becomes secondary in their lives.

Formal Group Settings: Crèches and Nursery School

Like other developing nations, India faces the challenges of providing adequate childcare for working women with young children. With an increasing number of women choosing to work in professional jobs and the concomitant changes in family social-structural organization where extended family members are not as available to assume the responsibility of caring for young children, it is imperative that Indians work toward developing plans for accommodating the needs of families with young children. As of 1985, there were about 14.1 million mothers with children between 0-5 years who were in the labor force (Swaminathan 1985). The demand for early childcare services for the 43 million children who need them far exceeds the number of available crèches. With few exceptions, conditions within crèches are uniformly poor. More specifically, appropriate developmental activities that include play, adult-child interaction, space and equipment, caregiver or *ayah* training are lacking or are of poor quality. Most crèches possess few toys and play materials and, if available, are rarely used; children are not encouraged to engage in play activities and instead may sit or wander aimlessly. Formal and informal games and language stimulation are not central to day-to-day activities (Swaminathan 1985). This is due in part to the lack of awareness of the value of play in early child development and to ill-trained crèche workers.

These conditions not withstanding, India is quite cognizant of its early childhood education needs. Historically, India has made provisions for the education of young children. From the inception of the first kindergarten school in 1879 through the introduction and use of Montessori education, the commitment to stimulating the social, intellectual, and emotional development of young children has remained a priority for India. During the 1960s, child welfare programs aided by the Ministry of Education established about 20,000-25,000 centers for young children. As of 1985, in Tamil Nadu alone there are preschool programs to cover almost all of the 13,000 villages (Swaminathan 1985). The concept of "disadvantaged children" also took on greater meaning and early intervention programs that emphasize play as a major component have been implemented in some parts of the country.

Today, preschool and kindergarten programs are beginning to implement play as a major part of their curriculum. At this juncture, we would like to briefly describe one such program at Lady Irwin College at the University of Delhi. We should warn the reader that programs of this nature are still rare in India. The Saraswati Puri Nursery School (SPNS) at Lady Irwin College was established with the objective of providing practical experience to graduate and undergraduate students studying Child Development at the college and to provide a creative unpressured environment in which young children's social and cognitive growth could flourish. The program is guided by Piagetian principles of self-discovery-based learning coupled with native cultural practices. What distinguishes the program from other preschools in the city is its emphasis on nonformal education (i.e., the school's philosophy of education through play and other creative means such as art, craft, dramatization, and experimentation that exemplify the concept of learning through doing). A major proportion of the preschool programs in India teach children the regiments of the alphabets or how to count in order to prepare children for higher schooling. In the SPNS nursery, socioemotional, cognitive, and physical development are deemed to be equally significant aspects of development and are emphasized in the school's goals and policies. The program, although influenced by western concepts of child development, weaves into its curriculum the traditional/local context using mainly indigenous and simple materials for art and play activities (e.g., matchboxes, broom sticks, leaves, clay).

Activities at the SPNS are based on specific topics that are designed for the week. The topics may include animals, fruits, festivals, a particular season (e.g., monsoon), various people who help others (postman, washerman, etc.) and so on. The idea behind this approach is to focus attention on one particular subject a week and build upon it. As activities evolve and build on previous experiences, it is hoped that children's understanding of the topic will become increasingly complex. Children engage in role playing and art activities that emphasize construction, both stimulated through oral (story telling, songs, rhymes) and visual (flash cards, books, flannel graphs, puppets) means. Children are also actively involved in both indoor and outdoor free play activities related to the topic.

In a somewhat related vein, in more academically inclined programs, children may engage in diverse games in the school yard or in the available play spaces surrounding the school. For the most part, children imitate games that they may have learned at home or by observing their peers at school. In quite a few games a leader is selected after which children sit in circles or follow the leader's interactions (e.g., *Kaalla Gajja*). Most games are played in large groups and require high levels of cooperation, imitation, or pretense (see Muralidharan et al. 1981). For example, in *Atiya Patiya*, children sit in a circle and place their palms upwards on each others palms and swing together while they sing a jingle. On the second line, they raise their arms in flying motions imitating the movement of birds in the air. In "follow the leader" children are required to imitate a leader and in "in the pond-in the bank" children briskly follow directions of a leader. Hopping games are usually accompanied by singing, whereas in some enactment games such as in *Bhatto, Bhatto*, children act out a trip to the market.

First player:	Yes
Second player:	Where have you been?
First player:	To the market
Second player:	What did you buy there?
First player:	Kathal'
Second player:	Was it raw or ripe?
First player:	Ripe
Second player:	*(Feeling the hands of the first)* Shall I cut from here, Is it raw or ripe?
First player:	It is ripe, but don't cut from here.
Second player:	*(Pretending to cut at the elbow)* Shall I cut it here?
First player:	No-No!
Second player:	*(Aiming at the folded hands)* Shall I cut here?
First player:	Yes!

(From Muralidharan et al. 1981)

Subsequently, the second child then pretends to prepare the vegetable and shares it with the other children.

As was the case with infant games, a striking feature about the games of preschool-aged children, regardless of whether they are enrolled in school or not, is the close physical contact and holding manifested in them. In our perusal of twelve urban/rural preschool games, six (50%) involved a good deal of holding or touching parts of another child's body. Again, touching and holding are encouraged in India and this practice continues in children's groups beyond the preschool years.

PLAY, CELEBRATIONS, AND ORAL TRADITION

While play has been viewed as an integral part of rituals and celebrations, there are few societies in which religious and non-religious celebrations evoke such playful participation as in India. During festivals such as *Diwali*, the festival of lights, and *Holi*, children engage in gleeful activities with peers and adults. Diwali permits children to welcome the Goddess of Wealth, *Lakshmi*, by lighting small clay containers, which is accompanied by elaborate fireworks. Holi allows children the liberty to sprinkle colors and water on their friends. Children can be heard shouting and yelling amidst bursts of laughter as they converge on their peers to squirt them. In other celebrations (e.g., *Janmashtami*) and at Melas children enact important figures in Hindu religious philosophy through songs, dance, and mime, and puppetry is used to tell tales about kings, queens, and courtiers of well-known stories (Baig 1979). Undoubtedly, the puppetry arouses children's imagination while infusing themes that are seminal to the transmission of cultural values.

Although distinctions have been made between oral and literate cultures in the play literature (Sutton-Smith & Heath 1981) the links between story telling and imagination are sketchy. In societies such as India, children may rely equally on tales and stories as play as a medium to stimulate imagination. Thus as stories are orally transmitted and enacted children have opportunities to use their imaginations in solitary situations and may conjure up things not present in the immediate environment (Johnson, Christie, & Yawkey 1987; Sutton-Smith & Heath 1981). For instance, in portrayals of the central figures in the *Ramanaya*, children's imagination may force them to historically contextualize images and events from a different period in India's history. Simultaneously, children are able to fuse ideological notions of their culture with the present and future. The depth of these cognitive extensions and transformations are rarely assessed.

OBJECTS AND PLAY

In the absence of abundant materials and toys, Indian children and parents improvise a good deal when it comes to using objects during play. From as far back as 2500 B.C., clay cycles and different kinds of animals were built for children. In earlier times, animal toys such as horses and elephants were cast in brass and bronze but these projects were primarily for wealthy children (Baig 1979). Today, toys are modeled after traditional toys and household objects that have a native flavor while others are imported from western industrialized societies. Toys for infants include mobiles, rattles, balls, paper objects, tins, containers, spoons, birds and animal figures, and dolls. These toys provide opportunities for the infant to reach, manipulate, chew, push, pull, and because of their colors and the interesting sounds they make, they can enhance visual-motor, cognitive, and manipulatory skills (Sharma 1989).

For preschool-aged children, too, there exists a range of playtime objects. Clay carts on wheels, clay monkeys that climb on a string, clay elephants that drink water, drum carts that move levers to beat a drum, paper snake objects that are fastened to wood, rattles made of gourds and pebbles, half-coconut shells that are made into tortoises, acrobatic dolls on sticks, bamboo flutes, child-sized brass or wooden utensils and dolls are some common Indian toys (Baig 1979). It is obvious that these objects draw upon dimensions within the immediate environment. The snake-charmer and the man who brings his monkeys or bears to perform have thrilled Indian children for centuries. Drums and flutes also are common musical instruments used in celebrations and during religious ceremonies. Quite often, then, the use of these toys is connected to everyday life experiences and children do expand on their usage beyond what they have observed. Some of the objects such as elephants, kings, and queens allow children to engage in pretend marriages, processions, and other celebrations.

As noted previously, Indian children build toys from discarded materials, clay, or materials gathered while accompanying their parents to work in the fields. Such creative use of materials can only enhance intellectual growth and problem solving (Johnson et al. 1987).

PLAY AND STIMULATION OF COGNITIVE GROWTH

In previous sections of this chapter, we hinted that for the most part low-income parents were not aware of the value of parent-child play and that play was not an integral part of most early childhood programs in India. Recognizing these tendencies, some Indian psychologists and educators have begun to emphasize the value of play in young children's intellectual and social development. Accordingly, a few intervention programs were implemented with play as a central part of the curriculum. For the most part, these programs have attempted to link play intervention to increases in performance on standardized tests.

One of the early studies that emphasized the importance of maternal stimulation demonstrated that infants who performed well on the Casati Lezine and Bayley Scales of Infant Development had mothers who would label and point to objects, had playthings within reach of their children, and engaged in parent-infant games. By contrast, infants who had scored poorly on these instruments had mothers who rarely played with their infants even though they held them most of the day (Misra 1977).

In a large demonstration project (Anandalakshmy 1979) the relationship between early maternal stimulation and performance on infant scales of development was further established. In examining mother-infant play and in assessments of cognitive and motor development using the Bayley Scales of Infant Development, it was found that infants who had low motor development index (MDI) scores had mothers who did not encourage play and engaged in little interaction with their infants. This trend was noticeable even when toys were present in some homes. Middle-income parents were more likely to provide cognitive stimulation for infants than low-income parents.

Of the 512 infants who participated in the abovementioned study, fifty-nine who had low MDI scores were selected for an intervention project. Twenty-nine were provided with maternal stimulation in the form of verbal and social interaction and were exposed to ample play materials in the home during ten play sessions over the duration of a month. The other thirty children served as controls. Although the experimental group showed gains in cognitive functioning, differences between the experimental and control groups were not significant. Perhaps the intervention was not intense enough and was too short in duration in order to realize dramatic changes in maternal behavior and infant competence. Nevertheless, the stimulation exercises did provide additional opportunities for exploration and mother-child interactions (Sharma et al. 1989).

In other work on early play intervention (Patri 1988), infants exposed to intense mother-child interaction and play activities that focused on fine- and gross-motor skills and block-building over a ten-month period showed significant gains in IQ when compared with infants who did not receive any additional stimulation than they normally would at home.

Taken together, these findings demonstrate the possible benefits of early parent-child play stimulation. Undoubtedly, as Indian child development experts continue to emphasize the value of play in early social and cognitive development, there should be an increased awareness of play as a vital part of early childhood curricula. In particular, India needs to reorient its thinking and approach to early childhood education in this direction because it has so many children who need early cognitive and social stimulation.

PLAY AND IMPLICATIONS FOR
EARLY CHILDHOOD EDUCATION

Judging from recent accounts of conditions within most crèches in India and given the accent placed on academic pursuits early in children's lives, early childhood programs that emphasize play and exploration as critical to Indian children's cognitive functioning make good sense. Why emphasize play at this point in time, and are Western conceptions of play necessarily relevant in the Indian context?

During the last two decades, there have been several advances in our understanding of the importance of play in early childhood education. These advances have not been accidental. As Western play researchers began to explore the playful activities of young children—their modes and developmental content— we soon realized that play provided lenses through which we could observe the unfolding of requisite childhood social and cognitive skills. Simultaneously, the absence of play or low levels of play in young children signaled problems in growth and development. The early efforts at understanding the value of play coupled with theoretically guided early childhood curricula brought to the forefront the necessity of play for development. Practitioners, educators, and parents in the West soon showed thoughtful appreciation for play as a chief aspect of young children's everyday cognitive and social experiences (Johnson et al. 1987). Intervention studies that targeted disadvantaged children showed the positive outcomes of play stimulation and thus further exemplified the significance of play and objects in children's cognitive development (Saltz, Dixon, & Johnson 1977).

Today, most Western and Indian scholars would hardly question the value of play. Does this mean that Western approaches to play intervention and play as a central theme in early childhood education would be appropriate for Indian society? The answer to this question is "not entirely." In some segments of Indian society, for instance urban areas, it is highly plausible that traditional conceptions of play intervention and ideologies regarding self-discovery-based learning would work in an exemplary fashion (e.g., in the,university nursery discussed earlier). But cultural factors should be strongly considered in designing early childhood programs. Too often, Western educational ideologies are imported into countries where the culture bends existing practices to fit the ideology (Roopnarine & Carter 1992) instead of modifying the educational ideology to fit the culture.

There are several factors that may conspire against maintaining the fidelity of early childhood curricula imported from the West and implemented in India. Parental belief structures about early socialization, the oral tradition, perceptions of schooling and achievement orientation, long-range goals of the society and political ideology, use of native themes and materials are but a few issues that are embedded in attempts to assimilate nonnative approaches to early childhood education. Thus, preschool programs and parent-child intervention efforts will have to deemphasize the rigorous learning of basic mathematics, language, and science facts in toddlerhood and the preschool years and instead use folk tales, puppetry, and celebrations to infuse playful themes that would influence ideational fluency and representational thinking. Additionally, the construction of native objects and toys should enhance problem solving and present culturally relevant themes to families and children.

In short, cognitive and social stimulation through play can be accomplished by means that are culturally appropriate and sensitive to the demands of a given society. In the case of India, one would assume that both highly structured and loosely structured early childhood environments may be required depending on educational background factors and general living conditions. Teacher, Ayah, and parental training on basic concepts of child development and developmentally appropriate curricular issues must go hand-in-hand with educational ventures into play stimulation.

REFERENCES

Ainsworth, M. D. S. (1969). Object relations, dependency and attachment: A theoretical review of the infant-mother relationship. *Child Development, 40,* 969-1025.

Anadalakshmy, S. (1979). Recent research on the young child. *The Indian Journal of Social Work, 40,* 295-309.

Baig, T. A. (1979). *Our children.* New Delhi: The Statesman Press.

Bharati, Y. (1982). *Hindu views and ways and the Hindu-Muslim interface.* Santa Barbara, CA: Ross-Erikson.

Easterbrooks, M. A. & Lamb, M. E. (1979). The relationship between quality of infant-mother attachment and infant competence in initial encounters with peers. *Child Development, 50,* 380-387.

Hewlett, B. S. (1987). Patterns of parental holding among aka pygmies. In M. E. Lamb (Ed.), *The father's role: Cross-cultural perspective* (pp. 295-330). Hillsdale, NJ: Lawrence Erlbaum Associates, Publishers.

Johnson, J. E., Christie, J. F., & Yawkey, T. D. (1987). *Play and early childhood development.* Glenview, IL: Scott, Foresman and Company.

Kakar, S. (1978). *The inner world: A psycho-analytic study of childhood and society in India.* New Delhi: Oxford University Press.

Kakar, S. (1979). *Identity and adulthood.* New Delhi: Oxford University Press.

Lamb, M. E. (1985). Observational studies of father-child relationships in humans. In D. Taub (Ed.), *Primate paternalism* (pp. 407-430). New York: Van Nostrand Reinhold.

Laosa, L. & Sigel, I. (Eds.) (1982). *Families as learning environments for children.* New York: Plenum Press.

Lu, M. (1987). *Maternal and paternal assessments of their activities with their infants in Kuching, Malaysia.* Unpublished master's thesis, Syracuse University.

Mandelbaum, D. G. (1970). *Society in India: Continuity and change* (vols. 1 and 2). Berkeley: University of California Press.

Misra, N. (1977). *Cognitive and motor development of infants (6-12 months): Nutritional and socioeconomic status correlates.* Unpublished master's dissertation, University of Delhi.

Muralidharan, R., Khosla, R., Mian, G. M., and Kaur, B. (1981). *Children's games*. New Delhi: Child Study Unit of National Council of Educational Research and Training.

Ogbu, J. V. (1981). Origins of human competence. A cultural ecological perspective. *Child Development, 52,* 413-429.

Patri, V. (1988). *An intervention program of early stimulation in a group of disadvantaged children.* Unpublished research report, New Delhi, India.

Ranter, N., & Bruner, J. S. (1978). Games, social exchange, and the acquisition of language. *Journal of Child Language, 5,* 391-402.

Roopnarine, J. L. & Carter, D. B. (1992). The cultural context of socialization: A much ignored issue. In J. Roopnarine & D. B. Carter (Eds.), *Parent-child socialization in diverse cultures.* Norwood, NJ: Ablex.

Roopnarine, J. L., Hooper, F. H., Ahmeduzzaman, M., & Pollack, B. (1993). Gentle play partners: Mother-child and father-child play in New Delhi, India, In K. MacDonald (Ed.), *Parents and children playing.* Albany, NY: SUNY Press.

Roopnarine, J. L. & Hossain, Z. (1992). Parent-child interaction patterns in urban Indian families. Are they changing? In J. Roopnarine & D. B. Carter (Eds.), *Parent-child socialization in diverse cultures.* Norwood, NJ: Ablex.

Roopnarine, J. L., Church, C. C., & Levy, G. D. (1990). Day care children's play behaviors: Relationship to their mothers' and fathers' assessments of their parenting behaviors, marital stress, and marital companionship. *Early Childhood Research Quarterly, 5,* 335-346.

Roopnarine, J. L., Talukder, E., Jain, D., Josh P. & Srivastav, P. (1990). Characteristics of holding, patterns of play, and social behaviors between parents and infants in New Delhi, India. *Developmental Psychology, 26,* 667-673.

Roopnarine, J. L., Lu, M. W., & Ahmeduzzaman, M. (1989). Parental reports of early patterns of caregiving, play, and discipline in India and Malaysia. *Early Child Development and Care, 50,* 109-120.

Rubin, K., Fein, C. G., & Vandenburg, B. (1983). Play. In P. H. Mussen (Ed.), *Handbook of child psychology, vol. 4: Socialization, personality and social development* (pp. 393-474). New York: Wiley.

Saltz, E., Dixon, D., and Johnson, J. E. (1977). Training disadvantaged preschoolers in various fantasy activities: Effects on cognitive functioning and impulse control. *Child Development, 48,* 367-380.

Sharma, J. (1989). The nuclearization of joint-family households in West Bengal. *Man in India, 44,* 193-206.

Sharma, N., Shrinawas, S., Anandalakshmy, S., & Capilia, A. (1989). *Infant stimulation: Documentation of research in Delhi.* New Delhi: Lady Irwin College, University of Delhi.

Sigel, I. (1982). The relationship between parental distancing strategies and the child's cognitive behavior. In L. M. Laosa and I. E. Sigel (Eds.), *Families as learning environments for children* (pp. 47-86). New York: Plenum.

Stern, D. (1974). Mother and infant play: The dyadic interaction involving facial, vocal, and gate behaviors. In M. Lewis and L. Rosenblum (Eds.), *The effect of the infant on its caregiver.* New York: Wiley.

Stern, D. (1977). *The first relationship.* Cambridge: Harvard University Press.

Straus, M. A. & Winkelmann, D. (1969). Social class, fertility and authority in nuclear and joint households in Bombay. *Journal of Asian and African Studies, 9,* 61-74.

Sutton-Smith, B. & Health, S. B. (1981). Paradigms of pretense. *Quarterly Newsletter of the Laboratory of Comparative Human Cognition, 3,* 41-45.

Swaminathan, M. (1985). *Who cares? A study of child care facilities for low-income working women in India.* Center for Women's Development Studies. New Delhi: Indraprastha Press.

3

Children's Play in Taiwan

Investigations of cultural differences in play derive from the assumption that play serves as an enculturative mechanism (Schwartzman 1978). That is, through play children learn societal roles, norms, and values. Despite the limited and narrow focus of the literature on children's play across cultures, a number of psychologists have recently proposed that children's play differs across cultures and socioeconomic status groups. In this chapter, an attempt has been made to examine the play behaviors of Chinese children in Taiwan, the Republic of China. The chapter aims to cover four major issues: (a) the Chinese perspective on play; (b) Chinese children's play behavior within a developmental framework; (c) current play behaviors of Chinese children and play differences across cultures; and, finally, (d) adults' perceptions of children's play.

CHINESE CULTURE AND BELIEFS ABOUT EDUCATION

Although Chinese culture is made up of a number of philosophical systems such as Confucianism, Taoism, Buddhism, Mao-

Tzu's theory of universal love, and Legalism, Confucianism has been the most influential in Chinese society. In order to understand Chinese philosophy on play and its role in education, an examination of the spirit of Confucianism is necessary.

Humanism had been in existence long before Confucius' time (551-479 B.C.). But it was Confucius who determined this outstanding characteristic of Chinese philosophy. He was concerned with understanding people, human values, and how these are to be realized both in individual and societal life. To create a good society based on good government and harmonious human relations, Confucius thought that filial piety and fraternal love were essential. These concepts served as the cornerstone to the social-structural organization of Chinese life. To enhance the fabric of Chinese society, Confucius advocated proper conduct of *li* (propriety, rites). He proposed *jen* as the heart of his educational ideal of humanism. To Confucius, the man of jen is the superior man (*Chun-tzu*), who is distinguished by love of humanity and by piety towards his parents and who possesses wisdom and is well-versed in courtesy, ceremony, poetry, and music. Further, Confucius believed that "personal cultivation begins with poetry, is established by rites and is perfected by music" (Waley 1938). Confucius viewed music as a civilizing force and poetry a moral force since music may harmonize our sentiments and restrain our passions, while poetry may moderate our nature and inspire our ethical feelings. The above descriptions suggest that the educational goal of Confucianism was to foster a superior man (Chun-tzu), which might be actualized through immersion in the traditional cultural spirits of poetry, rites, music, and the languages or arithmetics.

Following the path of Confucius' philosophy, Mencius proposed the theory of the original good nature of man. What Mencius meant was that human nature is the essential nature of man as distinguished from that of beasts. It is man's moral and intellectual nature that constitutes his very essence, without which he would be no better than a horse or a dog. Mencius maintained that human nature has the seeds or beginnings of four cardinal virtues—humanity, justice, propriety, and prudence—of which full development in these areas results in perfection. In addition to Mencius' theory of good nature, another Confucianist, Hsun Tzu, suggested that human nature was evil. The spirit of gain, envy, and the desire of the eyes and ears all existed at birth. Both Mencius and Hsun Tzu, however, emphasized the necessity of education, rites, and music as the tools of acquiring good values.

In short, Confucianism has provided Chinese society with the ideal of educational philosophy. Today, some of the tenets of Confucianism are preserved while others have been transformed or discarded. Within schools, certain traditional Chinese values such as filial piety, respect for the old, adherence to rules, the emphasis of submission, and the virtue of cooperation are still stressed. In the family, the main aim of education is to raise obedient children devoted to the family, working hard at school and maintaining harmonious relations with brothers, sisters, and neighbors. Perceptibly, with the influence of Western thought on modern Chinese society, some of the traditional values are being transformed. More communicative and democratic, rather than authoritarian, approaches are now being adopted by the younger generation of educators and parents.

EARLY CHILDHOOD EDUCATION AND PLAY IN TAIWAN

To better understand the role of play in young children's lives, a brief consideration is required of the early childhood educational institutions that are in place in Taiwan and the evaluation of modern efforts in early childhood education. As will become apparent, play still may not be accorded the importance it deserves in early childhood educational practice.

Types of Institutions

There are two types of preprimary institutions for young children in Taiwan: the kindergarten and nursery school. The earliest Chinese kindergarten was called "Meng Yang Yuan" and established during the late Ching Dynasty in 1902. At that time, the early education system and curriculum were patterned after those found in Japan. After the Republic of China was founded in 1912, Western models and ideas were imported, which strongly influenced kindergarten education. Even today, the Western impact still exists. The first formal nursery school was established in 1931 in Shanghai. It was a welfare-based experimental institution for children of laborers (Ding 1975).

Kindergarten and nursery schools were initiated for different functions. Kindergartens emphasized education while the nursery school focused on nurture and care. Furthermore, the two institutions are supervised by different authorities: the Ministry of Education oversees the kindergartens and the Ministry of Interior the nursery schools. The two branches of government have different regulations for the operation of the two programs. The goals, equipment criteria, teacher qualification, teacher/pupil ratio, age at which children should enroll, and the curricular contents of the two institutions are mandated through related legislation. The Early Childhood Education Act, the Kindergarten Curriculum Standard, and the Kindergarten Equipment Standard are used to guide and regulate the operation of kindergartens. The Establishment Regulation for Nursery School, the Manual of Education and Care for Nursery School and the Establishment Criteria for Nursery School are used to guide the nursery programs.

Among the above legislations, the Kindergarten Education Curriculum issued in 1987 and the Manual of Education and Care for Nursery School issued in 1979 are now the guidelines for teaching practice in kindergarten and nursery school, respectively. Thus the curriculum in kindergarten should cover five areas: health, play, music, work, language, and common sense (natural, social and mathematics concepts), while the curriculum of the nursery school includes play, music, work, story, song, and common sense. Furthermore, teachers are encouraged to use play as a tool for children's learning. Because play is listed as a separate subject in the curriculum, however, it can lead to confusion in pedagogy.

During the past forty years, there has been rapid growth in the number of kindergartens in Taiwan. After the Chinese government moved to Taiwan in 1951, there were only 280 kindergartens and 17,111 children enrolled in them; by 1988 there were 2,548 kindergartens and 248,498 children enrolled in them (Ministry of Education 1989). In 1990, the figures dropped a little to 2,505 kindergartens with an enrollment to 237,285 children (Ministry of Education 1991). Still, among kindergarten-age children, the enrollment rate was 21.81% in 1988 (Pan 1990). Because of the lack of active efforts by the government to set up public kindergartens, the private sector accounted for 12.81% of the total kindergartens in 1951, while it accounted for 72.22% in 1990 (calculated from Educational Statistics 1991).

There were three types of nursery schools: general nursery, community nursery, and harvest nursery. The harvest nursery was initially set up for children of farmers but its role became insignificant after 1970. None of it exists now. By contrast, the number of general and community nurseries has increased significantly during the past twenty years. In 1965, there were 325 general and community nurseries and 34,652 children enrolled in them; in 1988 there were 4,247 nurseries and 247,944 children enrolled in them. The enrollment rate for general and community nurseries in Taiwan was 21.76% in 1988 (Pan 1990).

With the increasing number of children enrolling in kindergarten and nursery school in Taiwan, early childhood educators face the challenge of implementing play as an integral part of children's classroom activities. Both kindergarten and nursery school emphasize educational pursuits more so than caregiving. In order to promote the ideal of equal educational opportunity, the Ministry of Education launched a six-year plan of early childhood education. Important to this policy is the setting up of public kindergartens in order to recruit all five-year-olds. Within the framework of this pursuit, the arrangement of the learning contexts and the contents, whether in the Kindergarten Curriculum Standard or in the Manual of Education and Care for Nursery School, play is listed as a separate subject. This has the potential of misleading teachers who adopt an approach that imparts specific knowledge to children rather than using play as a general tool to integrate the acquisition of knowledge in all learning areas.

A HISTORICAL PERSPECTIVE ON PLAY

Contemporary views of play are different from those espoused during earlier periods in Chinese history. As noted earlier, Confucianism remains a dominant force in Chinese philosophy and penetrates into Chinese lives, shaping Chinese ethics. According to Confucius, play incorporated the functions of education, called the polite arts: basically, this entailed the sublimated forms of play and physical education. These polite arts referred to six art forms: ceremonies, music, archery, charioteering, the study of characters or language, and the figures or arithmetics. In essence, Confucius gave Chinese philosophy its humanistic foundation, which can be seen in the twelve Chinese words in the Confucian Analects (Legge 1971).

Let the will be set on the path of duty. Let every attainment in what is good be firmly grasped. Let perfect virtue be accorded with. Let relaxation and enjoyment be found in the polite arts.

Confucius maintained that the development of the civilian character must be based on immersion in the polite arts, which essentially are the active aspects of play.

In earlier epochs (e.g., *Spring and Autumn* [722-481 B.C.]), emphasis was on physical education and the polite arts. Children learned sweeping, socializing, and language or arithmetic, which were passed down as a viable way of educating the youth in Chinese society. Among the aforementioned educational contents, sweeping and socializing were termed "playing rites," which meant that children enacted the roles to learn social rules and adult customs.

Education in the six arts emphasized both physical and intellectual development and suggested that the educated play and learn. But later, in the Sung dynasty (960-1279), now influenced by Buddhism, Confucianism also proposed "silence" as the way to develop one's personality and morality. Physical activities and play were depreciated in favor of a strict curriculum that valued a rigorous examination system. Following the Sung dynasty, the mainstream of Chinese culture viewed play as the antithesis of work. But throughout modern Chinese history, parents allowed their children to play when their work was completed. One consequence of the deviation from the depreciation tradition was that a variety of play forms evolved in Chinese history, some of which are currently observed. Nonetheless, the emphasis on hard work rather than play is still apparent in Chinese society.

Contemporary Chinese scholars, influenced by Western educational philosophy, maintain a different attitude towards play than that of the past. Currently, play is deemed important in that it may contribute to the child's psychological and physical development. However, this view is not shared by all educators. In school settings, free play sessions are assigned by only some kindergartens. Besides, the Kindergarten Curriculum Standard lists play as a separate subject, which may in part reflect the philosophy of Taiwan's academy. Play is viewed by some scholars as a subject rather than a means for achieving academic goals. Ideally, play should be viewed as a teaching method for curriculum instruction instead of being treated as a subject with specific teaching materials.

CHILDREN'S PLAY BEHAVIORS

Currently, the study of children's play in Chinese society focuses on two categories of play. One category includes traditional play forms, which primarily involve cultural connotations. The second category encompasses modern play forms. Modern play forms are influenced by Western culture and have fewer cultural boundaries. Let us consider each category in more detail.

Traditional Play Forms

Some traditional play forms were handed down through the generations and are exercised by children during special festivals in China. For example, during the Chinese New Year, children light firecrackers. The lighting of firecrackers is related to a myth that symbolizes the "year" as a "fierce monster." The monster usually appeared during the end of the year, injuring people. It then disappeared after New Year's eve. The next morning, the Chinese people would say "congratulations" to each other for surviving the previous "year's" disaster. During one particular year, firecrackers and drums were used in driving out the monster. This tactic was successful and thus the lighting of firecrackers was handed down as a play form of the New Year holidays.

Following the Chinese New Year holidays is the Lantern Festival. During this festival, children prepare their own lanterns and when night falls they go outside in groups lifting lanterns. Traditionally, the topic of lantern design usually corresponded to the year's animal. There are twelve animals used by the Chinese to symbolize the different years. But, because of scientific and technological influences, commercial lanterns often employ TV or movie heroes in their designs instead of the traditional Chinese symbols. With the advent of modern science, battery lamps have replaced the candle in the lantern.

Another activity that engendered favorable participation among Chinese children was kite flying. It is said that kites were used to send messages to assist armies thousands of years ago. In addition, the significance of the kite is illustrated by the saying, "let the kite fly away in tomb sweeping day." During "tomb sweeping" day, one may write down all of one's sorrows, pain, and sickness on the kites and let the kites fly away (*Han Sheng Magazine* 1984). This symbolized the disappearance of all bad luck. Kite flying remains a popular summer play activity for children. Nowadays, kites are increasingly being used as toys, and the designs on the kites reflect the versatility of Chinese designs—kites are shaped in the forms of dragons, tigers, butterflies, one-hundred-leg worms, and other figures.

Other traditional games include chopsticks games, top games, Chinese chess, cock kicking, Chinese yo-yo, and rope jumping. These may invite individual or group participation and are rule-oriented. The rules, however, have been modified over the years. Despite their long history, these traditional play' forms are gradually vanishing. The government has taken note of this state of affairs and has been advocating traditional folk sports, especially in elementary schools.

Modern Play Forms

With the increasing industrialization and urbanization of Taiwanese society in the past decades, the different forms of children's play have reflected associated dramatic changes. Two decades ago, children had larger playgrounds, and outdoor play was prevalent. Children often used ingredients from their natural surroundings, such as coconut leaves to weave grasshoppers, pigeons, cattle as leaves to make a horn that was used as an instrument to produce sound. Hopscotch play by children had different versions: spiral hoppy, strawman hoppy, robot hoppy, and square hoppy. Children utilized the shadows of hands to shape different figures such as an eagle, pig, dog, or rabbit on the wall. Rubber bands and puppets were used to engage in pretend play. Additionally, marble games and sand pocket games were favored by children.

There is the assertion that children's play preferences in Taiwan have been changing in recent years (Lee 1973; Lu 1978; Ho 1990). In an examination of play preferences among kindergarten children in Taipei, Lee (1973) found that slides and swings were children's favorite play structures, followed by kites, electrical toys, tricycles, and ball play. Gender differences were seen to emerge regarding the types of play. Boys preferred playing with electrical toys, followed by slides and swings, tricycles, toy guns, and kites. For girls, slides and swings were most popular, followed by kites, color paper folding, singing, and house playing.

In another study on play preferences of three- to six-year-olds, Lu (1978) found that the most popular toys in kindergarten were storybooks, drawing materials, and blocks. Boys were found to prefer transportation toys, whereas girls preferred story-books and drawing. Subsequently, Ho (1990) found that the most popular materials were symbolic play materials (e.g., puppets and dolls), followed by structured-construction play materials (e.g., blocks, Legos, and puzzles), fluid-construction play materials (e.g., clay and paints), sensorimotor play materials (slide and climbing construction), and sign play-numbers and letters (e.g., alphabetic cards and arithmetic cards). Gender differences were found only in children's selection of structured-construction play materials with boys preferring blocks, legos, and puzzles.

In sum, during the 1970s, slides, swings, and kites were favored by children, while puppets, dolls, blocks, Legos, and puzzles became the preferred play materials for kindergarten children in the 1990s. Further, when children play indoors more than outdoors, construction and symbolic play materials tend to be the preferred activity. This change of preference in play materials may be due to the urbanization that has resulted in smaller playgrounds for city children. Simultaneously, increasing affluence may have provided greater access to more technical or mechanical material goods.

ILLUSTRATIVE STUDY

In order to further explore Chinese children's play behaviors in current Taiwanese society, an observational study was conducted by the author. The Parten/Smilansky play framework (Smilansky 1968) was utilized to examine the assumptions concerning play deficits or play differences. The assumption of play deficits derives from studies indicating that children from low-income families engage in less pretend play, which may be caused by deficiencies in play stimulation in the children's environmental condition. This assumption has been generalized to children in Third World countries (Ebbeck 1973) and is supported by a number of cross-cultural studies that suggest that pretend play varies in quality in some societies (Seagoe 1971; Whiting 1963), while it is virtually nonexistent in others (Ebbeck 1973; Whiting 1963). By contrast, some anthropologists and folklorists offer a counter proposition—play difference. This perspective suggests that all children can engage in imaginative play, although this may be displayed in varying styles for children of different socioeconomic classes and cultural environments (Schwartzman 1978; Sutton-

Smith & Heath 1981). Consequently, Sutton-Smith and Heath (1982) propose that what appear to be developmental deficiencies in imagination may be differences in imagination style (cf. Johnson, Christie & Yawkey 1987, p. 138). Alternatively, assumptions of play deficit may arise due to the researcher's class bias or ethnocentrism (McLoyd 1982).

The present investigation was conducted on sixty-two children ranging in age from forty-one to seventy-eight months and drawn from middle-class families whose children attended two Taipei kindergartens (thirty-two boys and thirty girls). One kindergarten was attached to the National Taiwan Normal University; the other was private. They shared a similar educational philosophy in that the child was viewed as an active learner and play activities were encouraged. Units were planned for children's learning that lasted for a week or two. Different activity areas were set up for the learning units with time for free play. The teachers had graduated from junior teachers college or from secondary school with credits earned in the preschool education program at the junior teachers college.

A nonparticipant observational time-sampling technique was utilized to observe children's indoor play behaviors during free play sessions. Twenty one-minute observations were conducted for each child, each one-minute observation subdivided into fifteen-second periods with ten seconds for observation and five seconds for recording. The order of observations was randomized. The observations were conducted within a two-month overall period.

A mutually exclusive and exhaustive code catalogue was used to record the data based on a hierarchical three by four nesting of Parten's (1932) social play categories (solitary, parallel, interactive) and Smilansky's (1968) cognitive play categories (functional, constructive, dramatic, games with rules) first used by Rubin, Maioni, and Hornung (1976). Codes for onlooker behavior, unfocused behavior and nonplay behavior (i.e., teacher-assigned tasks, reading, exploratory, transitional behaviors) were also recorded. A procedure rule was followed in coding each fifteen-second interval according to the predominant play state occurring, with the higher state credited in the case of equal occurrence of two or more states.

An interobserver agreement of .90 was established prior to data collection. During observations, the interobserver agreements between observers were checked intermittently throughout the duration of the study encompassing 12% of the observation data. The overall interobserver agreements ranged from .90 to .95.

Results from the study indicated that (a) the most frequently occurring category of cognitive play was constructive play followed by functional play, dramatic play, and games with rules; (b) in the social play category the most frequently occurring play was parallel play, followed by solitary play and interactive play; (c) in nesting social and cognitive play, the most frequently occurring behavior was parallel-constructive play, followed by solitary-constructive play, solitary-functional play, parallel-functional play, interactive-dramatic play, interactive-functional play, parallel-dramatic play, interactive-constructive play, solitary-dramatic play, and interactive games with rules; (d) children's age was significantly and positively correlated with constructive play, parallel play, parallel-constructive play, and interactive games with rules; in contrast, it was negatively related to functional play, solitary play, solitary-functional play, solitary-constructive play, and parallel functional play; (e) children's mental age was positively related to parallel play, interactive play, parallel-constructive and interactive games with rules; while it was negatively correlated with functional, solitary, solitary-functional, and solitary-constructive play; (f) children's role-taking abilities were found to be correlated with interactive games with rule; and (g) children's sex, IQ (measured by the Binet test) and socioeconomic status were not found to be significantly correlated with play behaviors (table 3.1).

These findings suggest that the variety of cognitive and social play behaviors displayed by Chinese children do not deviate significantly from those of children in Western cultures in relation to the Parten/Smilansky framework (table 3.2). In both cultural settings, for example, a good deal of constructive play is exhibited by preschool and kindergarten children. With respect to the relationship between age and play, the findings are in agreement with other work in the area (Rubin et al. 1976; Rubin, Watson & Jambor 1978; Johnson, Ershler & Bell 1980). Rubin and his colleagues (1976) found that age was positively related to constructive play while negatively correlated with functional play. Similar findings have been reported by Johnson et al. (1980) in their work on white middle-class American children. In related work, it was found that preschoolers exhibited more solitary-functional and parallel-functional play and less parallel-constructive, parallel-dramatic, and interactive-dramatic play than

TABLE 3.1
Correlations of Play Activities with Age, Mental Age,
Role-taking Abilities, Sex, IQ, and SES

Variables	Age	Mental Age	Role-taking	Sex	IQ	SES
Functional play	-.441***	-.349**	-.142	.142	.091	.154
Constructive play	.307*	.218	.120	.155	-.096	-.106
Dramatic play	-.096	-.108	.009	.007	.104	.128
Solitary Play	-.547***	-.490***	-.166	.002	.073	-.036
Parallel play	.363**	.296*	.087	.088	-.084	.120
Interactive play	.175	.299*	.230	-.090	.189	.018
Solitary-functional play	-.352**	-.395**	-.055	.033	-.061	.232
Solitary-constructive play	-.359**	-.284*	-.093	.078	.084	-.244
Solitary-dramatic play	-.249	-.136	-.254	-.245	.197	.037
Parallel-functional play	-.395**	-.236	-.190	-.146	.146	.009
Parallel-constructive play	.550***	.411**	.151	.121	-.140	.049
Parallel-dramatic play	-.025	-.046	.104	.141	-.051	.225
Interactive-functional play	.039	.105	.016	-.163	.123	.006
Interactive-constructive play	-.010	-.013	.138	-.080	-.054	.055
Interactive-dramatic play	.004	.072	.079	.047	.080	.025
Interactive games with rules	.315*	.420***	.276*	-.034	.204	-.036

* p<.05
** p<.01
*** p<.001

kindergartners, which lend support to the notion that younger children engage in qualitatively less mature play than older children (Rubin et al. 1978).

The findings regarding the relationship between mental age and different play modes are partially consistent with those found in other studies. Previous research shows that constructive play is positively associated with intelligence, functional play is

TABLE 3.2
Percentages of Play Activities

Variables	Pan 1991 (Taiwan) %	Rubin, Watson & Jambor 1978[a] (USA)	
		Preschool %	Kindergarten %
Solitary-functional play	12.89	9.60	2.73
Solitary-constructive play	14.30	16.95	14.90
Solitary-dramatic play	2.82	2.35	1.95
Parallel-functional play	12.26	8.15	1.52
Parallel-constructive play	35.10	20.61	24.16
Parallel-dramatic play	4.14	1.70	7.70
Interactive-functional play	4.49	2.88	2.65
Interactive-constructive play	3.47	22.39	18.55
Interactive-dramatic play	7.81	13.09	23.54
Interactive games with rules	2.73	2.28	2.31

[a]Percentages calculated from Rubin et al. (1978), excluding unoccupied and onlooker percentage.

negatively correlated with cognitive ability, and that solitary play does not show a relationship with cognitive functioning (Johnson 1976; Johnson, Ershler & Lawton 1982).

Similarly, the findings on the relationship between children's role-taking ability and play are in partial agreement with previous research (Rubin & Maioni 1975). Gender differences in play patterns were not discernible in the present study, which contradicts the findings of previous research (Moore, Evertson, Brophy 1974; Rubin et al. 1976), but it is consistent with other results (Barnes 1971; Cheng 1984; Parten 1932; Rubin & Maioni 1975; Smilansky 1968). Furthermore, no differences emerged as a function of social class, which lends support to the findings of Golomb (1979). The lack of relationship between play and social class may be due to the fact that a majority of the children in the present study were very homogeneous in terms of middle-class socioeconomic status.

ADULT PERCEPTIONS OF CHILDREN'S PLAY

In a related study, Taiwanese mothers' attitudes toward play were assessed. A number of researchers (e.g., Johnson 1986;

Kooij & Hurk 1991) suggest that attitudes toward play and parental encouragement of play within the home provide children with opportunities for learning requisite cognitive and social skills. Accordingly, mothers (N = 68) were recruited from two Taipei private kindergartens in order to assess their attitudes towards children's play. Most of the mothers were well educated (four with a master's or doctoral degree, twenty-nine with a four-year college degree, nineteen junior college graduates, and sixteen high-school graduates). The participants were administered the Maternal Attitudes towards Children's Play Questionnaire, derived from Bishop and Chase (1971), by the kindergarten staff or by mail. Mothers were instructed to complete the questionnaire without advice from others.

The questionnaire was made up of two sections. The first part addresses what mothers perceive to be the function of play. That is, does play for the mother imply an activity that contributes to children's cognitive, mental, physical, or social development or is it merely a frivolous pursuit? The mothers were required to rate their degree of agreement for each item on a five-point scale. There are three items for each cognitive, physical and social category, and two items for a mental domain as well as the possible unproductiveness of play.

The second part of the questionnaire explores how mothers arrange children's play, which includes how mothers promote play, the role of mothers in children's play, and the amount of time mothers arrange for children to play. A five-point scale was used to assess the frequency of each item description.

Comparisons of mothers' responses on the five domains of play functions revealed that mothers had the highest mean score (M = 4.36) on the cognitive domain, followed by the social domain (M = 4.32), physical domain (M = 4.25) and mental domain (M = 4.04). The mean score for the perception that play is useless was only 1.81. Most mothers responded that they usually or sometimes provided children with toys and took them to a playground. More than half the sample reported that boys were not forbidden to engage in "girl's play" or gender-specific activities and vice versa. A majority of the mothers reported that they either sometimes or usually arranged opportunities for children to engage in functional, constructive, or dramatic play. However, mothers were more likely to arrange constructive play situations for children and let children engage in arithmetic and alphabetic play. In contrast, mothers were less likely to arrange games with rules for kindergarten children as they may perceive children to be too immature for such games. The average time mothers allowed children to play per day was about one to two hours.

Most of the participants of the present study were from middle-class backgrounds, and their attitudes may reflect those prevalent among today's adults living in urban Taiwan. Play is not viewed as useless anymore; on the contrary, it is perceived as being conducive to children's cognitive, social, mental, and physical development. Mothers in home settings often provide children with a variety of toys, letting children play for an average of one to two hours per day. Furthermore, sex stereotypes regarding the types of play were not discerned.

As far as the types of play that mothers arrange for children are concerned, the present study demonstrates that constructive play was the predominant activity arranged for kindergartners. This may be due to the fact that the markets are abundantly laden with imported constructive toys such as blocks, Legos, and puzzles. On the other hand, constructive toys require mature mental participation, which is perceived as being a significant aspect of play by mothers. Finally, because of insufficient play space in Taipei, constructive play may be encouraged by mothers since it is suitable for individual pursuit.

TEACHER TRAINING AND A
PLAY-ORIENTED CURRICULUM

Quite obviously, Taiwan is moving toward a strong emphasis on early childhood education. This direction was influenced, in part, by two forces: (a) the increased understanding of the importance of early social and cognitive stimulation for preparation for school entry and for children's development during the school years; and (b) sociopolitical changes that are occurring within Taiwan in terms of challenges to patriarchy as well as maternal employment. Since kindergarten and nursery education are regulated by different governmental bodies and play is listed as a separate subject in the prescribed curricula, it becomes imperative that the Taiwanese take a serious look at how play can be integrated more fully into classroom activities and teacher training.

For the most part, teacher qualifications for working in nursery school and kindergarten vary. In general, nursery school teachers are less well trained than kindergarten teachers. And although both kinds of teachers have training in the areas of preschool education, the value of play as an activity that is rich with social and cognitive activities is only now being emphasized. Thus, preschool and kindergarten teacher training programs should stress play as an integral part of early childhood curricula, especially during practicum experiences and in courses that pertain to educational practices and working with young children.

At the same time, the value of play versus more academic activities should be articulated more fully in Chinese society. Given the long history of the appreciation of music, poetry, ceremony, and the virtue of cooperation among the Chinese people, these themes could be enacted through pretend play and puppetry, for example. Likewise, cooperative and constructive play can be encouraged to boost friendship formation, respect for others, and to enhance problem-solving skills. These activities are already valued by parents and are gradually being reinforced in schools. The challenge for the Taiwanese, then, is to continue to stress play and exploration as central to early development over a more rigorous academic curriculum.

CONCLUDING SUMMARY

Play has been sublimated to the forms of polite arts, incorporating the functions of education before the Chinese Sung dynasty (960-1279). Afterwards, the traditional Chinese perspective on play shares distinct similarities to the Puritan ethic that dichotomized work and play in some respects. In the Chinese context the value of play was depreciated. More recently, contemporary scholars have espoused a more positive attitude towards play, encouraging play in kindergartens and home settings.

In examining children's play in Taiwan, two distinct categories of play types may be distinguished. One is the traditional play form employed during special festivals such as the lighting of firecrackers during the Chinese New Year, and the lifting of Lanterns during the Lantern Festival. The other traditional play forms are kite flying, top games, chopsticks games, Chinese chess, cock kicking, rope jumping and Chinese yo-yo. Some popular modern play forms are hopscotch play, marble games, and sand pocket games. Two decades ago, outdoor and gang play were widely prevalent. However, due to increasing industrialization and urbanization, most children tend to play indoors because of the limited size or location of playgrounds. Kite flying, marble games, top games, chopsticks games, and swing and slide play have been replaced by construction and symbolic play materials.

The illustrative investigation of children's play behaviors utilizing the Parten/Smilansky play category revealed that Chinese children's play activities were similar to those observed among Euro-American children. In addition, older children with higher mental abilities and better role-taking abilities were found to engage in qualitatively more mature play than their younger less mature counterparts.

Of further consequence are adult perceptions of children's play. The survey conducted by the present author indicates that mothers perceive play as a positive activity that may contribute to children's cognitive, social, physical, and mental development. In addition, most mothers preferred to arrange constructive games or play for their children. Another significant finding is that mothers did not discriminate or employ gender stereotypes in children's games, thus revealing an increased opportunity for interaction and exploration in different games and play forms for both boys and girls.

Lastly, educating a whole child is now commonly recognized as the goal for schools, and play is an important tool in this process. Children's cognitive, affective, and physical development are promoted through play in that children learn how to take another's point of view, to cooperate with others, to adhere to the rules, to use their own bodies, and to use their minds to think. Chinese educators are beginning to take a serious look at play as it relates to growth and development in their efforts to provide early childhood education for large numbers of young children.

REFERENCES

Barnes, K. E. (1971). Preschool play norms. *Developmental Psychology, 5,* 99-103.

Bishop, D. W., & Chase (1971). Parental conceptual systems, home play environment and potential creativity in children. *Journal of Experimental Child Psychology, 12,* 319-338.

Cheng, J. J. (1984). *Children's play and social interaction.* Unpublished master's thesis. National Taiwan Normal University.

Connolly, J. (1980). *The relationship between social pretend play and social competence in preschoolers: Correlational and experimental studies.* Unpublished doctoral dissertation, Concordia University.

Christie, J. F. & Johnsen, E. P. (1983). The role of play in social-intellectual development. *Review of Educational Research, 53,* 93-115.

Connolly, J. A. & Doyle, A. (1984). Relation of social fantasy play to social competence in preschoolers. *Developmental Psychology, 20,* 797-806.

Ding, B. Y. (1975). *The introduction of child welfare.* Taipei: Cheng Chung.

Ebbeck, F. N. (1973). Learning from play in other cultures. In J. L. Frost (Ed.), *Revisiting early childhood education.* New York: Holt, Rinehart & Winston.

Fein, G., & Stork, L. (1981). Sociodramatic play: Social class effects in integrated preschool classrooms. *Journal of Applied Developmental Psychology, 2,* 267-279.

Freyberg, J. T. (1983). Increasing the imaginative play of urban disadvantaged kindergarten children through systematic training. In J. L. Singer (Ed.), *The child's world of make-believe.* New York: Academic Press.

Golomb, C. (1979). Pretense play: A cognitive perspective. In N. Smith, & M. Franklin (Eds.), *Symbolic functioning in childhood.* New York: Wiley.

Han Sheng Magazine (1984). Chinese toys. Taipei: Han Sheng.

Ho, D. (1980). *The study of play preference in young children.* Unpublished masters thesis. National Taiwan Normal University.

Ho, H. L. (1987). Fatherhood in Chinese culture. In M. Lamb (Ed.), *The father's role: Cross-cultural perspectives* (pp. 227-245). Hillsdale, NJ: Erlbaum.

Johnson, J. E. (1976). Relations of divergent thinking and intelligence test scores with social and non-social make-believe play of preschool children. *Child Development, 47,* 1200-1203.

Johnson, J. E. (1986). Attitudes toward play and beliefs about development. In B. Mergen (Ed.), *Cultural dimensions of play, games, and sports.* Champaign, IL: Human Kinetics Publisher.

Johnson, J. E., Christie, J. F., & Yawkey, T. D. (1987). *Play and early childhood development.* Glenview, Ill: Scott, Foresman & Company.

Johnson, J. E., Ershler, J., & Bell, C. (1980). Play behavior in a discovery-based and a formal-education preschool program. *Child Development, 51,* 271-274.

Johnson, J. E., Ershler, J., & Lawton, J. T. (1982). Intellective correlates of preschoolers' spontaneous play. *The Journal of Genetic Psychology, 106,* 115-122.

Kooj, R., & Hurk, W. S. (1991). Relations between parental opinions and attitudes about childrearing and play. *Play and Culture, 4,* 108-123.

Lee, (1973). *The study of children's play interests.* Research report of Taipei Municipal Junior Teacher College.

Legge, J. (1971). *The Chinese classics.* Taipei: Wen Shih Che Publisher.

Lu, S. B. (1978). *The development and guidance of young children.* Taipei: Wen Jing.

McLoyd, V. (1982). Social class differences in sociodramatic play: A critical review. *Developmental Review, 2,* 1-30.

Ministry of Education (1989). Educational Statistics of the Republic of China. Taipei: Ministry of Education.

Ministry of Education (1991). Educational Statistics of the Republic of China. Taipei: Ministry of Education.

Moore, N. V., Evertson, C. M., & Brophy, J. E. (1974). Solitary play: Some functional reconsiderations. *Developmental Psychology, 10,* 830-834.

Pan, H. L. W. (1990). *Early Childhood Education in Taiwan, the Republic of China.* Paper presented at the 14th Conference on Comparative Education Society in Europe, Madrid, Spain, July 2-7.

Pan, H. L. W. (1991). *The study of children's play.* Funded research report of National Science Council of Taiwan, the Republic of China. No. NSC 79-031-h003-07.

Parten, M. B. (1932). Social participation among preschool children. *Journal of Abnormal and Social Psychology, 27,* 234-269.

Piaget, J (1962). *Play, dreams and imitation in childhood.* New York: Norton.

Rosen, C. E. (1974). The effects of sociodramatic play on problem-solving behavior among culturally disadvantaged preschool children. *Child Development, 45,* 920-927.

Rubin, K. H., Maioni, T. L. (1975). Play preference and its relationship to egocentrism, popularity, and classification skills in preschoolers. *Merrill-Palmer Quarterly, 21,* 171-179.

Rubin, K. H., & Maioni, T. L., & Hornung, M. (1976). Free play behaviors in middle- and lower-class preschoolers: Parten and Piaget revisited. *Child Development, 47,* 414-419.

Rubin, K. H., Watson, K., & Jambor, T. (1978). Free play behaviors in preschool and kindergarten children. *Child Development, 49,* 534-536.

Schwartzman, H. B. (1978). *Transformations: The anthropology of children's play.* New York: Plenum.

Seagoe, M. V. (1971). A comparison of children's play in six modern cultures. *Journal of School Psychology, 9,* 61-72.

Smilansky, S. (1968). *The effects of sociodramatic play on disadvantaged preschool children.* New York: Wiley.

Sutton-Smith, B., & Heath, S. B. (1981). Paradigms of pretense. *Quarterly Newsletter of the Laboratory of Comparative Human Cognition, 3,* 41-45.

Waley, A. (1938). *The Analects of Confucius.* New York: Random House.

Whiting, B. B. (1963). *Six cultures—studies of childrearing.* New York: Wiley.

MICHIO TAKEUCHI

4

Children's Play in Japan

This chapter addresses some aspects of children's play in Japanese society. Initially, it briefly outlines some common Japanese belief structures and views of the nature of the child, as well as theories on education and their relation to play. The second part of the chapter discusses some traditional theories on Japanese children's play and their influences on contemporary preschool education. Finally, the chapter describes some changes and problems associated with increased urbanization and technological growth in Japan after World War II and how these changes have influenced children's play.

JAPANESE BELIEFS AND THE NATURE OF THE CHILD

Japan has enjoyed tremendous economic prosperity since World War II. Its 121 million people are well-educated and highly motivated (Schwalb, Imaizumi, & Nakazawa 1987). Fully 94.4% of men and women in Japan classify themselves as middle class

(Sorifu 1982); and the quality of Japanese life has steadily improved during the postwar period as evidenced in the accumulation of material goods and the emphasis placed on educational achievement. Current day Japanese men are more educated and better off economically than their own parents (Sorifu 1980).

The Japanese people have lived in a tightly knit society as basically one people with one language. Whereas traditionally the Japanese family was organized along linear extended lines, today most families live in smaller nuclear units (Asahi Shinbun 1984). Even so, the Japanese have maintained some aspects of the stem family; parents still live with their eldest sons and about 27.6% of Japanese families have grandparents living with them (Sorifu 1982). Mothers assume a major role in caregiving and are responsible for children's education (*Kyoiku Mama*). Fathers are viewed as economic providers and are often absent since they work a good deal of the time. Such intense involvement in work does prevent men from becoming involved in the day-to-day aspects of family life (Schwalb, et al. 1987).

Japan's unique traditions are exemplified in *Sabi* or refined simplicity and *Wabi* or quiet elegance. *Cha-no-yu* or tea ceremony, *Haiku* or a seventeen-syllable poem (*tanka*), and *Waka* or a thirty-one syllable poem are literature born in the pursuit of these spirits. Buddhist arts, literature in the Heian period, the Japanese language, manners, religion, and technology have all influenced Japanese cultural history and the process of Japanization (Nippon Steel Corporation 1982; Reischauer 1977).

Buddhist discipline, Confucian thought, and the belief in Shinto Spirit are key in understanding current-day Japanese society. Buddhism, which entered Japan in the 6th century via China and Korea, has no god; it emphasizes tolerance, equality, and love, rejecting hate and jealousy. Most Japanese are served by Buddhist rites after death and are given Buddhist names posthumously. On the other hand, the philosophy of Confucianism stresses the rational natural order by which man lives in harmony within strict ethical principles. While many of the characteristics of Confucianism were transmitted to Japan between the sixth and ninth centuries, they did not survive the Meiji restoration of the nineteenth century. Nonetheless, the Japanese still pursue Confucian ethical values in morality, politics, in interpersonal relations, and in their faith in education and work. Similarly, Buddhism continues to have a tremendous impact on Japanese culture affecting its art, literature, architecture, morals, and thought.

The natural indigenous religion of Japan, however, is Shinto. Shinto Gods or so called "Kami" are present in all objects and phenomena. Although not all Japanese show an interest in the thought of Shinto, the Japanese go to Shinto shrines when children are born, and marriage ceremonies are conducted according to Shinto rites. Shinto beliefs suggest that children are gifts from the Gods and therefore should be treated with leniency with adults being kind and tolerant of them.

HISTORICAL VIEWS OF THE CHILD

Within a historical context, from the Archaic Age to the present, views of children progressed from adults' personal hopes and feelings about children towards more child-centered and society-centered principles as to the role of children in Japanese society (Ishigaki, 1991). By the early Modern Age (Edo period) through the Meiji period the importance placed on early education certainly influenced early views on children. During this span of Japanese history, overall the focus was on the conditions of children, their expressions, their education, and adults' views on children (Ishigaki 1991).

Traditionally, the Japanese people have regarded the child as a "jewel" (Kodakara). This view of the child has been expressed in certain early literary works. For example, in *Manyoshu*, originally published in the eighth century, Yamanoue Okura (660-737), a middle-rated official worker, composed the following Japanese Tanka poem that emphasizes the preoccupation with and the value placed on children:

Thinking of children

When I eat melon,
I remember my children;
When I eat chestnuts,
Even more do I recall them.
Whence did they come to me?
Before my eyes they will linger,
And I cannot sleep in peace.

Envoy

What use to me
Silver, gold and jewels?
No treasure can surpass children!

Further, the child was viewed as an object of adult love. In the old style Japanese poems, Imayo, originally published in the 1170s during the Heian Period (A.D. 8th century-A.D. 12th century), Ryo-Jin-Hisho wrote of the child:

Born to play with each other,
Romping to play with each other,
If I hear the shout of joy of children,
Only then is my heart touched to move myself.

Two representative views of children during the Edo Period (1603-1867) were those espoused by Toju Nakae and Ekiken Kaibara. Toju thought that the world of children and their minds were different from those of adults; children should not be treated as toys and forced to do what is not suitable for them. Children should be given great liberty to play and to learn from calm adults. In this context, children will acquire good manners and a sense of morality (Ishigaki 1991). Yet other views found in published documents around this period stressed the inherent good nature of children. One writer of the Edo period, Ekiken Kaibara, described a theory of childhood education and discipline wherein every child was perceived to be born with a potential ability for five perfect virtues: humanity, righteousness, decorum, wisdom, and sincerity. To foster these virtues, learning and the cultivation of discipline (Shinto) were deemed necessary for the child. Kaibara's views were similar to those of the Chinese Confucian, Zhu Xi (1130-1200), an idealist. These views were intertwined with the Froebelian kindergarten education movement during the Meiji period (1868-1912) which basically emphasized the self and involvement in spontaneous activities in order to promote the latent abilities in children. The similarities in Froebel's thinking and Japanese scholars' thinking will become clearer in the next section.

During the Meiji period (1868-1912), marked by enlightenment and civilization, the view that children should be obedient to their parents was still common and parents struggled with the notion of children as individuals (Ishigaki 1991). But newer views of the child were introduced. Yukichi Fufuzawa and Masano Nakamura posited more liberal conceptual frameworks of parent-child relationships. They believed that parents should encourage children to be independent beings. Nakamura, in particular, emphasized the plasticity of childhood, a period during which children could be shaped by parents and educational ideas (Ishigaki 1991). Through the Tashio democracy to the present time, liberalism, individualism, internationalism, and individuality assisted in placing children at the center of Japanese society. The instincts and activities of children became increasingly recognized as the Japanese began to vigorously develop principles of early childhood education and adopt a society-centered view of the child (Ogawa 1977).

A HISTORICAL LOOK AT PLAY IN JAPAN AND THE IMPACT OF WESTERN EDUCATIONAL THOUGHT

The Meiji period marked the transition from a feudal society to a more modern Japanese state. During this period, a number of developments occurred in the domains of caring for and educating young children. Special schools (*Komori gakko*) were set up to care for the children of poor families in 1875, day nurseries (*Takujisho*) were also established for poor children, and factory- (*Kojo takujisho*) and Christian church-run nurseries were built around the turn of the century. In 1876, the first kindergarten (*yochien*) was developed at the Tokyo Women's normal school, and kindergartens that were entrenched in Buddhist and Christian philosophy emerged after the turn of the century (Shwalb, Shwalb, Sukemune, & Tatsumoto 1992).

Inextricably tied to the evolution of different perceptions of children and the need to provide formal settings for their education was the value of play. While the importance of play for the cognitive and social development of children was not clearly spelled out, the different activities of children were mentioned by early Japanese writers. For example, during the Edo period, play was seen as central to children's lives and many games such as playing house and tag, and many toys that we know today such as the top, bamboo horse, kite, battledore, mask, toy drum, firework, and a shell top emerged during this period. The children of warriors were told fairy tales and nursery stories (Ishigaki 1991).

In the same vein, Ekiken Kaibara, who discouraged the practice of forcing children to learn, also noted the importance of play during childhood. Kaibara argued that playing with bows and arrows, balls, dolls, tops, and flying kites was akin to childhood only (Ishikagi 1991). In the Meiji period, too, children played make-believe games along with other traditional games (Naka 1977). By the Tashio period, children were playing competitive games such as basketball and catch (Ishikagi 1991).

The Taisho and Showa era (1912-1926) witnessed considerable developments in *jiyu kyoiku*. Minouru Wada (1876-1954), one of the leading preschool education scholars, contributed significantly towards the development of early childhood education in Japan. Of consequence are his publications, *Yoji-Kyoiku-Ho* (*Theories of Early Childhood Education*, with Goroku Nakamura, 1907) and *Jikken-Hoiku-Gaku* (*The Experimental Preschool Education and Care*, 1932). Wada emphasized the developmental and educational meaning of children's play and maintained that preschool education should be based on the child's developmental needs. The aims of early childhood education, Wada reasoned, should accentuate liberal education through free play and not rigid instruction. Early education should be amusing and playful and contain individualized instruction. Wada's thoughts reflect views also expressed in the writings of Locke, Rousseau, Froebel, Mencius (a Chinese Confucian), Schiller, Spencer, Groose, and Baldwin. His theory of "yudo-hoiku" (liberal education through free play) emphasized the following goals:

• to expand children's interests in new experiences,
• to use profitably pretend play behavior of children,
• to use quarrels and troubles among children to educational advantage and,
• to use children's various habits to foster learning in other areas.

Furthermore, Wada perceived children's play as a spontaneous activity enabling children to develop sound bodies and minds. Wada described play as a pleasant feeling or as ecstasy satisfying various interests. Satisfactory feelings derive from interesting play, and freedom was based on pleasant feelings and interests. If children were forced to play, it was not viewed as play but as a task or as labor. Play was thus viewed as fostering abilities for social interaction and facilitating the development of artistic, musical, and language expressions. Table 4.1 pre-

TABLE 4.1
Wada's Classification on Children's Play

1. Experienced play: intuitive play (observation, experiment, appreciation, collaboration); reflective play (listing the story)
2. Pretended and expressive play: pretending play; imaginative, constructive play
3. Expressive play: musical play (songs, dances); draft play (handicrafts, drawing, handplay)
4. Cognitive play: story telling, discussions, riddles, twenty-questions
5. Plays with little labor: natural collection, fishing, gardening, breeding insects, fish, birds, constructions by blocks
6. Physical play: tag, jog, jumping, sumo-wrestling, swing, slide seesaw, chin-up

---

sents Wada's typology of children's play. For the various modes of play, Wada emphasized their role in the development of children's different but integrated abilities—cognitive, social, moral, emotional, and physical. His philosophy of child-centered education, based on Yudo-Hioku, was later adopted and elaborated by Sozo Kurahashi.

The contributions of Sozo Kurahashi (1882-1955) in influencing play and early childhood education in Japan is duly noted. Viewed as "the father of early childhood education" in Japan, Kurahashi started as a Froebelian educator working on child-centered education as the main aim of kindergarten. However, he criticized the formalization of Froebel's "gift" education as it applied to the Meiji period. In his books *Yochien Zasso* (*Essays on Kindergarten* 1926) and *Yochien-Hoikuho Shintei* (*Essence of Kindergarten* 1934), he emphasized the education of "life experience" derived from child-centered education in kindergartens.

Kurahashi termed his theory "Kyoiku no Seikatsuka" (learning from life), or education derived from children's everyday experiences. This perspective was strongly influenced by John Dewey's views on education and childhood development. Moreover, Kurahashi deemed four characteristics as essential to the new kindergarten: (1) respect for the importance of children's spontaneous life; (2) necessity of the interactional life of children; (3) respect for the total life of children including the various elements; and (4) respect for the emotional life of children. All four characteristics superseded any kind of exclusive or dominant concern with a conceptual or structural life.

These four points basically marked the beginning and remained the backbone of Kurahashi's educational thought. Essentially, Kurahashi expanded Wada's existing conception of "yudo-hoiku," maintaining that kindergarten was the place for children to display self-fulfillment and that kindergarten facilities should allow for a sense of liberty in children under the watchful guidance of sensitive teachers. The teacher should provide the child with topics and play themes in accordance with children's interests. Kurahashi deemed children's play in kindergarten as essential and maintained that kindergarten teachers should learn from children's experiences and activities. He further stated, "Nature has the best teaching materials for the activities of children." He considered the necessary ingredients for play freedom, vast play space, fresh air, and sunshine.

The preceding discussion of children and play suggests that historically play was accorded importance in Japanese society. However, its degree of consequence, as far as child growth and development is concerned prior to the twentieth century, is difficult to ascertain. Nonetheless, the value placed on children does indicate that childhood activities engendered respect for play by adults. The perceptions of the child as a "different being" from the adult, and the child as "a playing being" or "a free being" during the Tokugawa period still remains.

Today, influenced by Western conceptual frameworks on play (Johnson, Christie, & Yawkey 1987), teachers in kindergarten and day care stress symbolic and constructive play and their importance in the everyday experiences of young children (Takeuchi 1988). Play is viewed as central to intellectual abilities, flexible thinking, imagination, and creativity. Furthermore, children acquire social norms, learn cooperation and leadership skills, develop friendships, and become less egocentric through peer conflicts (Rubin, Fein, & Vandenburg 1983). Children also acquire emotional stability, a sense of beauty, goodness, truth, cultural mores, and the exquisiteness of the hands and legs (Takahashi 1984; Takeuchi 1988).

CHILDREN'S PLAY IN CONTEMPORARY JAPAN

Increasing nuclearization and gentrification of the Japanese family has been attributed to various social developments including significant domestic economic growth after World War II. Children's play in Japan has changed enormously over this period. This is partly due to technological growth and to the deluge of information provided by television. Japanese children appear to spend more time viewing television and performing other sedentary indoor activities, more so today than ever before. Figure 4.1 displays in hours the daily activities of children in 1955 and in 1975.

As can be seen in figure 4.1, although the total number of hours children engaged in play has barely changed (boys playing an average of 4.9 hours and girls 4.3 hours, compared to 4.7 and 4.2 for boys and girls twenty years ago), changes are evident in the content of children's play. The number of hours of outdoor play for boys and girls has decreased (from 3.2 hours to 1.8 hours for boys, and 2.3 to 1.0 hours for girls). Furthermore, TV watching has increased for both boys and girls. Over 10% of Japanese children's lives are spent viewing television. In short, children in contemporary Japan are born into a TV society with television viewing a central part of their lives.

The data presented in figure 4.2 also lends support to the notion that children's social activities have changed. Japanese children spend far more time doing homework than children in select other countries.

In the United States, France, the United Kingdom, and Thailand, forty to fifty percent of children do one hour's worth of school assignments at home each day. By contrast, in Japan and Korea over fifty percent of children do two hours worth of after-school assignments, while about twenty percent of children study for more than three hours. With respect to after-school play, about thirty percent of Japanese children do not play or play less than thirty minutes compared with three percent in the United States and five and a half percent in the United Kingdom. Thus, a good number of Japanese children play only for short periods when they get home from school.

Data on the utilization of free-time are also indicative of changes in the social activities of Japanese children. The data in table 4.2 show that during free time, seventy-five percent of Japanese children watch television, sixty-four percent spend their time reading comics while only forty-two percent engage in outdoor activities. Children in the United States, the United Kingdom, and France are far more likely to engage in outdoor activities.

More recent cross-cultural comparisons (e.g., Stevenson,

FIGURE 4.1
Changes in the Lives of Children from 1955 to 1975
(Units are in hours)

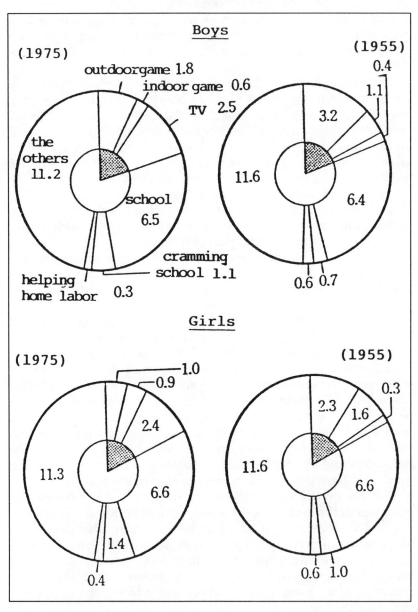

(Senda, 1984)

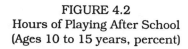

FIGURE 4.2
Hours of Playing After School
(Ages 10 to 15 years, percent)

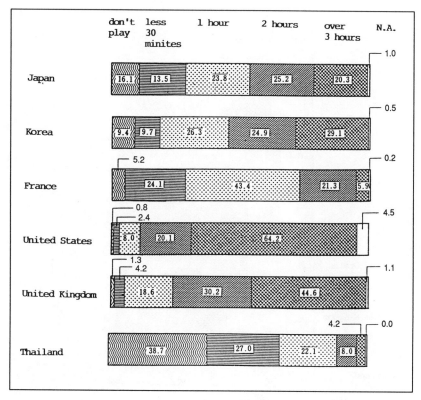

(Management & Coordination Agency, Central Government, Japan, 1987)

Lee, Chen, Stigler, Hsu, & Kitamura 1990) also confirm that Japanese children's lives at home are different from those of American children. There is a general tendency for American children to be more involved in nonacademic activities, and Japanese and Chinese children to be more involved in academic activities after school. Japanese children spend twice as much time doing homework as American children but play as much as American children. Moreover, Japanese children were far more likely to be enrolled in nonremedial after-school classes or to have tutors for academic subjects than children in Taipei or Minneapolis. As far as reading is concerned, comic books (*manga*)

FIGURE 4.3
Hours of Studying After School
(Ages 10 to 15 years, percent)

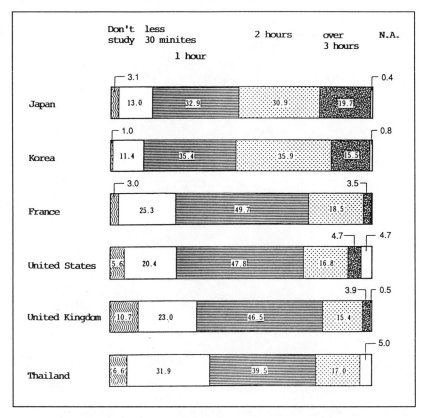

(Management & Coordination Agency, Central Government, Japan, 1987)

occupy a special place in Japanese children's lives, and about a third of reading time is devoted to comic books.

Some of the data mentioned point to a decrease in outdoor activities among Japanese children. Rapid technological growth and the loss of play space have partially contributed to this state of affairs. Presently, traditional forms of group play, such as hide-and-seek, blindman's buff (or tag), rope skipping, play-house, and spinning a top, which have been recorded during different periods in Japanese history have virtually vanished.

TABLE 4.2
How Children Use Free Time (plural answers: percent):
International Comparisons

	Japan	United States	United Kingdom	France	Thailand	Korea
Watch TV	75.6	76.9	79.4	74.0	62.7	69.4
Read magazines, comics	64.2	24.9	44.7	52.3	41.1	34.9
Outdoor game and sports	42.4	76.6	72.1	74.5	43.8	51.3
Listen to music	34.4	59.1	54.5	50.4	22.6	17.4
Reading books	27.5	45.8	55.3	57.9	22.9	47.8

(Management & Coordination Agency, Japan, 1987)

These forms of play share certain common characteristics: they occur outdoors with peers of various ages, they involve the use of natural materials and physical movement, and they are more spontaneous, away from the control of parents and other grown-ups.

The disappearance of the traditional forms of play is closely related to the disappearance of the peer group. From early childhood to early adolescence, peer groups essentially assist in the mental, moral, and physical development of children (Johnson, Christie & Yawkey 1987). In modern day Japan, children are far more likely to play indoors with several friends in small groups and with ready-made toys and machines. This is more "isolation-type play" and there is speculation that it may impede the development of various abilities in children.

The Rise of Video Games

Video games are widespread throughout Japan. Currently, one-fifth of all households owns a video game set. There are various reasons for the rising popularity of video games in Japan. First, they are rapid moving, easy to operate, and dramatic. Video games are often characterized by the 4S's in Japan: speed, story, scale, and suspense. A second reason for their popularity stems from the fact that Japan is a custodial, controlled society. It has been argued that the basic design concept behind video games reflects the Skinnerian behavioral modification theory of variable interval and variable rate reinforcement schedules discovered from studying laboratory animals in the 1950s. The design features of the game provide intrinsic reinforcement to encourage player use for long periods (Loftus & Loftus 1983), and they use appealing as well as aversive reinforcement contingencies (Braun & Griox 1989).

The characteristics of video games for learning include three main concepts: challenge, fantasy, and curiosity (Malone). Games with the highest appeal contain the following features: score-keeping, audiovisual effects, high reaction time, and randomness of unpredictable changes. Additionally, interactive action is the key element of video games; it facilitates a flow of information to children (Greenfield 1984). Some games allow children to create characters while others allow for the creation of the game itself (Lasater 1990). Additionally, certain modes of social-cognitive play are incorporated in and manifested when playing with video games (e.g., Parten/Piagetian play categories).

Insights into children's video-game activities came from a nationwide survey of the life and awareness of modern elementary school children conducted in 1989 by the Nippon Hoso Kyokai (NHK). The top five play activities of boy students reported in table 4.3 were baseball and softball (forty-nine percent), video games (thirty-four percent), soccer (twenty-eight percent), dodgeball (twenty-four percent), and tag and hide-and-seek (twenty percent). Interestingly, as compared to a previous survey conducted in 1984, the rate of video-game play increased five times (from seven percent to thirty-four percent) by 1989. Table 4.4 depicts the number of hours children spend playing video games. These data suggest that boys engage in video game play more than girls.

Do video games pose any salient developmental problems for children in Japan today? Many parents whose children play video games for a large number of hours maintain that their children are unstable, perform poorly at school, and spend a great deal of money. Furthermore, ophthalmologists note that too much exposure to video games may have adverse effects on children's eyesight. Also, the long-term influences of video games may result in deficits in interaction between parents and children, the development of people feeling separated from the real world, and a decrease in cooperation and empathy towards others.

Furthermore, a number of shocking cases were reported at

TABLE 4.3
Elementary School Boy's Play by the Playing Hours of Video Game

Kinds of Play	Don't play (n = 36)	Less than 7 hours a week (n = 82)	Over 10 hours a week (n = 16)
1. Outdoor play: baseball, soccer, etc.	56%	78%	44%
2. Riding bicycles	56	43	44
3. Roller skating	0	1	0
4. Play at playground and amusement park	42	42	38
5. Picking flowers or collecting worms	17	15	13
6. Going fishing	3	0	6
7. Playing video game or game-watch	22	94	100
8. Playing miniature car or radio-controlled car	22	6	0
9. Playing plastic model	11	11	0
10. Collecting the small dolls made of eraser	22	10	31
11. Reading comics	45	64	91
12. Playing the learning toys	22	12	13
13. Playing cards, puzzles or shogi-chess	25	29	13
14. Window shopping	0	6	19
15. Chattering with friends	22	12	25
16. Outdoor group play: tag, etc.	22	22	0
17. Indoor play: origami, etc.	6	9	0
18. Walking on stilts or other play	0	2	0

(Yamazaki, 1986)

the end of 1992. Certain children with a photosensitive epileptic syndrome suddenly fell into convulsive fits, lost consciousness or experienced headaches in Japan and the United Kingdom. This is called "space invader epilepsy" (Jeavons 1985) or TV-game epilepsy. Two cases were first reported by a pediatrician in Japan (Maeda et al. 1988, 1989) and we have several additional reports (Sato et al. 1990; Muranaka et al. 1992). Over thirty cases were reported in Japan from 1992 through January 1993. Thus, a new controversial issue was brought on by video games as a type of children's play.

These speculative concerns have been addressed in part by research (Lasater 1992). For example, scattered data indi-

TABLE 4.4
Hours of TV-Game Play by Sex and Grade (percent)

Boys	N	*Don't play*	*Less than 4 hours a week*	*Less than 7 hours a week*	*Less than 10 hours a week*	*Over 10 hours a week*	*Unknown*
K-4 year-olds	116	75.0	12.9	4.3	2.6	0.9	4.3
K-5 year-olds	99	38.4	38.4	15.2	4.0	2.0	2.0
E.S. lower graders	100	19.0	28.0	31.0	17.0	5.0	0.0
E.S. higher graders	156	10.9	31.4	32.7	16.0	7.1	1.9
Girls							
K-4 year-olds	96	86.5	6.3	1.0	0.0	0.0	6.3
K-5 year-olds	104	95.2	3.8	0.0	0.0	0.0	1.0
E.S. lower graders	114	71.1	16.7	8.8	0.9	0.9	1.8
E.S. higher graders	180	41.7	33.9	13.9	2.8	2.8	5.0

(Yamazaki, 1986)

cate that about ten percent of the individuals in one study showed some addiction to the games but there were no other discernible problems associated with video-game playing (Elgi & Meyers 1984); children who played a violent video game were more aggressive and more likely to imitate the video character than children who played a nonviolent game (Schutte, Maloutt, Post-Gorden, & Rodasta 1988); video games may arouse children in the same manner that cartoons do (Silvern & Williamson 1987); and children's prosocial behaviors may be affected after playing aggressive video games (Chambers & Ascione 1987). But others (Greenfield 1984: Loftus & Loftus 1983) have pointed out the possible benefits of video games for storing information, parallel processing, and for improving cognitive transformation skills.

ORGANIZATION OF CHILDREN'S PLAY IN KINDERGARTENS (*YOCHIEN*) AND DAY CARE CENTERS (*HOIKUEN*)

With over ninety percent of five-year-olds attending kindergarten (*yochien*) and day care (*hoikuen*) and considering attempts being made to integrate kindergarten and day care in Japan, the main aim of education in *yochien* and *hoikuen* remains socialization through play. Towards achieving this goal the *yochien* and *hoikuen* are set up for individual children in a manner such that the child's development is influenced through play (pretend play, functional play, symbolic play, and group play). Even so, in some cases, such as in the private kindergarten classrooms for the talented, children are required to follow a strict academic curriculum. They learn the *Hiragana* (Japanese letters) *kanji* characters (Chinese characters), mathematics, and English conversations (Takeuchi 1988).

Presently, children's play, as listed in the recent course of study in kindergarten and day care center teacher preparation, emphasizes the following points:

Health

- spontaneous play with peers in various activities outdoors
- awareness of his/her own health and prevention of illness
- awareness of safety of self
- enjoyment in having lunch with peers
- dress and undress self and conduct toilet activities by self

Human Relations

- play with peer groups
- play games with rules
- interact with various people with affection and confidence
- learn social habits and attitudes
- show concern for foreign people and cultures

Environment

- play with the surrounding natural world (plants, animals, etc.)
- have concern for tools of play
- concern with number, quantity, quality, time, space and place in everyday life

Language

- enjoy conversations with peers
- express via language what child experiences/ed
- show concern for storybooks and to expand his/her images
- show concern with signs and signals using Japanese syllabary

Creative Expressions

- play using various materials
- play dramas with images and language
- play and enjoy drawing and making things
- play and enjoy color, sound, shape, feel, and the movement of materials
- play with individual creative joyfulness using available materials, toys, and the necessities of everyday life.

Currently, kindergarten and day care are under the jurisdiction of the Ministry of Education and the Ministry of Health and Welfare, respectively. Kindergarten is viewed as having educational functions, while day care is seen as a caregiving facility. Furthermore, there is a dual certifying system for teachers in kindergarten and day care. Kindergarten teachers are required to complete two to four years of study beyond high school to complete their teaching certificate. Most daycare center teachers have completed high school and some have attended junior colleges or universities (Takeuchi 1988). The early childhood education curriculum was updated in 1989 and 1990 so that kindergarten and day care have some common goals, and the two governing agencies are working more cooperatively in efforts to improve the standards of early childhood education and teacher training.

CONCLUSION

In this chapter I have attempted to examine the treatment of play from a historical perspective and its role in early childhood education. Moreover, the influence of urbanization and technological growth on the play activities of children was reviewed. Today, play is highly stressed as a central part of the early childhood curriculum. It will be interesting to see how Japanese educators meet the challenges of the changing social ecology of childhood in their efforts to further underscore the importance of play in early childhood development while simultaneously attempting to achieve equity in early childhood education that meets the child care needs of working women.

REFERENCES

Braun, D.,& Giroux, J.(1989). Arcade video games: Proxemics, cognitive and content analysis. *Journal of Leisure Research, 21,* 92-105.

Chambers, J. & Ascione, F. (1987). The effects of prosocial and aggressive video games on children's donating. *Journal of Genetic Psychology, 148,* 499-505.

Data-Bank Editorial Committee (1987). *Data bank for teachers.* Tokyo: Reimei-kenkyukai Publishing Co.

Elgi, E. & Meyers, L. (1984). The role of video game playing in adolescent life:Is there reason to be concerned? *Bulletin of the Psychonomic Society, 22,* 309-312.

Fukaya, M. (1985). Kodomo no asobi hyakunen (One hundred years of children's play). *Aiiku Magazine,* vol. *50,* no. *9,* 28-32.

Greenfield, P. (1984). *Mind and media.* Cambridge: Harvard University Press.

Hattori, S. (1985). *Oya to ko.* (Parents and their children). Tokyo: Shincho-sha Publishing Co.

Hendry, J. (1986). *Becoming Japanese: the world of the preschool child.* Manchester: Manchester University Press.

Ishigaki, E. (1991). The historical stream of early childhood pedagogic concepts in Japan. *Early Childhood Development and Care, 75,* 121-159.

Ishikawa, K. (1949). *Wagakuni ni Okeru Jidokan no Hensen* (A history of views of children in Japan). Tokyo: Shinrei-sha Publishing Co.

Johnson, J., Christie, J., & Yawkey, T. (1987). *Play and Early Childhood Education.* Glenview, Illinois: Scott Foresman.

Joko, G. (Ed.) (1933, originally published in the 12th century). *Ryo-jin Hisho.* (The collected ancient prose poems). Tokyo: Iwanami Book Publishing Co.

Kaibara, E. (1973/1710). *Wazoku-Doji-Kun.* (Essays on Child-rearing). Translated by M.Matsuda. Tokyo: Chuo-koron Publishing Co.

Kazuki, G. (1976/1703). *ShoniHitsuyo Sodategusa.* (Essentials on Child-rearing). Tokyo: Heibon-sha Publishing Co.

Kurahashi, S. (1965/1926). *Yochien Zasso.* (Essays on Kindergarten). Selected works vol.2. Tokyo: Fureberu Publishing Co.

Kurahashi, S. (1965/1934). *Yochien Hoikuho Shintei.* (Principles of Kindergarten Education). Selected works vol. 1. Tokyo: Fureberu Publishing Co.

Lasater, C. (1990). Nintendo: A modern play phenomenon in the U.S. and Japan. Unpublished manuscript, The Pennsylvania State University.

Loftus, E.& Loftus, E. (1983). *Mind at play.* New York: Basic Book Inc.

Maeda, Y., Sakamoto, K., Kurokawa, T., Igarashi, K., Kitamoto, I., Ueda, I., & Tajima, S. (1988). Two epileptic children induced by TV-game, a paper presented at the Annual Meeting of the Japan Neurology Society, Kyushu Branch, *Clinical Neurology,* vol.*28,* no. *2,* 28-29.

Maeda, Y., Sakamoto, K., Kitamoto, I., Mizuno, Y., Ueda, K., & Kurokawa, T., (1989). TV-game epilepsy and its background, a paper presented at the Annual Meeting of the Japan Pediatrics Society, *Journal of Japan Pediatrics,* vol. *93,* no. *3,* 93.

Maeda, Y., Kurokawa, T., Sakamoto, K., Kitamoto, I., Ueda, K., & Tashima, S., (1990). Electroclinical study of video game epilepsy, *Developmental Medicine & Child Neurology, 32,* 493-500.

Matsuda, M. (1988). *Waga shogai, Waga shiso.* (My life and my thought). Tokyo: Iwanami Book Publishing Co.

Mori, S. (1992). *Asobi no qenri ni tatsu kyoiku* (Education based upon the principles of play). Nagoya: Reimei-Shobo Publishing Co.

Muranaka, H., Nagatoshi, S., Kojima, M., Koide, S., & Shiotani, M., (1992). Four epileptic children with complaints of seizures induced by TV-game, *Journal of Clinical Electroencephalogram,* vol. *34,* no. *2,* 131-133 .

Naka, A. (1977). *Fukoku Kyoheika no kodomo, Nippon kodomo no rekishi,* vol. *5,* (Children in the age of prosperity and armament, History of Japanese children, vol. 5). Daiichihoki Publishing Co.

Nippon Gakujutsu Shinkokai (Ed.) (1965, originally published in the 8th century). *The Manyo Shu.* New York: Columbia University Press

Nippon Hoso Kyokai, Dept. of Public Opinions. *Gendai shogakusei no seikatsu to ishiki.* (Life and awareness of contemporary elementary school children in Japan). Tokyo: Nippon hoso kyokai Publishing Corp.

Nippon Shihoshoshi-kai Rengokai. (1991). *Kodomo no yume to genjitsu chosa.* (Survey on children's present and future). Nippon shihoshoshi-kai hakko.

Nippon Steel Corporation (Ed.) (1982). *Nippon: The land and its people.* Tokyo: Gakusei-sha Publishing Co.

Ogawa, M. (1977). *Sekai no Yoji Kyoiku.* (Early Childhood Education in the World). Tokyo: meiji Tosho Shuppan Publishing Co.

Peak, L. (1991). *Learning to go to school in Japan: The transition from home to preschool life.* CA: University of California Press.

Reischauer, E. (1977). *The Japanese.* New York: Charles Tuttle Co.

Rubin, K. H., Fein, G., & Vandenburg, B. (1983). Play. In E. M. Hetherington (Ed.), *Handbook of child psychology, vol. 4, Socialization, personality, and social development,* 693-774. New York: Wiley.

Sato, M., Ishizuka, T., Abe, T., Watanabe, T., & Oda, Y. (1990). Clinical observations of seven cases of video-game induced epilepsy, *Journal of Niigata City Hospital,* vol. *11,* no. *1,* 53.

Schutte, N., Maloutt, J., Post-Gorden, J., & Rodasta, A. (1988). Effects of playing video games on children's aggressive and other behaviors. *Journal of Applied Social Psychology, 18,* 453-462.

Schwalb, D., Imaizumi, N., & Nakazawa, J. (1987). The modern Japanese father: Roles and problems in a changing society. In M. E. Lamb (Ed.), *The father's role: Cross-cultural perspectives.* Hillsdale, NJ: Erlbaum.

Schwalb, D., Schwalb, B., Sukemune, S., & Tatsumoto, S. (1992). Japanese nonmaternal care: Past, present, and future. In M. E. Lamb, K., Sternberg, C., Hwang, C., & Broberg, A. G. (Eds.), *Child care in context.* Hillsdale, NJ: Erlbaum.

Seishonen koryu kyokai Yagai bunka kenkyujo (1988). *Yagai Densho-asobi no jittai chosa* (Survey on outdoor traditional play in Japan). Tokyo: Seishonen koryu kyokai.

Senda, M. (1984). *Kodomo no asobi kankyo.* (The environment of children's play). Tokyo: Chikuma-shobo Publishing Co.

Shields, J., Jr. (Ed.) (1989). *Japanese schooling: Patterns of socialization, equality, and political control.* Philadelphia, PA: The University of Pennsylvania Press.

Somu-cho. (Ed.) (1987). *Nippon no kodomo to hahaoya.* (Children and mothers in Japan: International comparisons). Tokyo: Okurasho Insatsukyoku (Department of Treasury Printing Office).

Sorifu. (1980). Japanese mothers and children: An international comparison. *Gekkan Yoron Chosa, 12,* 50-57.

Sorifu. (1982). *International survey of youth and the environment.* Tokyo: Prime Minister's Office.

Stevenson, H., Azuma, H., & Hakuta, K. (Eds.) (1986). *Child Development and education in Japan.* NY: W. H. Freeman and Company.

Stevenson, H. W., Lee, S., Chen, C., Stigler, J. W., Hsu, C., & Kitamura, S. (1990). Context of achievement. *Monograph of the Society for Research in Child Development*, vol. 55, nos. 1-2.

Takahashi, T. (1984). *Nyuyoji no asobi* (Play in early childhood). Tokyo: shinyo-sha Publishing Co.

Takeuchi, M. (Ed.) (1988). *Shocho asobi* (Symbolic play). Tokyo: Koreru Publishing Co.

Tobin, J., Wu, D., & Davidson, D. (1989). *Preschool in three cultures: Japan, China, and the United States.* New Haven, CT: Yale University Press.

Wada, M. (1978/1932). *Jikken-hoiku-gaku* (The experimental early childhood education). Tokyo: Nippon Raiburari Publishing Co.

Yanagita, K. (1960/1932). *Chiisaki-mono no koe* (Voices of small children). Tokyo: Kadokawa Book Publishing Co.

5

Peer Interactions in Polynesia: A View from the Marquesas

INTRODUCTION

Recent ethnographers (Kirkpatrick 1983; Ritchie & Ritchie 1979; D'Amato 1986; Howard 1974) have characterized Polynesians as self-reliant and autonomous in contrast to earlier accounts of Polynesians as group-oriented and constrained by the collectivity. The emerging view of Polynesian autonomy recognizes strong group orientations but also stresses that Polynesian self-understandings and behavioral patterns encourage self-reliance within group contexts.

Western concepts of autonomy stress the freedom of the person to pursue individual goals unencumbered by social obligations. Recent work suggests that Polynesians conceptualize autonomy differently and develop a different set of skills for governing their lives within the structures of the group. Marquesans, for example, value group participation but reject the idea of persons submitting to the will of others (Martini & Kirkpatrick 1992). The purpose of this chapter is to describe how young Marquesan children learn to balance autonomy with group participation.

A Play Group of Young Marquesan Children

Thirteen members of a stable play group were observed daily for four months and less systematically for another two months in a small valley on the island of 'Ua Pou, Marquesas Islands. Children ranged from two to five years old. They played several hours a day without supervision while their siblings attended school nearby.

They organized activities, settled disputes, avoided danger, dealt with injuries, distributed goods and negotiated contact with passing others—without adult intervention. They avoided adults, probably because adults disrupted their play.

The play area was potentially dangerous. A strong surf broke on the boat ramp. The large rocks on the shore were strewn with broken glass. The valley walls were steep and slippery. Children played on a high bridge and high, sharp, lava-rock walls. Machetes, axes, and matches were occasionally left around and young children played with these. In spite of these dangers, accidents were rare and minor.

Hitting, teasing, and scolding were frequent, but fistfights, tantrums, and prolonged crying were rare. Disputes were frequent but these dissipated after a few minutes. Children did not seek adults or older children to settle conflicts or direct their play.

Questions

The study was designed to answer the following questions:

1. How do young Marquesan children manage themselves so efficiently without adult help or supervision?
   (a) How do they organize group play?
   (b) How do they keep themselves safe?
   (c) How do they deal with children who are hurt or scared?
   (d) How do they settle peer disputes?
   (e) How do they distribute food or goods?

2. How do they teach each other the interaction rules and values of their group?
3. How do they learn to exercise autonomy within the structures and obligations of this stable group?

In answering these questions, the chapter shows how Marquesan children, while engaging in play—the "work" of childhood—develop autonomous selves and acquire sophisticated social skills.

ETHNOGRAPHIC BACKGROUND

Setting

The Marquesas Islands are located 2,000 miles southeast of Hawaii and about 900 miles northeast of Tahiti. More than 5,000 people live on the five inhabited islands. I conducted fieldwork on the island of 'Ua Pou from 1976-1977. 'Ua Pou is a high, volcanic island, without an encircling reef or coastal plan. Its steep valleys are separated by rugged ridges. In 1976, life within most valleys was self-contained, since travel between valleys was difficult.

The valley described in this chapter had about 200 inhabitants. Many of the twenty-five houses are built on steep slopes, set back from a loop path that runs upland on one side of a stream and then down to the sea on the other side. Near the rocky shore, a cleared flat area, a concrete bridge, and a boat ramp serve as public spaces.

This settlement is dispersed, with houses set back from the major path, facing away from each other. Marquesans state explicitly that they value distance between themselves and their neighbors, allowing them some freedom from others' observation and potential criticism.

Daily Life

Daily life is organized around work for the household. Men and adolescent boys leave in the early morning to go fishing in outrigger canoes. Women clean house, wash clothes, prepare breadfruit, work in the garden and, on some days, weave pandanus, iron, or fish from shore. Children get up, get their own breakfasts, do light chores, look after infants, and go to school.

By late morning men return from fishing, children return

from school and the family eats lunch in their cookhouse. The children play for a while, then return to school until 3:30. Adults sit, talk, or sleep for a while and then work in the upland gardens or do jobs around the house.

Adults finish work by late afternoon, shower, sit and talk in neighborhood groups, or go down to the public area by the sea to talk and watch volleyball. Adolescents and young adults play volleyball. Children play on the bridges, in the stream, or in the sea until dusk when family members return home, shower, and eat a light meal.

In the evenings, children play in or near the house, read, do homework, and listen to the radio. Adults talk and listen to the radio. Children go to sleep at dark with little coaxing. Adults follow soon after. Adolescent males gather in public areas to play guitar, sing, and talk. They reportedly sneak around the valley, climb into girls' houses, or meet girls in prearranged places to have sex.

Expanding Social Worlds

Throughout childhood and young adulthood, Marquesans move outward into larger and larger social realms. Young infants spend most of the time in or near the house. Older infants are carried around the valley by adults and children. One-year-olds play in the yard with siblings and cousins, supervised periodically by adults. Two- and three-year-olds play away from the yard with their peer group, under the wing of an older sibling, but away from adult supervision. Four-year-olds play away from home most of the day.

School-aged children go to the valley school for three years, but then move to the main valley to attend boarding school. They live at the boarding school for five or more years in groups of fifty children with one adult supervisor. They return home only for summer and Christmas vacations.

Children are permitted to quit school at fourteen and many boys return to the home valley to live. Teens who want to continue school move to other islands to do so.

Young adults expand their social realms as far as Tahiti and even France (for some young men doing military service). As adults, however, many Marquesans choose to settle down in their home valley, to live among the relatives and friends they grew up with.

Marquesans are seen as mature when they can maintain their own households and govern their own lives while still living harmoniously within the community of associates. They have learned how to exercise autonomy within the obligations of these networks.

In this chapter I describe the transition of toddlers into their first nonfamily peer group. Many elements of this transition process will be repeated again and again for these children as they move from smaller to larger social realms.

PEER INTERACTIONS IN POLYNESIA

Hierarchical versus Egalitarian Relations

Polynesian children learn two sets of rules for interacting with others. One applies to hierarchical relationships—such as between parent and child—and the other applies to interactions among age-mates and status-equals (Boggs 1985; D'Amato 1986; Franco 1987; Howard 1970, 1974; Ritchie & Ritchie 1979).

In hierarchical relationships,

> the rules . . . require that individuals be restrained and compliant when dealing with persons of senior rank. . . . [The senior-ranking individual has the right] to initiate inter-action, to direct one's activities and to set the general tone for the relationship (Howard 1974, p. 206).

Relations among status-equals, on the other hand, are characterized both by reciprocity, "a continual willingness to share what one has with others," (Howard 1974, p. 206) and by status-rivalry.

Separation of the Generations

The hierarchical system leads to separation of the generations (D'Amato 1986). Adults come to interact mainly with other adults, children, with other children. In this system, for example, adults discourage children from talking back, including expressing their own views, so children turn to peers for self-expression (Boggs 1985).

Hawaiian parents discourage children from participating in adult conversations with rules such as "You need [to] shave [to] sit at this table" (D'Amato 1986). They also deal with their children as a group rather than as separate negotiators. They set clear guidelines for the sibling group and then hold all children responsible for the behavior of each. If one child disobeys, the whole group is punished—the one for misbehaving, the others for not controlling this child (D'Amato 1986).

Similarly, parents assign large jobs to the sibling group but then leave it to the children to decide how to perform the tasks. They do not insist that children organize or do the work in particular ways; rather, they judge the outcome. Siblings learn they are all in the same boat, and they develop strong bonds. Rivalry for parents' attention is ineffective and rarely occurs. (See Martini & Kirkpatrick [1992] for a discussion of similar processes among Marquesans.)

Stages of Social Learning

D'Amato (1986) describes stages of social learning for Hawaiian children. Other researchers confirm at least some of these stages for other Polynesians (Levy 1973; Martini & Kirkpatrick 1981, 1992; Ritchie & Ritchie 1979).

Appetite for social interaction. First, Polynesian infants develop an appetite for constant social interaction. Babies are the centers of attention of their families and tend to be totally indulged. Marquesan infants, for example, are rarely left alone to entertain themselves and are redirected to interact with others whenever they become too self-involved (Martini & Kirkpatrick 1981). Infants learn that life involves being with other people and that being alone is uncomfortable.

Self-reliance. Toddlers experience a shift from adult indulgence to adult intolerance. They learn that valued group members are self-reliant. Parents scold and punish them for dependent behavior but show pleasure when they "do for themselves." Toddlers learn to make their own snacks, dress themselves, and keep themselves out of danger. They also resolve their own peer conflicts. They learn that their personal plans, feelings, and interests are less important than adult and family plans and needs.

Emotional control. Preschoolers learn to control their emotional reactions to social frustration. They suffer a period of hazing in which they are criticized and attacked without provocation. They are provoked to anger and then punished for becoming angry.

Martini (1984a) notes that young Marquesan children, also, are criticized and attacked for making mistakes, being inattentive, endangering themselves, or showing less deference than expected. For example:

A plane flies overhead and children jump up and down, yelling "avion, avion." Stephanie (2 1/2) falls off a wall in the excitement. Children stop yelling and watch silently until Stephanie sits up and begins to cry. At this point they begin to point, laugh and chant "Ste-pha-nie! Ste-pha-nie!" Her older sister climbs down, yanks her to a standing position and slaps her. Her 4-year-old brother picks up a rock and threatens to heave it at her. She cries louder and tries to crouch. Her sister makes her stand and says, with disgust, "tuitui" ("[too much] noise"). She takes her home (Martini 1984a).

At other times, Marquesan children are attacked for becoming too attached to their personal projects or objects. For example:

Twenty young adolescents play soccer by the sea. A seven-year-old runs along the nearby road, flying a handmade kite. One fourteen-year-old stops playing, picks up a rock and throws it at the kite. Five others join him. They pelt the kite until it falls, then rip it apart and break the sticks. They laugh and return to playing soccer. The boy picks up the sticks and paper, crouches on the road, and cries.

On still other occasions, children are attacked without provocation, or serve as scapegoats for other children's status problems.

Martini (1984a) concludes that hazing:

1. causes children to attend vigilantly to the most dominant members of the group;
2. socializes children to be careful and competent (if somewhat cautious and conservative);
3. punishes children for breaking social rules; and,
4. teaches children that their own plans, projects, and products are less important than those of the group (see also Boggs 1985; D'Amato 1986).

Withstanding social frustrations to remain in the group. Through social criticism and hazing, children learn to depersonalize attacks and withstand the frustrations of social life. They learn to deal with social binds and to recognize that others experience these as well. They do not give in to the group, nor do they withdraw. Instead, they "deflect attacks with humor and mount their own playful attacks" (D'Amato 1986).

Early Peer Interactions

At three or four years, Polynesian children move out from the family group into the nonfamily peer group. Whereas sibling relations were organized around an age hierarchy, with younger deferring to older siblings, peer groups do not have a clear age hierarchy. Peer interactions involve status rivalry as children struggle for equality. Gradually, "children learn . . . how to treat one another as equals, something they do not learn in the hierarchical relationship among siblings at home" (Boggs 1985, p. 39).

Activities. Because Polynesian children are extremely sensitive to status, they avoid play that requires distinct leaders, being singled out from the group, or extensive negotiation of rules or roles (Martini 1977, 1984b; Ritchie & Ritchie 1979). They prefer activities that "do not require much coordination, influencing, or individual competition" (Boggs 1985, p. 40).

Organization by consensus. Children who are sensitive to relative status reject leaders or bosses who tell them what to do. A single boss who decides on activities, assigns roles, directs behavior, and enforces rules would threaten the fabric of status equality among age-mates. Instead, children organize themselves consensually. Each child voluntarily agrees to follow a suggested game, and the group activity crystallizes (Martini 1977, 1984b; Ritchie & Ritchie 1979).

Contributions of this Study

Status rivalry, hazing, peer reciprocity, and consensual group process have been repeatedly observed in Polynesian peer groups. In the current study I demonstrate how these processes work together to shape the dynamics of a group of young Marquesan children. I also show how these processes shape the messages about social life that children send to each other. In particular I show how hazing and social criticism, which, seem to destroy self-esteem, may actually build up resilient concepts of self in these Marquesan preschoolers.

METHODOLOGY

The thirteen children were observed in rotating order for ten-minute periods while the observer wrote stream-of-behavior records. Behavior records focused on children's interactive exchanges. For each exchange, the observer described:

1. what the focal child was doing;
2. who initiated the exchange;
3. who was involved in the exchange;
4. how the initiator initiated the exchange; and
5. how the other responded to this initiation.

Actions and language were described in as much detail as possible, given the field conditions. The observer lived in the household of one of the children and was familiar to all. Children became uninterested after about two weeks. Twelve hours of behavior records were coded and analyzed for this chapter.

Behavior records were formatted as lists of interactive exchanges involving the focal child. An exchange consisted of an initiation by one person and a response by another. Lists were made of the ways in which children initiated interactions and the ways in which they responded to other children's initiations. Categories were generated from these lists and tallies were made. The behavior records were coded and analyzed in terms of:

1. forms of play;
2. size of play groups;
3. who interacted with whom;
4. how children initiated interactions; and
5. how children responded to others' initiations.

FINDINGS: FEATURES OF PLAY

The Play Environment

In these observations, the children play in a large, diverse space. It covers about an acre and includes the rocky shore, a boat ramp, thatched boathouses, a dry-docked boat, several outrigger canoes, a stream, bridge, retaining walls, fences, rope swings, the valley walls, goats, pigs, a dog, and numerous trees.

Parents place few limits on children's play and children repeatedly violate the few rules they do set. Mothers worry that young children might drown, fall from trees, or damage property. They occasionally shoo children away from playing in the surf, on the boats, or near the church. But children filter back to these areas as soon as the mother leaves. When asked why she does not enforce the rules, one mother says, "What can you do? Children will do what they want anyway."

Adults worry that children will damage tools, such as machetes, and waste materials, such as matches, so they take these away from them and scold them. Parents say, however, that they are not worried that children might hurt themselves.

The children play with natural and discarded objects (mud, sticks, stones, plastic bottles, wheels, and batteries). Parents rarely buy toys for their children, in part because these are expensive, in part because toys that were bought in the past were quickly destroyed by playmates. Yet, young children rarely fashion toys out of available materials.

Autonomy of the Peer Group

Children have little contact with adults during the observed play. The group moves away from adults whenever they are near, probably because adults disrupt their play. During the twelve hours of play, a mother shooes the children away from the surf twice; a mother scolds them for playing too close to her house twice; a father scolds them for playing in the boats twice; and a bored adolescent heckles them once. Children do not go to adults for help in resolving conflicts or structuring play. They do not ask parents to provide food or objects or to comfort them when hurt.

Forms of Play

Thirty percent of the play episodes of this group consist of group object play, twenty-four percent consist of fantasy play, nineteen percent consist of fighting and negotiating, and eighteen percent consist of sitting and talking (table 5.1).

Object play. During group object play, each person performs the same actions at the same time. For example, everyone in

TABLE 5.1
How Marquesan versus American Children Spend Their Play Time

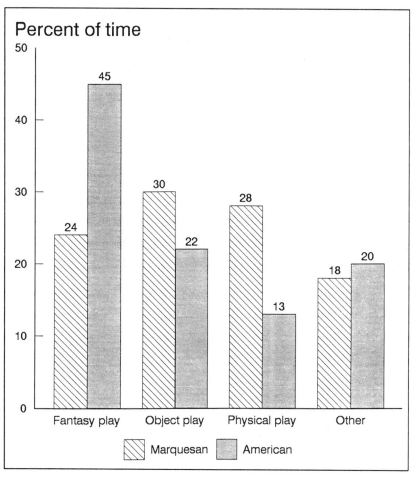

Source for American data is Segal et al. 1987, in which fantasy = fantasy play; constructive = object play; rough-and-tumble = physical play.

the group gathers lemons, picks up leaves, sorts and lines up rocks, smashes match heads, and pounds rocks together to make different sounds. Groups of children roll wheels down the boat ramp and throw stones for the dog to fetch. They dig in the dirt and plaster rocks with mud. They search for eels and insects, smash glass bottles, drop objects from the bridge, and throw rocks at cans. Because everyone performs the same actions at the same time, children do not need to negotiate game plans or assign roles. Like the Hawaiian children studied by Boggs (1985) and older Marquesan children observed by Martini (1977, 1984b), these children prefer activities that do not require extensive coordination or negotiation of rules.

Fantasy play. Garvey (1977) notes that in fantasy play children negotiate "two kinds of social constructs" or "socially shared views of the way life is."

> One is an action plan, a sort of blueprint for arranging actions and events into a coherent episode. The other is the role or identity assumed by the pretender (p. 80).

About half the fantasy play episodes in this sample (twelve percent of all play episodes) involve scripts and roles. The other half consists of isolated incidents of using objects symbolically, such as making mud bananas.

Scripted fantasy play in this sample includes "ship" play, "fishing," "hunting," and "preparing feasts." In ship play, children pretend to drive, dock, anchor, load, and unload the drydocked motor boat, as a copra ship. They also fix the motor, fight off invaders, and save drowning shipmates. Children pretend to launch and paddle the outrigger canoes and to fish and shoot goats from these. They pretend to hunt and kill the valley goats, pigs, and dogs. They also prepare and "eat" mud meals.

Children engage in fantasy play only occasionally, and they follow the same fantasy scripts from one performance to the next. Children may prefer simple scripts and unchanging roles because these do not require extensive one-to-one negotiations.

Fighting and negotiating. In nineteen percent of the play episodes children fight or negotiate with each other. They tease each other aggressively and engage in "status leveling" in which one child tries to "lower" another who has claimed dominance by trying to command, direct, or scold him. Older children also haze younger ones by attacking and disrupting them, without provocation, until they cry. In these fights, children throw lemons, stones, and mud at each other, usually missing. They chase each other with spears. They argue over food, and insult and exclude each other from play. They also organize "war games," (*keu tou'a*), with teams, rules and roles, but these are included in the category of organized games.

Typically, no one clearly wins or loses the status conflicts. Rather, children turn them into games or jokes, dissipating the group tension. Children do not ask adults to resolve conflicts, but sometimes tattle on each other in hopes the adult will scold the other.

Sitting, talking, and/or watching. In eighteen percent of the play episodes, children sit and talk. Typically, they comment on ongoing events that everyone can see: the arrival of a copra ship, fishermen landing their canoes, or adults loading copra into a whale boat. They also talk about past and future events they all know about—that their siblings will soon return from boarding school, that certain adolescents will go with the singing group to another island, or that a certain family will run a candy booth during the July festival.

Occasionally, a child high in the dominance hierarchy repeats a story s/he has heard, recounts a film s/he has seen, or talks about events that none of the other children have experienced. Talk that deviates from the observable here-and-now or the shared past is tolerated only from dominant children. When new or recent initiate members try to talk about events that are not already familiar to the others, they are silenced with shouts of *tivava* ("lies").

Physical play. In five percent of the play episodes, children engage in physical play. They run up and down the boat ramp, chasing the waves. They swing on rope swings, swim in the stream, and sway on the schoolyard fence. They run back and forth under the bridge, yelling to hear their echoes. They climb walls and jump to the ground. They run, gallop, and jump.

Organized games. Occasionally, children organize games with routines or rules (four percent of all episodes). *Keu tictoc* ("the tictoc game") is a chase game learned from older siblings in which captured children join hands and form a swinging line, resembling the hands of a clock. *Keu toua* consists of one team chasing the other with spears or other weapons. Children also sing, dance, and play group circle games.

Size of Play Groups

In contrast to the American sample of Segal et al. (1987), these Marquesan children almost never play alone (table 5.2). Very occasionally a child fails to follow the group as it moves to a new

TABLE 5.2
Size of Play Groups for Marquesan versus American Samples

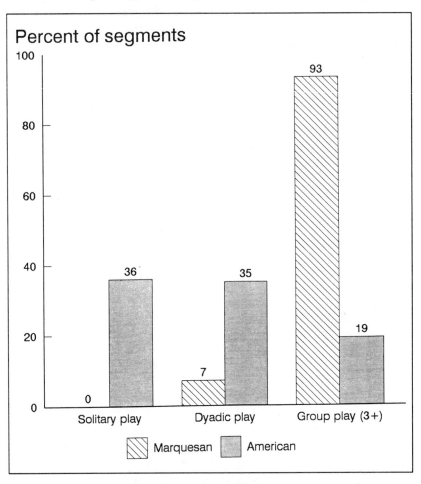

Source for American data is Segal et al. 1987. Percent of segments in which focal child is in groups of these sizes.

location, and plays by himself or herself for a short time. Dyadic play is also rare and often consists of an older and younger sibling taking time away from the group (only seven percent of the observed play groups consist of dyads). Children tend to play in groups of three to six children (seventy-five percent of the play groups). In eighteen percent of the behavior records, children play in large groups of seven to ten children.

Comparative Analysis

A brief comparison to American data highlights the significance of the above findings. American toddlers and preschoolers are almost always supervised by adults who set limits, direct activities, schedule eating and resting, comfort children, and resolve children's conflicts. American toddlers play in restricted, baby-proofed settings, are not exposed to dangerous objects or areas, and are not held responsible for younger siblings.

American preschoolers spend much of their play time in fantasy play (see table 5.1) (Garvey 1977; Segal, Peck, Vega-Lahr & Field 1987; Corsaro 1985). During pretend play they spend much time deciding on shared scripts, setting up the play environment, distributing roles and elaborating the expected course of events. Much of the fun of pretend play appears to be the process through which the players develop and elaborate a shared reality.

Because much of their play involves self-explanation, negotiation, and development of shared realities, American preschoolers tend to play in dyads, if not alone (see table 5.2). It is difficult to coordinate the plans of several children, distribute roles among many, and incorporate new children once play is set up, so American children avoid these problems by excluding other children (Corsaro 1985).

Also, the large group play of American preschoolers tends to be led by one or two dominant children who boss others around. Marquesan children are extremely sensitive to relative status and avoid play that requires bosses who set rules, decide on scripts, enforce rules and distribute roles. Marquesan groups crystallize, with followers joining the activity once dominant children have agreed on direction.

The children in the Marquesan group succeed in consensual coordination in part because (a) they engage in activities that are very familiar to all players, reducing the need for explanation and negotiation; (b) they play games the same way from one time to the next, with little elaboration of the scripts; and, (c) they engage in activities in which everyone performs the same actions at the same time, reducing the need for negotiation of specialized roles or leadership.

But how do the children organize themselves so efficiently? To answer this I analyze group dynamics.

FINDINGS: PEER DYNAMICS

Group Organization

The group. Children in the group come from ten different households and five different areas of the valley. Some children walk a quarter mile to play with these friends.

For most, participation in the group marks their first continuing peer relations outside the family. However, due to the small population of the valley, most children in the group are related. Ten of the fifteen children have a sibling in the group. Also, nine of the fifteen children have several first cousins in the group.

The composition of the group was relatively stable throughout the six months of observation, but it changes at the beginning and end of the school year. At the beginning of the year, the oldest members of the previous preschool group leave to go to school. At the end of the year, school-aged siblings begin to play in the area and the younger children often tag along with them rather than stay with their peers.

Toddlers join the group throughout the year, but there is a marked increase in toddlers after the festival period in July. During the festival period many families live by the play area and toddlers who normally stay home with their mothers are allowed to wander with siblings, since their mothers are nearby. The toddlers, mothers and siblings get used to them playing with the peer group and they continue to do so after the festival.

Group structure. Children occupy one of four roles or positions in this group. Each position is characterized by a particular set of behaviors. Children in each position interact with children in other positions in characteristic ways. The positions are:

1. the peripheral toddler position (children in this position are labeled "D children");
2. the initiate member position ("C children");
3. the quiet leader position ("B children") and;
4. the noisy leader position ("A children").

The positions form a Y-shaped dominance hierarchy as depicted in table 5.4, page 95.

The Roles

Peripheral toddlers. Children join the group at about two years of age, almost always under the wing of a three- or four-year old sibling. At first, they play on the periphery and watch the group intently. They are not encouraged to join group play, since they can not physically keep up. If they endanger themselves, get in the way, or demand too much attention, their siblings take them home.

Initiate members. Children remain peripheral to the group until they can keep up with the play. At that point they are obligated to participate. Older children disrupt them if they engage in self-contained play. Older children also tease them without provocation, in an apparent process of hazing. Children move up to the leadership roles when (a) they master emotional self-control in reacting to the hazing; (b) the oldest children in the group leave to attend school, creating a need and openings for leaders; and, (c) their own toddler siblings join the group. Children become either "quiet" or "noisy" leaders, depending on their personalities and probably a number of other factors.

Noisy leaders. Noisy leaders are the most vocal and active members of the group. They introduce many of the play ideas and persuade others to participate. Noisy leaders engage in constant status rivalry with other dominant members.

The noisy leaders are noted for their toughness. They-stand up to teasing by older children and even by adults. The noisy leaders of this group are considered to be particularly brash, rambunctious, and *va'avo.* They are seen as more likely than other children to claim superiority and to intrude on others' affairs without concern for social rules or the opinions of others.

These children tend to be youngest or special children (e.g., adopted) in their families. In three of the four cases, their parents are seen as having particularly forceful personalities. The noisy leaders in this group also have the fewest kin-connections in the group, so are relieved of caregiving duties.

Quiet leaders. Quiet leaders are high in the dominance hierarchy but are less vocal, bossy and self-promoting than the noisy leaders. They are seen as tough but nonintrusive. They often shame noisy leaders for being too bossy, aggressive, or impolite. They play on the edge of the group and unlike other members are not pressed to participate. In this position they innovate new forms of play. They have numerous younger cousins and siblings in the group, whom they carefully care for.

Group Process

Children in this group engage simultaneously in two kinds of group process: (1) they organize group activities and maintain group solidarity; and, (2) they fight for status within the group. To organize group activities, they persuade each other to act in particular ways and they use shame techniques to keep each other on track. To maintain group solidarity, they help and support each other.

The actions they perform to solidify the group also improve their status within the group. Children negotiate status by varying the intensity with which they try to persuade others, the intensity with which they try to shame others, and the intensity with which they resist or accept others' attempts to control them.

How Children Initiate Contact

Children initiate interactions in four main ways:

1. they try to persuade others to act in particular ways;
2. they try to prevent others from acting in particular ways;
3. they support others' activities by watching and joining in; and,
4. they help, comfort, and protect others.

The first two ways of initiating contact (persuading and limiting/shaming) consist of trying to control others. The second two ways (cooperating and helping) consist of trying to support others.

In coordinating group activities, some children perform social control actions that keep the group on track, while other children perform social cohesion actions that keep the members emotionally involved. Children in the four roles differ in terms of the extent to which they try to control vs. cooperate with others.

Social Control

Persuasion. Persuasion techniques range from strong to weak forms. Strong forms include forcing, commanding, or directing another to act in a particular way. Weak forms include inviting, suggesting, or requesting another to act in a particular way. The following examples range from strong to weak forms of persuasion:

1. Teri (A1) pushes Justin (A2) away from the steering wheel and takes over driving;
2. Atai (A3) commands Justin (A2) to bring him some lemons;
3. Teresi (A4) directs Teri (A1) to give candy to Justin (A2), Fere (B1) and Niki (C3) but not to Atai (A3);
4. Atai (A3) says he will give Sorike (B2) a potato chip if Sorike will show him his cut;
5. Fere (B1) yells "tictoc game" to suggest to the group to play that game;
6. Teri (A1) touches Atai (A3), jumps on deck and begins tying up ropes. Atai joins him and they pretend to dock the ship.

Shaming. Children use shaming techniques to stop others from acting in particular ways. Children shame others for endangering themselves, accidentally hurting others, making mistakes, going beyond the limits of acceptable social behavior, and for acting too bossy or self-centered. Shaming techniques range from strong to weak forms. Strong forms include hitting, shoving, or insulting a child for his or her actions. Weak forms include lecturing the child or showing disgust with the child's actions.

Sometimes older children attack initiate members, with no provocation. This appears to be part of a process of hazing the initiate members. The following examples range from strong to weak forms of shaming:

1. Atai (A3) hits Teri (A1) for hitting Justin (A2) too hard;
2. Tive (C1) threatens to throw a stone at Stephanie (D3) when she slips and falls off a wall;
3. Atai (A3) swears at Teva (C2) when he accidentally hits Tive (C1) with a stone;
4. Fere (B1) taunts that Atai (A3) is a coward for running away from older boys;
5. Four children chant "your pants are wet, your pants are wet" when Atai (A3) slips in the mud;
6. Teri (A1) lectures Atai (A3) and Teresi (A4) about not being careful when they accidentally hit Sorike (B2) with a rock; and
7. Atai (A3) scowls and says "oh-u" with disgust when Sorike (B2) accidentally splashes him while bailing a canoe.

Social Cohesion Actions

Social control is used to focus group members on a common goal or activity. Children remain in the group, however, because they feel included, liked, and supported, and because they like including and supporting others.

Following. Children actively support each other by watching, imitating, and joining each other's play. For example:

1. Maiore (D1) watches her brother, Tive (C1), and then joins his play;
2. Teva (C2) watches a group of leader children load the ship. He climbs on deck and begins playing the role of "deck hand";
3. Josephine (D2) watches the group move toward the school-yard. She stands up and follows.

Helping. Children actively help and comfort each other. They share food and objects, help each other carry out plans, stand by each other when teased, and greet and include each other in play. For example:

1. Justin (A2) tries to lift Maiore (D1) into the boat, when he sees she cannot reach;
2. Sorike (B2) puts his arm around Stephanie (D3) when she cries after falling down;
3. Tive (C1) shares his mud with Maiore (D1);
4. Sorike (B1) greets Joseph (C4) and invites him to come play; and
5. Tive (C1) stands by Maiore (D1) when Justin (A2) tries to persuade her to give him her mud.

How Children in the Different Roles Initiate Contact

Children in different roles initiate contact differently (table 5.3). Children at the top of the dominance hierarchy (A's and B's) try to control others more than do children at the bottom of the hierarchy. Children at the bottom of the hierarchy (C's and D's) support others more than do children at the top.

Noisy leaders. These children initiate most of their contacts (71.2%) by trying to control others. Of these, 41.6% consist of shaming others and 29.6% consist of trying to persuade others. Only 12.9% of their initiations consist of trying to help or support others.

TABLE 5.3
Extent to Which Marquesan Children in Different Roles
Control Others versus Cooperate with Others

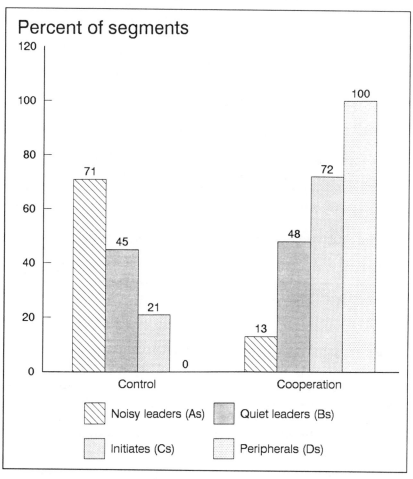

Control includes attempts to persuade others. Cooperates includes helping, watching, sharing and following.

Quiet leaders. These leaders present a more balanced profile. They initiate half their contacts by trying to control others, the other half, by supporting them. Of the control initiations, 33.9% consist of shaming others and 10.7% consist of trying to persuade others. Of the support initiations, 37.5% consist of watching and following, and 10.7% consist of helping.

Initiate members. Initiate members initiate most contacts (71.5%) by cooperating with other children. They watch, imitate, and join others' play 56% of the time and offer help 15.5% of the time.

Peripheral toddlers. Toddlers initiate all contacts by supporting others. They watch and join others' play 96.4% of the time and offer help 3.6% of the time.

In summary, as indicated in table 5.3:

1. Noisy leaders initiate most of their contacts (71.2%) by trying to control others and only a few contacts (12.9%) by trying to cooperate with others.
2. Quiet leaders, on the other hand, try equally to control and support others (44.6% and 48.2% respectively).
3. Initiate members, in contrast, initiate most contacts (71.5%) by supporting others, and only a few contacts by trying to control (20.7%).
4. Peripheral toddlers initiate virtually all contacts by cooperating with others.

As children move up the dominance hierarchy they shift from predominantly supportive to predominantly directive roles.

How Children Keep the Group on Track

To determine how children keep the group on track, I analyze who does what to whom. As indicated in table 5.4, noisy and quiet leaders (A and B children) perform most of the social control actions (trying to persuade or shame others). On the other hand, initiate and peripheral members (C and D children) perform most of the social cooperation actions (watching, imitating, following, and helping others).

Who persuades whom? Noisy leaders do most of the persuading in this group (76% of all observed instances of persuasion, correcting for unequal numbers of behavior records per child). Half the time they try to persuade each other, the other half, they try to persuade initiate members. Typically, they encourage others to follow them in play. First they try to secure the cooperation of other leaders. Once other leaders agree to play, most lower status children join in. Then noisy leaders encourage straggling initiates to join the play, to round out the group. In this way group activity is decided in consensus by the dominant children.

TABLE 5.4
Roles in the Marquesan Peer Group and Who Does What to Whom

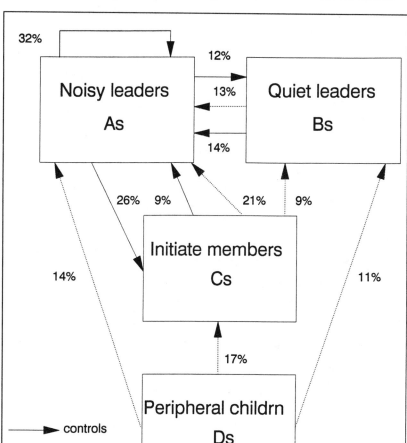

Who shames whom? Noisy leaders do most of the shaming (69% of all instances). They shame initiate members about half the time, and other noisy leaders somewhat less than that. They shame initiate members for not joining group play, for making mistakes, and for endangering themselves or others. Noisy leaders also attack initiate members without provocation, in an apparent process of hazing. For example:

1. Atai (A3) pulls on Teva's (C2) extended navel and laughs when he winces. Teva backs away, nervously.
2. Teresi (A4) grabs Teva's penis, shoves him backwards and tells him to go home, the same way one would tell a baby to go home to Mama. Teva looks away, nervously.
3. As Joseph (C4) approaches the group, Atai (A3) calls to Sorike (B2) to throw a stone at him. Joseph squats down and begins to cry. Sorike calls to him, in a comforting tone, to "come play."
4. Atai (A3) tells Tive (C1) to go away, claiming he stinks. Tive slinks away.

At times noisy leaders frustrate initiate members until they cry and then show them more appropriate ways to deal with frustration. They encourage the frustrated child to stand up and attend to the group. They show him how to make light of the attack. For example,

> During ship play, Justin (A2) and two other leaders pretend to load the ship. Rora (C5) plays nearby, washing down the deck. Justin (A2) runs up to him and knocks the container of water out of his hands. Rora angrily swings at him. Justin laughs and hits him hard. Rora squats and begins to cry. Justin pats him on the head, gently lifts him to a stand and gives him a can to load on the ship. Rora joins their play.

Noisy leaders shame each other for "putting on airs," for presuming superiority, and for going beyond the bounds of acceptable behavior. They scold and lecture each other for being too bossy, rough, stingy, or impolite. For example:

1. Atai (A3) and Teresi (A4) say "oh-u" and look disgusted when Justin (A2) hits Niki (C3) hard.
2. Teri (A1) scolds Atai (A3) when he refuses to share his candy.
3. Teri (A1) calls Teresi (A4) and Niki (C3) "dogs" when they mock the observer's English by talking with their noses plugged.
4. Atai (A3) gives Fere (B1) a lecture about cutting himself with a knife. He copies the adult lecture form: "Who told you to play with knives?"

Quiet leaders perform an additional 22% of the shaming attempts. Mainly, they scold noisy leaders for being too bossy, brash, stingy, or rough. In this way they protect the group against brazen, self-centered leadership. For example:

1. Fere (B1) scolds Atai (A3) for teasing children with his raisins. Atai had encouraged children to beg for these and when they did, threw the raisins on the ground. He then taunted them to eat them like dogs. Fere taunts Atai that a friend of Atai's father will beat him for stealing and giving away the family's raisins. Other children take up the taunt: "Damasi's going to beat you. Damasi's going to beat you." Atai begins to whine and cry.
2. Sorike (B2) scolds Atai (A3) and Teresi (A4) for "putting on airs," when they conspire about whom to give crackers to.
3. Fere (B1) scolds Teri (A1) for playing with the observer's clipboard.

The Function of Social Control

Children keep each other in line and socialize each other into following group norms by scolding each other for:

1. making mistakes;
2. endangering themselves or others;
3. not attending to the group process;
4. transgressing the bounds of acceptable behavior, e.g., by hurting a child through teasing;
5. being impolite to outsiders; and,
6. being too bossy, stingy or self-centered.

Social control techniques are used to steer group members in the same direction, to keep members from drifting off into self-centered play, and to keep members within acceptable bounds of comportment. The group uses sophisticated checks and balances. No one leader, for example, becomes the sole "boss" since noisy leaders compete for having their ideas followed. Consequently, the group follows first one then another leader. The quiet leaders keep the noisy leaders from becoming too aggressive.

How Children Hold the Group Together

The flip side of peer constraint in Polynesian groups is peer solidarity. Young children in this group solidify their ties by helping, comforting, and supporting each other.

Who helps whom? Initiate members and noisy leaders do most of the helping. Typically, children help others who are at or below their status level. Initiate members help each other and peripheral toddlers. Noisy leaders distribute help evenly among the lower three groups. Almost half the observed instances of helping are directed toward peripheral toddlers.

The initiate members stand by each other through the process of hazing. They do not fight each other's battles but they stay near a child being teased or frustrated. If the child cries they wait quietly and then re-engage him in play.

Initiate members take care of toddlers almost as much as the toddlers' siblings do. They share food with them, sit near them, groom them, look at their sores, and show affection.

Helping less skilled others is associated with maturity in the Marquesas. Children like to help others and gain status in doing so. Preschool children, for example, beg their mothers to bring the toddler sibling to play. Toddlers seem to realize that being helped lowers their status to dependent babies while it elevates the status of the helper to that of an autonomous caregiver. Sometimes they reject help.

Helping, sharing food, and comforting also provide a break from the tension of status rivalry. Children sometimes leave the group during conflicts in order to help their younger siblings. They sit and play with the toddler for a short while, until the group resolves the conflict, at which point they rejoin the group.

Who follows whom? Followers hold groups together by following the leaders. In this group younger children tend to watch and follow older ones (see table 5.4). Peripheral toddlers watch older children to imitate their actions and learn the activities. Initiate members watch noisy leaders to know what to do next and to avoid gratuitous attacks or hazing. Quiet leaders watch noisy leaders to know what to do next and to monitor their actions—correcting leaders who become too bossy or aggressive. Significantly, noisy leaders do the least watching in this group (7%).

SUMMARY

Children in this group play specialized roles to coordinate group activity. Noisy leaders introduce activities, direct group play, and keep players on track. Quiet leaders invent new play, monitor the bossiness of noisy leaders, and care for peripheral toddlers. Initiate members follow the leaders and support each other as they go through the process of hazing. They also care for peripheral toddlers and generally hold the group together from the inside. Peripheral toddlers are interested observers. Their incompetence highlights the skills of the older children. Older children gain status by helping and teaching dependent toddlers.

The children usually follow group norms about safety, sharing, conflict resolution, and emotional display. Children who go beyond the limits of appropriate behavior are shamed and chastised. This leads to children generally avoiding danger, caring for their own needs, settling disputes efficiently, and distributing goods fairly.

Children pass through peripheral, follower, and leader positions as they gain tenure in the group and as they acquire social skills. In each position, they learn crucial lessons about how to do the functions associated with that role and how to deal with others in the other positions. They learn how to be members of a group and about how to exercise autonomy within the tight group structure.

Comparative Analysis

Compared to Marquesan children, middle-class American children may suffer what Thomas (1979) calls a "cooperation deficit" (as cited in Ritchie & Ritchie 1979, p. 78). They may also develop a rigid conception of the self as solely a goal-oriented agent. This rigid sense of self may become stressed when a child is frustrated in reaching his or her goals as is often the case in complex social situations. In these cases, American children may retreat to carefully negotiated social contacts or to solitary play.

American children learn to value goal-directedness. They learn that a main goal in life is the achievement of individual potential (Bellah, Madsen, Sullivan, Swidler & Tipton 1985).

> The ideal is that each individual be able to develop his abilities to maximum potential. . . . Persons are supposed to set high but realistic standards for task performance and to feel a sense of self-gratification when achieving these goals. (Howard 1974, p. 212).

They see their own goals, plans, and interests as special and worthy of being protected.

Group life poses the problem of how to coordinate the goal-directedness of the many people in the group. Problems in American preschools center around clashes of wills and goals (see Reynolds 1990 for a review of these problems). Children want the same toy at the same time; they want to be in the same space at the same time; they hurt each other to reach their goals; they exclude each other to remain focused on their play (Corsaro 1985).

American preschool teachers and parents see their jobs as making sure each child has the opportunity to plan and implement plans. So adults monitor the peer group to make sure that it operates in a fair and just manner. They try to make sure no child's efforts are blocked unless these conflict directly with the efforts of another child. Adults help children take turns, share and alternate goal-directed behavior.

American parents and educators also teach children to resolve their own conflicts by negotiating interests (Fisher & Ury 1983; Gordon 1976; Poppin 1989; Reynolds 1990). Each person is to explain his or her own interests, listen to the interests of the other and then invent options to satisfy the needs of both. Giving up personal goals to comply with the group or to preserve a relationship is considered to be "soft bargaining" and is seen as counterproductive.

Because American children believe in the sacredness of the individual and of personal plans, they react strongly and self-righteously to any attacks on their ideas, interests, or property. They have been led to believe that social life should be fair and that the individual should be allowed to pursue his interests as long as these do not impinge on the interests of others. This is not the message received by the Marquesan boy who watched the adolescents destroy his proudly made kite.

American children invest enormous energy to maintain a fair world. They argue endlessly about who is at fault in a conflict. They appeal to adults to restore justice by judging who is right and wrong. They are more concerned with the principle of justice than with resolving the conflict or restoring the relationship. In fact, these children are seen as justified in bearing long-term grudges based on even minor injustices, since "it is the thought that counts."

American children's concern with the sanctity of self makes them vulnerable to the vagaries of social life. The everyday social hazing that Marquesan four-year-olds learn to handle with poise and humor would devastate most American preschoolers and would be considered emotional abuse by our courts.

The Marquesan children learn not to take these events personally and not to assume that others' attacks are aimed directly against their persons. They learn to define their selves as something more stable than their (frustrated) plans of the moment and as something more worthy than how they are portrayed by their tormenters.

In this sense, although Marquesan children attend and respond extensively to the group, they seem less vulnerable to the inevitable disappointments of social life. In the end they may be less affected by shame and group opinion than are their American counterparts.

Marquesans view mature adults not as those who give up personal goals and the valued goal-direction process to conform to the group, but rather those who coordinate their own goals with those of the group. The valued person knows a lot about the group and shapes personal goals around this information. Ritchie & Ritchie (1979) note for Maoris:

> For individuals, the trick is to enhance their status vis-a-vis others (for example by sensing the disposition of the group and making appropriate suggestions) in the context of arriving at a consensus (p. 106).

Highly valued children in this group, and the most popular children in a group of Hawaiian preschoolers (Martini 1991), are both highly imaginative and goal-directed and highly responsive to the group.

REFERENCES

Asher, S. & Gottman, J. (1981). *The development of children's friendships*. Cambridge: Cambridge University Press.

Bellah, R., Madsen, R., Sullivan, W., Swidler, A. & Tipton, S. (1985). *Habits of the heart: Individualism and commitment in American life*. Berkeley: University of California Press.

Boggs, S. (with the assistance of K. Watson-Gegeo & G. McMillen) (1985). *Speaking, relating and learning: A study of Hawaiian children at home and at school*. Norwood, N.J.: Ablex Publishing Corp.

Corsaro, W. (1985). *Friendship and peer culture in the early years.* Norwood, N.J.: Ablex.

D'Amato, J. (November 1984). Doorways: Coping with interactional facts of life. Paper presented at the Annual Meeting of the American Anthropological Association, Washington, D.C.

D'Amato, J. (1986). "We cool, tha's why": A study of personahood and place in a class of Hawaiian second graders. Unpublished Ph.D. dissertation, University of Hawaii at Manoa, Honolulu, HI.

Fisher, R. & Ury, W. (1983). *Getting to yes: Negotiating agreement without giving in.* New York: Penguin Books.

Franco, R. (1987). *Samoans in Hawaii: A demographic profile.* Honolulu, HI: East-West Population Institute.

Garvey, C. (1977). *Play.* Cambridge, MA: Harvard University Press.

Gordon, R. (1976). *Parent effectiveness training in action.* Toronto: Bantam Books.

Howard, A. (1970). *Learning to be Rotuman: Enculturation in the South Pacific.* New York: Teachers College Press.

Howard, A. (1974). *Ain't no big thing: Coping strategies in a Hawaiian-American community.* Honolulu: University of Hawaii Press.

Kirkpatrick, J. (1983). *The Marquesan notion of the person.* Ann Arbor, Michigan: UMI Research Press.

Kirkpatrick, J. (1985). How personal differences can make a difference. In K. Gergen and K. Davis. (Eds.), *The social construction of the person.* New York: Springer.

Martini, M. (April 1977). Patterns of social interaction among Marquesan children. Unpublished manuscript.

Martini, M. (March 1984a). Gentleness and violence among Marquesans. Paper presented at the annual meeting of the Association for Social Anthropology in Oceania, Molokai, HI.

Martini, M. (November 1984b). Peer dynamics among Marquesan school-aged children. Paper presented at the Annual Meeting of the American Anthropological Association, Washington, D.C.

Martini, M. (January 1991). Succeeding among peers vs. succeeding at school: Decisions made by young Hawaiian children. Paper presented at the annual meeting of the Hawaii Educational Research Association, Honolulu.

Martini, M. & Kirkpatrick, J. (1981). Early interactions in the Marquesas Islands. In T. Field, A. Sostek, P. Vietze & P. Leiderman, (Eds.), *Culture and early interactions*. Hillsdale, N.J.: Lawrence Erlbaum.

Martini, M. & Kirkpatrick, J. (1992). Parenting in Polynesia: A view from the Marquesas Islands. In J. L. Roopnarine & D. Carter (Eds.), *Parent-child relations in diverse cultures*. Norwood, N.J.: Ablex Press.

Poppin, M. (1989). *Active parenting* (audiocassette program). Nightingale-Conant Corporation.

Reynolds, E. (1990). *Guiding young children: A child-centered approach*. Mountain View, CA: Mayfield Publishing Co.

Ritchie, J. & Ritchie, J. (1979). *Growing up in Polynesia*. Sydney: George Allen & Unwin.

Segal, M., Peck, J., Vega-Lahr, N. & Field, T. (1987). A medieval kingdom: Leader-follower styles of preschool play. *Journal of Applied Developmental Psychology, 8,* 79-95.

Weisner, T., Gallimore, R., and Jordan, C. (1988). Unpackaging cultural effects on classroom learning: Hawaiian peer assistance and child-generated activity. *Anthropology and Education Quarterly, 19,* (4), 327-354.

LOURDES DIAZ SOTO
LILLIAN NEGRON

6

Mainland Puerto Rican Children

Puertorriquenos or *Boricuas* originated from the Caribbean island of Puerto Rico, settled by the Spanish in the late 1500s. Spanish settlers arrived in Puerto Rico prior to the Pilgrims landing on Plymouth Rock. In their quest for gold, the Spaniards virtually destroyed the native Indian population; disease, conflict, and overwork took a toll on the native Indians. Later, African slaves were imported by the Spaniards to work in the gold mines and the sugar cane fields. The island was eventually ceded to the United States in peace treaties. The Puerto Rican people and their accompanying languages and cultural practices were involuntarily incorporated into the larger American society in a manner similar to what occurred to Mexican American, native American and African American citizens.

Puerto Ricans were granted official citizenship in 1917 as a result of the Jones Act. Dramatic changes in Puerto Rico's economy took place between the 1940s and 1960s as a result of Governor Munoz Marin's leadership in a collaborative venture with the mainland entitled "Operation Bootstrap." The drafters of this venture had not anticipated that United States interests would leave the island when cheaper labor was available elsewhere or when tax incentives expired. The mainland's economy continues to affect island employment, tourism, industrial growth, and debt.

Citizenship affords islanders the opportunity to migrate to the mainland. Cycles of migration have included professionals, yet most migrants are laborers employed as farm workers, factory workers, or in menial jobs. Puerto Rican children are among the most seriously disadvantaged population in the United States today (Santiestevan & Santiestevan 1984). Puerto Rican children in fifty states and the District of Columbia have the highest poverty rates of any other race or ethnic group (Miranda 1991).

Data from the United States Census Bureau (1991) paint a grim picture of a people who originated from a rich cultural and linguistic heritage, have experienced colonization, tended farm lands, labored in factories, and participated in a variety of professional endeavors. The educational gap between Hispanics and non-Hispanics continues to be wide. In Valdivieso's (1986) words in a piece entitled, *Must they wait another generation?*, this sentiment was echoed:"A shocking proportion of this generation of Hispanic young people is being wasted because their educational needs are neither understood nor met, their aspirations are unrecognized, their promising potential is stunted" (p. 1).

FAMILY CHARACTERISTICS

Puerto Ricans make up 11.1% of the total 21.4 million Hispanic population (U.S. Census 1991). The United States Department of Commerce characterizes Latinos as younger and as family households (80%) more than non-Latinos (70%). In spite of the fact that Latino families are playing by the rules since Latino males have the highest job participation rates (78%) in our nation (U.S. Census 1991), one in three Latino children are poor and one in two Puerto Rican children are poor. Puerto Rican children constitute the poorest children of any racial/ethnic group in this country (57%) with heads of households overrepresented in economic vulnerability.

My (L. Soto) extended family, like many other Puerto Ricans, migrated to the mainland prior to World War II. They settled in New York as factory workers and participated as soldiers in the war. Today, there are sizable Puerto Rican populations in New York, Illinois, Florida, and New Jersey (Duany & Pittman 1990).

Despite the many challenges, Puerto Rican families continue to act as role models for our society by providing a caring curriculum of community-centered life, extended family support networks, and respect for the inner worth of human beings. Yet an ERIC search conducted in 1992 (152 citations) indicates that Puerto Ricans continue to be portrayed in a deficit manner as having mental health problems, special educational needs, being unable to adjust to society, and lacking Eurocentric values. The lack of insight into the Puerto Rican experience indicates a need to explore the strengths of this culture (Soto 1992a), its childrearing and family socialization patterns, issues of language maintenance (Soto and Smrekar 1992), generational cohorts, and societal assimilation.

At the heart of the issue is that most studies are conducted from the perspective of the American majority culture, including some of our own work, since we too have been affected by prevailing educational research methods and perspectives. Puerto Rican children are socialized within families who continue to address a variety of issues including socioeconomic status, educational attainment, power and influence, limited assimilation, selective retention of ethnic cultural values and beliefs, native language loss, mainland societal discrimination, and cyclical migration. Researchers unable to gain insight into the complex issues faced by Puerto Rican children and their daily life experiences will continue to portray a whole group of children in a deficit manner.

PUERTO RICAN CHILDREN'S PLAY

In the next few sections of this chapter, we describe existing empirical research on Puerto Rican children's play, contemporary views of play by a group of mainland (migrant and nonmigrant) Puerto Rican parents, the play activities of their primary school-aged children, and how play relates to issues that pertain to early childhood education. It is our feeling that play researchers need to experiment with assessments and observations of children, parents, and teachers if they are to gain more complete insights about culturally and linguistically diverse populations. Moreover, alternative research paradigms are necessary to more accurately study diverse ethnic groups.

The extant literature on play and culture point to possible cultural continuities and discontinuities in early parent-child and peer group socialization (Slaughter & Dombrowski 1989). The culturally continuous contexts studies include families who have resided for at least two generations within the United States while the culturally discontinuous studies include immigrant, refugee, or migrant children whose families have resided less than one generation within the United States and whose families are not yet enmeshed or embedded in the newly adoptive culture. Slaughter and Dombrowski (1989) note that: "Much research is needed into the play behaviors of American minority (and majority) children from the perspective of their cultural identities" (p. 302). The idea proposed aligns with the notion that since culture may influence behavioral competence and performance differently, research needs to consider the participant's cultural point of view.

We feel that research studies comparing and contrasting Puerto Rican children's play behaviors to those of children in the majority culture or in diverse ethnic groups run the risk of disseminating value judgments. Inevitably, a deficit interpretation will be afforded to one group when another group is used as the yardstick comparison. The assumption in such studies is that one group serves as the norm (usually the majority culture). Udwin and Schmukler (1981) issue a stern warning to researchers regarding the tendency to generalize from white middle-class (American) samples to samples in other cultural or ethnic groups, particularly on issues of play and culture. Within-group comparisons appear more appropriate and should shed more light on children's play; between-group comparisons require more careful culturally relevant interpretations.

Most of the studies that have attempted to describe Puerto Rican children's play have employed a between-group comparison design. For example, a small-scale investigation of the spontaneous free play behaviors of twenty Puerto Rican and twenty Anglo five-year-old children from middle-class socioeconomic backgrounds was conducted, using a topology of either simple/functional, fantasy, or reality-oriented, and suggested a developmental play hierarchy (Yawkey & Alvarez-Dominguez 1984). This study revealed that: (a) Puerto Rican girls had significantly higher reality-oriented play scores than Anglo girls; (b) Puerto Rican boys had significantly higher simple play scores than Anglo boys; and (c) Anglo boys had significantly greater fantasy play scores than Puerto Rican boys.

In an attempt to determine if there were common activity preferences among Hispanic children, Cintron de Esteves and Spicola (1982) interviewed 225 Mexican American, 23 Puerto Rican, 20 Cuban, and 17 Venezuelan children. The children were found to differ in the way they prefer to engage in quiet games. Eighty-eight percent of the children interviewed preferred to engage in activities that require more energy and movement. However, most of the children indicated a preference for playing outside, in activities such as running, riding tricycles, playing with balls, cars, and other toys. There was also a heavy use of television (twenty-five hours per week) for recreational and educational purposes (Citron de Esteves & Spicola 1982).

In another study (Trostle 1988) that employed play therapy interactions among four- and five-year-old Puerto Rican mainland children, it was found that children receiving group play sessions outperformed control groups on self-control and free play rating scales with boys outscoring all children on a sociometric measure.

We found no previous research documenting Puerto Rican parents' attitudes about play. Evidence exists, however, that children's play behaviors can be limited, enhanced, or facilitated by the significant adults in their lives (Johnson, Christie, & Yawkey 1987). This chapter will not attempt to review the literature on play behaviors and adult roles. We would like to highlight, however, that:

(a) Values and beliefs, as well as cognitive attributes of parents, may enhance children's play and creative potential (Bishop & Chase 1971);
(b) There is a relationship between parental and teacher attitudes toward play and learning (Johnson 1986);
(c) The culture plays a significant role in influencing how parents and teachers view the effect of play on children's development (Bloch & Wichaidit 1986); and,
(d) Socioeconomic variables influence the level of imaginative play (see Udwin & Schmuckler 1981 for a discussion of Israeli and African preschool children).

Research has shown that within a variety of cultural contexts significant adults can mediate and impact the participatory play activities of young children. Significant adults can facilitate, organize, and have ultimate control of much of the daily experiences provided for young children. Johnson (1986) notes that "adult groups within a society have different access to mainstream ideological beliefs, values, and attitudes concerning play and development in children" (p. 99).

Country Town and Steel Town

In this study we present data on Puerto Rican migrant and nonmigrant families' attitudes about play. This was done to avoid yardstick comparisons and to highlight within-group differences in perceptions. Additionally, we observed children in differing contexts at home and at school, in order to compare and contrast opportunities for play offered in these two settings. We chose prevailing methods and instruments that have been found to be reliable and valid by play researchers (Howes 1980; Johnson 1983, 1986); an observational checklist was designed to view congruence among parental attitudes about play and actual child play behaviors. Although our quantitative approach was successful in documenting play, we see the need to propose alternate research paradigms in order to gain additional insights into Puerto Rican children's play practices.

Our study focused on twenty migrant and twenty nonmigrant families. Both home visits and school observations were conducted. Parent interviews and child observations were conducted at home. A comparison of play in the different contexts (home and school) was not possible because we found that young Puerto Rican children were not provided opportunities for play at school. Ten visits to the school sites during the spring semester by graduate bilingual teachers revealed that classroom activities were highly structured without opportunities for play, including playground time. The home became the sole site for data collection and provided data which, to the best of our knowledge, have not been reported elsewhere.

The migrant families (N = 20 dyads) reside in "Country Town," an urban east-central area of Pennsylvania and are recent arrivals (five years or less) to the mainland. Country Town is comprised of diverse city dwellings such as apartments, row homes, a historical area, and spacious suburban areas. All of the families we visited lived in either apartments or rented row homes. The neighborhood was mostly Latino with nearby schools, *bodegas* or grocery stores, with access to health care and shops in the historical section of town. The larger suburban food chain stores were not accessible to the families. The fruit and vegetable markets with a variety of Amish goods were interesting to the families but not frequented by them. Most of the families shopped at the ethnic food stores or shops that were within walking distance.

The migrant families created an extended family situation for themselves as a result of collaborative efforts provided by the Migrant Education office. Families relay information to each other about health services, educational opportunities, and social events. These families were closely knit in a manner that simulated the traditional extended family system on the island.

Sixteen of the mothers maintained housewife roles in spite of economic sacrifices because of a desire for family stability. The seasonal nature of the migrant life was relegated largely to the fathers who traveled from farm to orchard or to factories in search of employment. The labor and economic needs of the families dictated their length of residency in any one area. At the time of our visits, the parents noted their occupations as follows: among mothers, there were sixteen housewives, two laborers, two secretaries; among fathers, there were three laborers, one community worker, one disabled individual, and six unemployed individuals. Eleven families were intact, while nine were single, female-headed households.

The nonmigrant families (N = 20 dyads) reside in "Steel Town," an urban eastern Pennsylvania setting. The nonmigrant families lived in a community which may be considered more stable in terms of length of residency. All of the children were born in Steel Town. Their parents were originally recruited as workers for the steel industry.

Steel Town is an ethnically and linguistically diverse setting affected by the virtual shutdown of the steel industry. All of the families we visited lived in a housing project and most of the fathers (N = 18) were unemployed. We did not find the cohesive and supportive capabilities among these families that we found among those who lived in Country Town. Though their proximity to the elementary school seemed to provide a link among the families, there was a feeling of isolation and segregation so that in spite of the community's attempt to increase economic advantages, these families were not benefiting from economic prosperity. The families described their occupations as follows: among the mothers, there were twenty housewives; among the fathers, there were two laborers and eighteen unemployed individuals. Ten families were intact and ten families were single female-headed households. These were poor families whose daily existence is based upon meeting basic needs of food, shelter, and health.

The home interviews were conducted in an individualized face-to-face manner with the assistance of graduate bilingual teachers participating in a teacher education program. The teacher trainees who visited the forty Puerto Rican families were of Puerto Rican heritage themselves. All expressed ethical dilemmas during their field experiences. First-year trainees expressed an initial concern about the delineation of parent roles and teacher roles. How involved should early childhood educators be in the personal lives of families? Should information be imparted or should collaboration be the norm? Is parent education of Hispanic or other minority families necessarily assuming a deficit stance when educators are the experts and parents are the learners?

For the purposes of this study, the parent interviews consisted of The Play Attitudes questionnaire (PA) (Johnson 1982); Attitudes about School and Play questionnaire (TAASP) (Johnson 1982); and four additional descriptive questions. Photographs were obtained of individual children's play space and play areas.

The instruments used to observe children's play behaviors were the Howes' (1980) Peer Play Scale (PPS) and an observational checklist designed as a companion to the parental attitudes about play scales (PA and TAASP). The observational checklist was constructed using the categories and items found in the PA and TAASP questionnaires. The following information describes the instruments contributing quantifiable information:

1. *Play Attitudes questionnaire (PA).* This instrument assesses attitudes about different types of play activities for young children (Johnson 1986). From a pair of play activities, parents select the one they believe to be the most important for young children. It consists of twenty items divided among five categories. The categories are convergent play, divergent play, physical play, game play, and expressive play.
2. *The Attitudes about School and Play questionnaire (TAASP).* This questionnaire assesses general attitudes about school

and play activities for preschool children. It consists of eighteen paired comparisons among twelve items, with three items each for four categories: content skills, process learning, convergent play, and divergent play (Johnson 1986). Mothers select the item that they believe is most important for their child.

3. *Howes' Peer Play Scale* (Howes 1980). This instrument examines children's social play behaviors. It is divided into five categories: simple parallel, parallel play with mutual regard, simple social play, complementary/reciprocal play with mutual awareness, and complementary/reciprocal social play. The observer needs to record the appropriate play behavior in a fifteen-second time sampling procedure.

4. *Combined PA-TAASP checklist*. This instrument was adapted by Soto, Negron and Moreno (1991) from the Play Attitudes questionnaire and the Attitudes about School and Play. It includes twenty-three play behaviors divided into seven categories: convergent play, divergent play, physical play, game play, expressive play, content skills, and process learning. Children's play behaviors were observed and recorded with a fifteen-second time sampling procedure. The intent is to compare and relate children's actual play behaviors and mothers' attitude toward play. This instrument was used along with four additional questions regarding children's play. These questions were: (a) what is your child's favorite toy?; (b) list five toys present in your home; (c) describe the space where your child plays; and, (d) indicate how often your child plays with friends.

Tables 6.1 to 6.4 summarize the quantifiable data and the comparisons among the migrant and nonmigrant families.

The mean rankings for the PA questionnaire (table 6.1) for both migrants and nonmigrants indicate a preference for convergent play while the mean rankings obtained with the TAASP questionnaire (table 6.2), indicate a preference for convergent play by migrant families and a preference for content skills by nonmigrant families.

The observations of children's play behaviors obtained with the Howes' Peer Play Scale indicate a variety of activities. Almost half (N = 9) of the nonmigrant children were engaged in television viewing, while four of the migrant children chose this activity. Repeated home visits indicated that the children participated in

TABLE 6.1
Mean Scores on Play Attitudes Questionnaire (PA)

Categories and Items	Means	
	Migrants	*Nonmigrants*
1. Convergent Play	5.50	5.05
(a) Making something from different materials	2.65	2.75
(b) Building something with table blocks	2.85	2.30
2. Divergent Play	3.20	3.10
(a) Make-believe with small people/animals	1.65	1.55
(b) Pretending to be a favorite character	1.55	1.55
3. Game Play	2.70	3.85
(a) Playing a board game like "Candyland"	0.80	1.65
(b) Playing a paper and pencil game like connect the dots	2.70	3.85
4. Physical Play	4.35	4.35
(a) Climbing and exercising	2.45	2.45
(b) Balance and coordination activities	1.90	1.90
5. Expressive Play	4.25	4.35
(a) Singing children's songs	2.35	2.05
(b) Dancing and movement expression	1.90	1.60

television viewing consistently for recreational purposes. This finding is congruent with that of Cintron de Esteves and Spicola (1982) who also found heavy television viewing among the children in their study (twenty-five hours per week). We did not clock the number of hours but noted that children would view television at the same time they were snacking or eating a meal. It appeared to us that the nonmigrant children, who have resided longer on the mainland, relied on television viewing to a greater extent. The role of television viewing in the lives of culturally and linguistically diverse Puerto Rican children may be an area of interest for future research.

The migrant, more recent arriving children, appear to participate in a more diverse set of activities and interact with multiple materials. The children's rooms, indoor play spaces, and outdoor play areas also appeared more elaborate to the observers. The parents and children were engaged in more activities together. In the migrant homes, there were higher levels of

TABLE 6.2
Mean Scores on Attitude About School
and Play Questionnaire (TASSP)

Categories and Items	Means	
	Migrants	Nonmigrants
1. Content Skills	5.55	5.80
(a) Counting out different numbers of objects	1.70	1.75
(b) Learning the sounds of the letters (alphabet)	1.85	1.80
(c) Learning color and shape names	2.00	2.25
2. Process Learning	2.75	3.40
(a) Figuring out how something is wrong	0.55	1.20
(b) Thinking about how two objects are alike	0.90	1.05
(c) Planning what to do next	1.00	1.15
3. Convergent Play	6.00	5.40
(a) Painting a picture of something	1.90	2.05
(b) Forming clay into different objects	2.00	1.85
(c) Making something with blocks	2.10	1.50
4. Divergent Play	3.70	3.40
(a) Make-believe using puppets	1.40	1.05
(b) Pretending with dress-up clothes	1.30	1.15
(c) Imagining with miniature toys	1.00	1.20

family involvement, parental aspirations, and concern for the use of language (Soto 1990a).

When the mean rankings (table 6.1) for both mothers and children are compared it can be seen that there is no apparent match between the mothers' responses and their children's actual play behaviors. For instance, using the PA questionnaire the migrant mothers indicated a preference for convergent play, followed by a physical play, expressive play, divergent play, and game play. By contrast, the means obtained through observations of children's play behaviors indicated a preference for physical play as a first choice, followed by game play, divergent play, and convergent play. *Expressive play was not observed during any of our visits.* In the nonmigrant home, it was found that children also engaged in physical play more than any other kind of play behavior with convergent play as a secondary choice,

TABLE 6.3
Migrants/Nonmigrants

Howes Peer Play Scale

Migrants	*Nonmigrants*
A. 7 children were playing alone	A. 6 children were playing alone
a. 1 was playing video	a. 2 children were riding bicycles
b. 2 were engaged in gross motor activities	b. 1 was playing with miniature toys
c. 2 were playing with miniature toys	c. 1 was playing with a doll
d. 2 were coloring	d. 1 was playing with pieces of paper
	e. 1 was playing with video games
B. 9 children were playing with one or more playmates	B. 14 children were angaged in a variety of activities
a. 2 girls were playing with dolls	a. 9 children were watching TV
b. 1 was roller skating	b. 2 "hosting" visitors
c. 3 were climbing and running	c. 2 children were completing their homework
d. 1 boy was playing with water in an outdoor setting	d. 1 was talking with playmates
e. 2 children were playing with video games	
C. 4 children were watching television	

and divergent, game play, and expressive play were not evidenced during home visits.

When asked what their favorite toys were, the following responses were obtained in the migrant homes: two children preferred roller skates, two, bicycles, one, a car, five, dolls, one, a book, one, a stuffed animal, three, home video games, two, balls, one, "My Little Pony," one, a model, one, a water-related toy. The nonmigrant responses include: four, bicycles, four, cars/trucks, one, a ball, one, a robot, one, Legos, six, Barbie dolls, one, a stuffed animal, one, a toy telephone, one, a home video game. A total of four migrant children preferred large motor activities while eight nonmigrant children indicated such a preference.

TABLE 6.4
Play Attitude and Behavioral Observational Checklist (PA-BOC)

Part A: PA	Migrants %	Nonmigrants %
1. Convergent play	8.3	28.09
2. Divergent play	17.8	13.48
3. Game play	29.9	5.60
4. Physical play	44.0	52.81
5. Expressive play	0	0
6. Content skill	4.6	13.95
7. Process learning	25.1	37.21
8. Convergent play	30.86	1.16
9. Divergent play	39.43	47.67

(Soto, Negron, Moreno, 1990)

The degree to which the families were impacted by the media juxtaposed against their own resources must be viewed in terms of parental beliefs and practices. Puerto Rican parents often sacrifice their own needs based upon child-centered beliefs and what some may consider doting behaviors toward young children. The Puerto Rican childrearing experience often incorporates the need to provide children's expressed material desires even when these are beyond the parental economic capacity. Because the children who view television to such an extent are also impacted by advertising commercials, it may be that families would appreciate ideas and suggestions about simple, handmade toys, and information about the creative aspects of sociodramatic play to offset aggressive marketing campaigns and mass-produced toys that can influence the degree of playfulness or imagination children exhibit (Aguilar 1985).

When parents were asked what was the preferred play space most parents responded by describing the living room. The living room was described as the safe haven for children and at the same time it was convenient for parental supervision. Parents expressed a concern for the lack of parks, playgrounds, and safe places for children to play in both communities. Nevertheless, parents indicated that their children had the opportunity to play with friends almost every day. Playing with friends was encouraged by many parents because it was better to allow children to play in a friend's home than to play in unsafe spaces. The literature (Harter 1989; Kritchevsky, Prescott & Walling 1987; Myers 1985; Phyfe Perkins 1980) reviewing the use of physical space and materials earmarked for play indicates that children can benefit from their environment. The parents we visited described a protective stance toward their young children resulting from fears regarding what "could happen" to children. The observers expressed concern about the amount of television viewing young children were engaged in, as well as the lack of potential play spaces. Most of the play materials (if not all) were commercially produced objects with a mix of toys for large motor and small motor activities. Outdoor play spaces were seldom used due to parental concerns about safety. These families lived in urban neighborhoods that motivated parents to protect youngsters from "societal ills" (e.g., drugs and crime). How much of the parental protectiveness is a result of real or perceived danger and how much is a cultural component is an intriguing issue for additional research and discussion.

DISCUSSION

This initial study highlights the fact that we know very little about the cultural continuities and discontinuities of Puerto Rican children's play. In our visits to homes of migrant, more recent arriving, and nonmigrant, longer mainland residents, we found somewhat elaborate provisions and opportunities for migrant children to play in the home. Differences among parental beliefs about play and the accompanying provisions for play were also noted. The daily experiences of the children differed in Country Town and Steel Town, with the latter residing exclusively in a segregated housing project and the former in rented apartments or rented row houses. The migrant families initiated a cohesive family network system. The nonmigrant families appeared somewhat isolated, in spite of the confines of a close-quartered housing project community.

In many ways the topic of "play" in our study may have served as a social bridge, facilitating communication between teachers (observers) and parents (Johnson 1992). The common interest in and around the language of play became a non-threatening topic and a common ground for establishing rapport and initiating discussions with parents. Even though there may be differing views among the participants, play became an area for reaching consensus on behalf of young children. Parents were keenly interested in the role of play in the lives of young children when discussing mainstream play research studies. We feel that additional insights and research are warranted in this area as a way of working collaboratively with parents in a manner that models mutual respect.

Our collaborative stance served our own search for a research agenda emanating from a nondeficit philosophy. We realize that this is an ongoing struggle between (a) proponents of interventions on behalf of young children as exemplified by a "family inadequacy model"; and (b) the need to consider the strengths and cultural practices of Puerto Rican children. We feel strongly that until genuine and authentic collaborative, mutual respect models are implemented, educators and researchers will find it difficult to relate to and be able to interact in a meaningful manner with families of culturally and linguistically diverse young learners.

The Bush administration proposed in its "America 2000" plan that "All children will be ready for school." It may be that schools need to be prepared to receive our young children from diverse backgrounds and that schools need to generate connections with families in a facilitative, collaborative, and culturally appropriate manner. The "lived" and unique experiences of young Puerto Rican children on the mainland need to be understood by educators, practitioners, administrators, and researchers. The successful and caring curriculum modeled by Puerto Rican families can be celebrated and applauded in light of current societal concerns.

An important issue that needs to be pursued is why young children were not playing in schools. What curricular evolutions are so vital that play has been deleted from both the indoor early childhood classroom and the outdoor traditional recess? Are such school practices the norm and are these practices developmentally appropriate? Janice Jipson (1991) raises questions about the ability of developmentally appropriate practice to respond to cultural diversity. Jipson asks: "Whose experiences are represented?" and "Whose ways of knowing are validated?"

The voices of Puerto Rican children and their families need to be represented within the early education developmentally appropriate framework, particularly in the cultural and linguistic domains. Caretaking practices capable of enhancing and retaining languages and cultures can benefit family stability and long-term societal interests.

What types of initiatives do we envision based upon our experiences with Puerto Rican children and their families?

(a) We have documented the need to improve our knowledge base in the field and recommend experimentation with alternative research paradigms. Patti Lather's (1986) model of "research as praxis" capable of energizing participants in what Freire (1971) refers to as "concientization" (p. 67) is an area for future consideration (Soto 1992b);

(b) Implementing knowledge into practice is a second needed initiative. Promising practices include Comer & Haynes' (1991) model that views families and schools as important sources of influence on children's development and must, therefore, work collaboratively; Cochran and Dean's (1991) model where mutual respect assumes the strength of both parents and teachers; and a follow-up to our own work where the nonthreatening topic of play is integrated into a collaborative early education model. Areas to be explored include the possibility of affording children choices and the re-definition of play by caretakers. The Deweyian notion of viewing play as a continuum (drudgery, work, play, chaos) may have implications for group dynamics. A carefully implemented model of mutual respect and collaboration is recommended; and,

(c) There is a strong need for early childhood teacher education models where guided field experiences include research and practica with culturally and linguistically appropriate "best practices." The continued exploration and implementation of nondeficit perspectives will enhance understanding within the field of early childhood education and the educational possibilities for Puerto Rican family systems.

Puerto Rican children, like all of our young children, have diverse experiences and capabilities. Children embedded in such rich, unique cultural strengths and linguistic contexts can provide needed leadership and talents for a changing society. The nonthreatening language of play provides an optimal opportunity for educators and parents to pursue. We need to continue to enhance our knowledge base of Puerto Rican family systems as these relate to the field of early childhood education.

REFERENCES

Aguilar, T. E. (1985). Social and environmental barriers to playfulness. In J. L. Frost & S. Sunderlin (Eds.), *When Children Play*. Wheaton, MD: Association for Childhood Education International.

Bishop, D. W. & Chase, C. A. (1971). Parental conceptual systems, home play environment, and potential creativity in children. *Journal of Experiential Child Psychology, 12*, 318-338.

Bloch, M. N. & Wichaidit, W. (1986). Play and school work in the kindergarten curriculum: Attitudes of parents and teachers in Thailand. *Early Child Development and Care, 24*, 197-218.

Cintron de Esteves, C. & Spicola, R. F. (1982). Four Hispanic groups: Oral and social traditions, education and play implications for educators. Paper presented at the Annual Meeting of the International Reading Association, Chicago, IL.

Cochran, M. & Dean, C. (1991). Home-school relations and the empowerment process. *The Elementary School Journal, 19*(3), 261-269.

Comer, J. & Haynes, N. (1991). Parent involvement in schools: An ecological approach. *The Elementary School Journal, 19*(3), 271-277.

Duany, L. & Pittman, K. (1990). *Latino youths at a crossroads*. Washington D.C.: Children's Defense Fund.

Freire, P. (1971). *Pedagogy of the oppressed*. New York: Herder & Herder.

Harter, L. (1989). *Preschool children's play behaviors associated with housekeeping equipment and blocks in an outdoor environment*. Unpublished Doctoral Dissertation. The Pennsylvania State University.

Howes, C. (1980). Peer play scale as an index of complexity of peer interaction. *Developmental Psychology, 16*, 371-372.

Jipson, J. (1991). Developmentally appropriate practice: Culture, curriculum, connections. *Early Education and Development, 2*(2), 120-136.

Johnson, J. E. (1982). The attitudes about school and play questionnaire. Unpublished manuscript. The Pennsylvania State University.

Johnson, J. E. (1983). Play attitudes questionnaire. Unpublished manuscript. The Pennsylvania State University.

Johnson, J. E. (1986). Attitudes toward play and beliefs about development. In B. Mergen (Ed.), *Cultural Dimensions of Play, Games and Sport: Association for the Anthropological Study of Play* (vol. 10). Champaign, IL: Human Kinetics Publishers, Inc.

Johnson, J. E. (1992). Personal communication. The Pennsylvania State University.

Johnson, J. E., Christie, J. F. & Yawkey, T. D. (1987). *Play and Early Childhood Development.* Glenview, IL: Scott, Foresman & Co.

Kritchevsky, S., Prescott, E. & Walling, L. (1987). *Planning Environments for Young Children: Physical Space* (2nd Ed.). Washington, D.C.: National Association for the Education of Young Children.

Lather, P. (1986). Research as praxis. *Harvard Educational Review, 56,* 257-277.

Miranda, L. (1991). *Latino child poverty in the United States.* Washington D.C.: Children's Defense Fund.

Myers, J. (1985). Perceived and actual playground equipment choices of children. In J. Frost and S. Sunderlin (Eds.), *When Children Play.* Wheaton, MD: Association for Childhood Education International.

Phyfe-Perkins, E. (1980). Children's behavior in preschool settings: The influence of the physical environment. In L. G. Katz (Ed.), *Current Topics in Early Childhood Education* (vol. 3). Norwood, NJ: Ablex.

Rogler, L. H. (1978). Help patterns, the family and mental health: Puerto Ricans in the United States. *International Migration Review, 12*(2), 248-259.

Santiestevan, H. & Santiestevan, S. (Eds.) (1984). *The Hispanic Almanac.* Washington, D.C.: Hispanic Policy Development Project.

Slaughter, D. & Dombrowski, J. (1989). Cultural continuities and discontinuities: Impact on social and pretend play. In M. Bloch & A. Pellegrini (Eds.). *The Ecological Context of Children's Play.* Norwood, NJ: Ablex.

Soto, L. D. (1990a). The ecological context of the home learning environment. Paper presented at the American Educational Research Association, Boston.

Soto, L. D. (1990b). The relationship between the home environment and motivational orientation of higher and lower achieving Puerto Rican children. *Educational Research Quarterly, 13*(1), 22-36.

Soto, L. D. (1991a). *Families as learning environments: Reflections on critical factors affecting differential achievement.* ERIC Document.

Soto, L. D. (1991b). Hispanic families as learning environments for young children. Paper presented at the American Education Research Association, Chicago.

Soto, L. D. (1992a). Bilingual families as educators. Research proposal funded by the Spencer Foundation.

Soto, L. D. (1992b). Success stories. In C. Grant (Ed.), *Research Directions for Multicultural Education.* New York: Falmer Press.

Soto, L., Negron, L., & Moreno, V. (1991). *Play attitude and behavioral observational checklist (PA-BOC).* Pennsylvania State University, University Park, PA.

Soto, L. D. & Smrekar, J. (1992). The politics of early bilingual education. In Kessler, S. & Swadener, E. (Eds.), *Reconceptualizing Early Childhood Curriculum.* New York: Teachers' College Press.

Trostle, S. (1988). The effects of child-centered group play sessions on social-emotional growth of three to six-year-old bilingual Puerto Rican children. *Journal of Research in Childhood Education, 3*(2), 93-106.

Udwin, O. & Schmukler, D. (1981). The influence of socio-cultural economic and home background factors on children's ability to engage in imaginative play. *Developmental Psychology, 17*(1), 66-72.

U.S. Census Bureau. (1991). *The Hispanic population in the United States.* Washington, D.C.: U.S. Government Printing Office.

Valdivieso, R. (1986). *Must they wait another generation?* ERIC Clearinghouse on Urban Education. NY: Teachers' College, Columbia University.

Valdivieso, R. & Davis, C. (1988). *U.S. Hispanics challenging issues for the 1990s.* Washington, D.C.: National Hispanic Policy Development Project.

Winetsky, C. S. (1978). Comparison of the expectations of parents and teachers for the behavior of preschool children. *Child Development, 49,* 1146-1154.

Yawkey, T. D. & Alvarez-Dominguez, J. (1984). Comparisons of free play behaviors of Hispanics and Anglo middle class SES five-year-olds. EDRS 274 460.

REBECCA S. NEW[1]

7

Child's Play—*una cosa naturale*: An Italian Perspective

There are many reasons to consider children's play from a cross-cultural or comparative perspective, not the least of which is to learn more about the range of play behaviors that might be included in the normal processes of development. As the importance of play to children's development gains credence among American educators and psychologists (Bredekamp 1987; Johnson, Christie & Yawkey 1987), the need also grows to better understand the role of environmental variables such as parental attitudes, the presence or absence of physical "props" such as toys, and characteristics and availability of playmates—variations of which may be readily examined in natural settings around the world. Finally, as educators struggle to meet the needs of children representing various ethnic groups within the United States, it becomes increasingly imperative to disentangle cultural diversity from minority status (Spencer 1990). Such a task is made more feasible by examining the lives of children growing up in settings where they represent the norm rather than the exception.

The goals of this chapter are several: to (a) briefly review the anthropological treatment of children's play; (b) describe the context and characteristics of infant and toddler play as observed in a small town in central Italy; and (c) consider the ways in which educators in a second Italian community have responded to children's play as a major component of the early childhood curriculum. The chapter concludes with a discussion of theoretical implications and future research directions regarding children's play.

ANTHROPOLOGICAL TREATMENT OF CHILDREN'S PAY

In the published proceedings of the first annual meeting of the Association for the Anthropological Study of Play, harsh criticism of the traditional anthropological treatment of play was expressed (Schwartzman & Barbera 1976). Two years later in a treatise on anthropological studies of play (Schwartzman 1978), the claim was reiterated that anthropologists in general have shown little interest in the study of children or their play, Margaret Mead's work notwithstanding. Schwartzman's review of ethnographies conducted in Africa and South America revealed that play was not included as a legitimate ethnographic topic, even in studies specifically directed to children and childrearing. The classic work of the Whitings, as represented by the *Six Cultures* series (1975), was not exempt from criticism since most studies made only brief mention of play, focusing instead on childrearing features such as feeding and toilet training and children's agonistic and prosocial behaviors.

In anthropological studies where the topic was considered, information on children's play was generally depicted from one of the following four perspectives: (1) play as informal preparation for adult life (the most common view); (2) play in the form of games or sports activity; (3) play as projection or expressive activity; and (4) play as simply "miscellaneous" diversion (Schwartzman & Barbera 1976; Schwartzman 1978). The level of interest among most anthropologists was seen as parallel to a general lack of interest in children's play in Western societies (Norbeck 1976).

Much has changed, and much has remained the same, in the time following those reviews. Certainly, the topic of children's play is no longer beyond the mainstream of scholarly investigations in either developmental psychology or anthropology, as is evident by the growing number of published articles and volumes on the topic (this one included). And while play as a sort of practice for adult activities remains perhaps the most common view among those who examine various cultural groups (Erchak 1980; Harkness & Super 1986; Wenger 1983), play is now also studied as both a context and a vehicle for social, emotional, linguistic, and cognitive development (see Kelly-Byrne's outstanding review and ethnographic study, 1989).

Differing approaches to play among anthropologists reflect two prevailing views of the relationship between play and culture: that of play as a contributor to the dynamic process of cultural renewal, and that of culture as a determinant of play through the provision of settings as well as norms for play behavior (Sutton-Smith 1977; Harris 1979). These two views have been combined into a dialectical model (Sutton-Smith 1977; 1978) that resonates with a transactional view of human development (Samaroff 1975)—one in which the developing organism influences and is influenced by his or her environment.

In spite of the recent proliferation of research on play, there remains very little research on the "context" of play. Studies of play in natural settings remain rare, and most such studies continue to neglect the very young child (Bloch 1989).

With these concerns in mind, the next portion of this chapter will consider the manner and extent to which play is woven into the fabric of daily life among a sample of young children growing up in central Italy during infancy and toddlerhood.

THE STUDY: CHILD CARE AND DEVELOPMENT
IN A CENTRAL ITALIAN TOWN

This discussion of infant and toddler play is based on a longitudinal investigation of child care and development conducted in a small town in northcentral Italy. The initial study, conducted during 1980-81, included the examination of the social and caregiving routines of twenty infants in conjunction with an ethnographic study of family life and child development in the community (New 1984). A follow-up investigation in 1982 focused on patterns of play and mother-toddler interaction. Subsequent return visits to the field site (1987, 1988, 1989, and 1991) were for purposes of continued investigation into parental beliefs regarding child behavior and temperament, the role of schooling, and strategies of care in the early childhood period.

The subjects. All two-parent resident families with a later-born infant of criterion age were invited to participate in the study. The resulting twenty families represented approximately seventy percent of similar families in the community. Socioeconomic levels ranged from lower- to upper-middle class; father employment positions varied from truck driver to surgeon. Three mothers were employed part-time, and the average family size was four members (two children and two adults). Three households included a widowed grandparent. Sample children were equally divided by sex, and approximately half were of southern Italian immigrant status.

The data. Sources of data to be integrated into the discussion reflect the multimethod approach to the study, and include two hour-long naturalistic home observations utilizing a microprocessing event recorder when sample infants were ten months old; daily routine interviews and a family social network questionnaire administered during the first year of life; audiotaped recordings of mother-child interactions during a free-play setting at two years; and a series of parental attitude interviews regarding beliefs, goals, and expectations for child behavior and development. Findings from these sources will be discussed within the framework provided by the ongoing ethnographic study.

The following discussion of results from the study is organized according to the "developmental niche" concept as a way of placing play behavior within its cultural context (Super and Harkness 1986).

Context As Content

The developmental niche concept entails examination of three distinct features of a given culture that are considered to play a vital role in contributing to the course of child development: (1) the physical and social settings in which a child lives; (2) the culturally determined strategies of child care and patterns of interactions; and (3) the "psychology" of the caregivers (those values, beliefs and goals that influence the ways in which individuals organize, perceive, and respond to children's behavior) (Harkness & Super 1986; Super & Harkness 1982; 1986). This conceptualization incorporates previous theoretical work outlining the relationship between environmental constraints, cultural values, and parental goals and behaviors (Bronfenbrenner 1979; LeVine 1974; Whiting 1980) and enables a rich and vivid depiction of the context in which a child develops.

The setting. The study was conducted in the small town of Civita Fantera,[2] approximately fifty kilometers (thirty miles) from Rome. Located amidst a rich agricultural zone, the town's major source of employment is the local ceramics industry. Two decades of immigration from southern Italy is apparent in the rapidly growing suburbs, condominiums, and public housing beyond the original town center (*Centro Storico*). In spite of modern supermarkets located in the newer parts of town, most residents continue to perceive the Centro Storico as the hub of their daily activities.

Residents of the Centro Storico, typically southern Italian immigrants, live in crowded apartments (often over storefronts) along cobblestone streets, with much of the exterior in continual disrepair. There is one small park in the Centro which is infrequently maintained and ill-equipped for children; its several water fountains are surrounded by gravel and an occasional shard of glass. The most frequent occupants of the park are gender-segregated groups of elderly men and women who converse from the park benches.

Most middle-class residents, as well as those eligible for public housing assistance, reside beyond the plateau in the more expansive suburbs. While apartments are small within the public housing projects, the grounds are spacious, providing in each case more territory and somewhat safer play spaces in the form of concrete patios and broad expanses of dirt-covered surfaces. There are also several parks, each larger than the one in the Centro Storico, with swings and other playground equipment.

Regardless of where children and their families reside, none are socially isolated; neighbors are typically well-informed of each other's whereabouts, and extended family members come and go freely from each other's homes, often making several visits in the course of a single day. Family life determines the daily routine, such that all businesses and schools (with the exception of the *scuola materna*, or preschool) close down to accommodate the mid-day meal (*pranzo*). Following this family meal time, fathers and young children nap, while mothers return to household responsibilities. By late afternoon, shops have reopened, and the streets are full of adults and children, including mothers and infants, joining in the traditional afternoon stroll. Grandmothers sit with restless toddlers in strollers in the small Centro Storico park. Elderly men congregate in doorways or at one of the town bars, while teenagers cavort around town on small but noisy mopeds. By the time the sun has set, most children are back inside their homes or are with their families at the home of extended family members, although on a warm summer day children may continue playing outside until well after dark.

There is a clear and articulated interest in children on the part of adults in this community, with the period of infancy described as one of indulgence. Yet in many instances there is less distinction made between adults and children than there is between males and females (New & Benigni 1987). Certain spheres of adult activity are off-limits to members of the opposite sex, yet little in the adult world is hidden from children. Until the age of two most infants share sleeping quarters with their parents. Children accompany their mothers to the markets, and are privy to the daily gossip shared by neighbors. Although less likely to be invited into the male-dominated work environment, young boys are frequently found in the company of their fathers at local bars, where pool tables and card games are the norm. Entire families attend weddings and funerals, as well as religious festivals and the perennial traveling carnivals that appear on the outskirts of town. In short, children in this community of 16,000 are an active part of the social order.

Infancy. Patterns of infant care have been described extensively elsewhere (New 1984; 1988; 1989; 1991). Maternal goals reflected a concern for physical health and well-being. While much of the mother's attention and effort was directed to feeding and grooming, the infant experienced a high degree of social activity as well. Interactions with mothers and others were predominantly verbal, with high levels of responses to infant frets and cries as well as nondistress vocalizations.

Physical and social characteristics of the infant care environment directly influenced infant opportunities for play and exploration. There was little effort made at childproofing the environment. A majority of infant caregiving as well as family socializing took place in the kitchen, where there was always the danger of coming into contact with a hot stove or cooking utensils. Dining and living rooms in both working and middle-class homes were rarely used except for formal occasions; filled with breakable objects, they were not considered safe for exploration by crawling infants. Floors throughout the home were tiled with ceramics from local factories, and carpets were uncommon; hence crawling on the cool surface was also discouraged. Outside, opportunities for infant exploration were not much greater; no outdoor space was considered safe for infants, nor were there efforts to create such a space. Even though infants were taken out daily for a stroll, the purpose was for fresh air and socialization, not physical activity. Throughout most of the first year of life, infant motor activity was restricted by use of infant seats, playpens, highchairs, and strollers.

Opportunities for play were created by the presence of others in the infant care environment. Infants had many and varied play partners in addition to nuclear family members. Home observations revealed an average of five to six people per two-hour observation period, several of whom were typically neighbors or relatives. Ethnographic observations as well as family network and daily routine questionnaires suggest that this figure grossly underestimates the number of individuals with whom these infants had regular, if not daily, contact (Miller, New, & Richman 1982). In fact, infants were rarely if ever observed solely in the company of their mothers.

Virtually everyone who came into the home initiated some sort of interaction with the infant. Yet even though play has been described as "easy to recognize" (West 1979), it was often difficult to determine when individuals were actually playing with an infant. Patterns of play and interaction with infants varied as a function of gender, age, and familial status. Rarely was the kind of play observed that matched Western descriptions in which "the child is in charge of the situation" (Sutton-Smith & Roberts 1981). Visiting women (neighbors as well as extended family members), for example, were often observed playing with infants in what might be described as the "rough and tumble" fashion previously ascribed primarily to Western fathers (New & Benigni 1987). Others would go so far as to pinch the cheeks of a sleeping infant to arouse him or her for play; teasing in the form of removing food or pacifiers was also common.

There was an element of vigor in these interactions that

often led to cries, clearly taxing the coping skills of some young infants. Even four-month-olds were occasionally jostled and bounced by adults until their laughter turned to tears. While this type of play was tolerated when engaged in by adults, children were often discouraged from too much direct physical contact for fear of hurting or soiling the infant (New 1987). Yet siblings, cousins, and neighbor children were all eager to hold, carry, and otherwise physically manipulate the infant, helping him or her perform *batti, batti le manini* (the Italian version of patti-cake), play peek-a-boo, and practice walking. These performances were often viewed with amusement by nearby adults. Another role of older children in the play of infants was to serve as a major source of household objects as well as toys. Such interactions were typically the source of much excitement on the part of the infant; they were also, however, a source of frustration as infants were frequently offered a toy only to be required to sit and watch as the older child played with it.

Unanimously declared to be the primary caregivers of infants, mothers were among the least likely to play with their infants, declaring that the role of playmate belongs to siblings and extended family members. While enjoying an occasional game of peek-a-boo, sample mothers rarely engaged their infants in the kind of one-on-one play sessions that have been observed in American mother-infant dyads, focusing instead on infant care tasks such as feeding and grooming and including the infant in domestic routines as well as social encounters. At no point did any mother suggest that play was an important contributor to infant development. Fathers were also unlikely to be infant play-mates, although not because they had other infant care priorities. Most fathers of young infants indicated a reluctance to handle their children, purportedly out of a fear of hurting them. Their attempts at play were characterized by whistles, making faces, and other distal efforts to elicit smiles. Both mothers and fathers occasionally utilized toys as sources of distractions—particularly during feeding or bathing routines—but play with objects was not seen as necessary for optimal infant development.

What was important was that the infant learned to cope with the demands of the group. In turn, children and adults gave infants much attention, occasionally in the form of teasing, often by teaching social routines such as the *ciao* greeting, or practicing motor skills. Cumulatively, such encounters served as invitations to become a "full partner of the social order" (Snow 1985).

Toddlers. For most of the sample, the period following the second birthday signaled a major change in caregiving concerns and strategies. In most cases, increased mobility and interest in the surrounding environment resulted in an expansion of play terrain as well as additional opportunities and partners for social exchange. Within the home, in contrast to the restricted crawling infant, the toddler was free to move about, typically following the mother as she moved from one part of the house to another. Still, no efforts at child-proofing the environment were noted. Instead, mothers relied on reprimands, hand-spanking, and threats of returning children to the playpen to keep them away from forbidden areas of the house.

While mothers did not relinquish their predominant role as caregivers, they became much more likely to share the supervision of the thirty-month-old toddler with others, including the mixed-age play groups of siblings. Thus toddlers who lived in the Centro Storico, for example, were often found outside in one of the narrow cobblestone streets which, barely able to accommodate a single lane of traffic, were full of small groups of children chasing balls and each other out of the way of passing automobiles. Toddlers living in the public housing and apartment condominiums played in the stairwells and surrounding yards, in the company of siblings and neighbor children. In each case, the children's play groups were often but not always visible from the apartment windows and balconies.

While maternal attitudes regarding the need to safeguard a child's physical well-being underwent a rather abrupt transition from the infancy to toddler periods, maternal beliefs and practices with respect to play remained consistent with those noted previously. When describing their child's daily activities, mothers gave more emphasis to the child's desire to play. But mothers saw this desire on the part of children as unrelated to their responsibilities as parents, other than to tolerate children's playful activity. Mothers rarely attempted to insert playful behavior into caregiving routines; if anything, they were more perfunctory in their feeding and grooming strategies. Their definition of play as *una cosa naturale* (a natural thing)—something children just do—precluded any active involvement on the part of adults.

This attitude of non-involvement was apparent even in settings focused specifically on play. When requested to play with their toddlers during an assessment of child language, symbolic play, and mother-child discourse at thirty-one months, sample mothers articulated a belief that had been described before: playing with a child is not part of the maternal role. When asked to "play with your child in any way that you choose," several mothers declared, "I never play with him. I don't know what to do;" and one refused outright to even attempt the task. Most mothers who obliged utilized the toys provided as props in their interactions with the child. Their patterns of play consisted of demonstrations (e.g., stacking blocks), prohibitions (warning the child not to touch the toys), followed by commands for the child to imitate ("watch . . . now you do it!"). For the most part, mothers preferred to sit back and watch the child play rather than become actively engaged in the activity. While it is certainly possible that sample mothers were inhibited by this "strange situation," ethnographic observations suggest that the mothers were hesitant to do more because to do so would be incongruent with their normal patterns of interaction. Cooperative play with their toddlers was neither a goal nor a characteristic of maternal interactions.

Toddlers' playmates, then, were most often older children, both males and females, ranging in age from four years and up. In fact, the play assessment we describe was frequently interrupted by siblings and neighbor children, many of whom attempted to direct the symbolic play activity of the younger children. While such interruptions were counter to attempts to standardize observations of mother-toddler play, they were valid indicators of toddlers' typical play patterns and play partners.

Issues of autonomy common to American parent-child dyads with two-year-olds were less often observed in these interactions. Given that the cultural press was more toward interdependent relationships with others than any form of independent behavior, toddlers in this sample appeared accustomed to the didactic nature of their mothers' and others' play interactions. Toddlers' arguments in their own behalf seemed consistent with the social norms rather than any indication of age-related expressions of independence. Furthermore, toddlers in this sample were allowed significantly more autonomony than they had been permitted as infants. Even though their comings and goings were under the commanding directions of older children who played in and out of each other's homes, and mothers as well as nearby adults frequently shouted warnings to their child caregivers, the toddlers themselves were removed from the close maternal supervision that had characterized the first year of life.

A majority of the siblings of toddlers attended the preschool, which—as noted previously—continued through the mid-day meal time. Thus the mixed-age groups of which toddlers were a part included extremes of age. Playmates during the morning hours for most of the sample toddlers were adults—men as well as women. The two- to three-year-old child might be observed on the floorboard of a teenager's moped, cruising up and down the street; on the shoulders of an uncle or grandfather as he took a stroll; or in the grasp of a female neighbor or relative at the market. The behavior of adult males now more closely approximated that of the females described earlier (with infants). Even the fathers of toddlers appeared more comfortable with a rough-and-tumble type play; adults of both sexes engaged in much tickling, jostling, and verbal teasing. In many of these encounters, the involvement in playful activity was initiated by the adult, and rarely continued to the extent that it would interrupt the predominant activity. School-aged children joined the scene at midday, assisting in the supervision of toddlers as the mothers finished preparations for pranzo. By shortly after four o'clock, when the preschool day ended and naptimes were over, toddlers joined their siblings and neighbors in widely mixed-age play groups that roamed from one home or apartment to another. Play in these settings included games of hide-and-seek and kickball, as well as dramatic play involving dolls, cars, weapons, and television cartoon drama figures. At this time preschoolers competed with school-aged children to share in the supervision of a toddler, perhaps but not necessarily the sibling of one member of the group. While the request to care for a toddler was somewhat more likely to be made by a female, males were also observed carrying two-year-olds about, teaching them how to kick a ball or shoot a toy gun. Involvement with younger children seemed more a function of proximity than gender at this age.

The scheduling of the evening meal for eight o'clock or later extended the number of hours available for play, and it was not at all uncommon to see children playing in one another's homes after dinner and/or after dark—especially if they were extended family members. In such cases toddlers were typically allowed to remain with the group, observing if not actively participating in the playful activities of other children. Toddlers' imitative attempts at more mature behavior during such sociodramatic play scenes were often viewed with interest and amusement on the part of older caregivers as well as nearby adults, yet few parents were observed to elaborate upon or purposely provide opportunities for such play behavior.

For the most part, the play of toddlers and other young children was not hindered by adult mandates or directions. When adults did engage toddlers in playful interactions, such encounters were typically characterized by a great deal of teasing, false threats, and requests to show off newly developing motor or verbal skills. Toddlers were also exposed, in their mixed-age peer groups, to teasing, taunting, and debate rituals (*discussione*) of the type described in Corsaro's studies of children's peer relations (1988; Corsaro & Rizzo 1988). These instances appeared to serve a function similar to that observed in other cultures, where it has been noted that children acquire both language and culture through such playful routines (Schieffelin & Ochs 1986).

What seemed most important to all concerned—the toddler included—was that he or she had left the confines of the infant care environment and was rapidly becoming a willing observer and active participant of the community at large.

Summary of Findings

The depiction of the developmental niche in which this sample of Italian children resides has revealed a number of environmental characteristics and cultural values that directly and dramatically influence the nature of infant and toddler play.

Physical and social characteristics. Throughout the study, children spent time in settings seemingly unconducive to playful activity, yet play of the sort described was interspersed throughout much of the infant/toddler's day. The physical restraints that were imposed on infants were removed after the second birthday, and social norms proved to circumvent any inhibition of toddler play imposed by the physical surroundings. By age two, children had access to the world beyond their front door, including the neighborhood streets and homes of many other children. This discontinuity between the period of infancy and toddlerhood is consistent with findings of a number of anthropologists who have noted that typically, after weaning, the toddler is out on his own, in the care of older children (Weisner & Gallimore 1977; Whiting & Whiting 1971).

Playmates and play locations reflected the toddler's membership in the larger community, such that people rather than objects were the more common vehicles for play activity. The highly social quality of the infant care environment has been projected to result in a qualitatively different learning environment than one which is characterized by the presence of a single caregiver with only one style of interacting (Lewis & Cherry 1977). Thus infants in this sample had opportunities to learn multiple modes of interaction. The frequent inclusion of toddlers into mixed-age groups, regarded as child caretaking by some (Weisner & Gallimore 1977), served to promote rather than inhibit playful activity. Rarely did mothers have to request older children to care for a toddler; they, like the adults, enjoyed showing off the *bella bambina*.

Adults throughout the community served as undesignated supervisors of young children's multiage and multisex peer groups. These findings are in contrast to those conducted in the United States, where adults are often directly engaged in children's play (especially with infants and toddlers) (Rogoff 1981).

Patterns of interaction. The overall pattern of child care observed in this study supports the hypothesis that early concerns for health and protectedness, coupled with high levels of responsiveness to vocalizations and an emphasis on social behaviors, are predictive of less restrictive demands in later years, including more free-time at some distance from home (Munroe & Munroe 1980). In this sample, the strong degree of dependency and group membership fostered during the first two years of life were associated with clear and stable patterns of play and caregiving, which enabled both toddlers and their parents to accept a transition into a less restrictive play setting.

In addition to the opportunities for observation, imitation, participation, and play provided by the large number and variety of individuals in the child's social environment, patterns of social interaction influenced the quality and type of play observed. There was often a lack of distinction between times for play and other activities. Throughout family meal times, as well as during social encounters, there was much teasing, cajoling, and playful verbal exchange. There was little emphasis on the kind of play typically advocated to foster cognitive development (e.g., guessing games, games involving the exchange of information). Yet the play that did take place surely promoted children's development in the intellectual as well as social domains. While the mixed-age play groups often took on the appearance of an insensitive and noncontingent environment for the younger members, comparative research suggests that there are many reasons why such play groups are ultimately more adaptive and conducive to development than either same-age grouping or the highly contingent adult-child dyad which characterizes the middle-class American child's play. Multiage groupings of children such as those observed in this study not only allow the older children to practice nurturing skills and gain status in the group; such arrangements are also beneficial to the younger members, who are protected from harm by the group as a whole, and exposed to multiple and varied learning opportunities within that context (Konner 1976). Even the varying degrees of contingent responsiveness exhibited by preschoolers and older children to infants and toddlers in this study have been deemed as adaptive, by way of providing a natural transition to more mature behavior and a more appropriate means of stimulating the development of the cognitive abilities not destined to mature until after the first year of life (Konner 1976; Munroe & Munroe 1974). As noted previously, many play sessions with infants and toddlers involved attempts to teach something—to play patti-cake, pronounce someone's name, or learn to walk—with numerous opportunities for the infant and toddler to demonstrate their own developing competencies as well as their knowledge of social rules and customs.

The high levels of verbal negotiation that characterized the play of children of all ages certainly contributed to children's linguistic development as well as to their acquisition of culturally valued forms of social behavior; even infants were included in these lively conversations with multiple and overlapping partners. As was the case with playful interactions, these verbal exchanges included few observed instances in which the child directed the course of the interaction. As such, these exchanges were consistent with the hierarchical relationships that have been noted to prevail throughout Italian adult life (Tannebaum 1980).

Attitudes. The psychology of the caregivers as elicited and observed in this study revealed a number of critical beliefs and cultural values that influenced children's play. Harkness & Super (1983) have noted that a primary function of culture is the division of human development into meaningful segments or developmental stages, with variations in both the timing of stages as well as the developmental issues seen as critical to each stage.

In the United States, beginning in infancy and continuing throughout the period of early childhood, there is a marked preoccupation with the educational value of play. Educational toys and creative playthings have become major industries in the United States, thanks to marketing strategists' abilities to capitalize on United States middle-class parental goals of academic achievement for their children. These attitudes regarding play and playthings are in direct contrast to those observed among this Italian sample. It has been observed that beliefs about development probably exist as part of a larger ideological system that encompasses broad philosophical views about the "very nature of mankind" (McGillicuddy-DeLisi 1982). To the families participating in this study, there was much about life that was beyond human control, and a certain fatalistic view permeated the long-term goals parents expressed for their children (New 1988). But there was also a belief in one's right to a certain quality of life, certain indexes of which were viewed as givens, including wine on the table and the pursuit of playful activity. Mothers' comments and minimal support of children's play reflected the belief that play would take place regardless of their involvement, not that play was unimportant. It was commonly understood that children should be allowed to play. It was just not considered necessary for parents to foster, in any overt fashion, something that is considered to occur naturally. Indeed, play was such a natural part of life that there was little or no stigma attached to adults behaving playfully, too. On more than one occasion, when adults did play with children, it appeared to be for purposes of their own pleasure, rather than the provision of an experience vital to the child's development. What was vital to the child's development was the growing sense of membership in the family and the community; patterns of play contributed to and reflected this cultural imperative.

These features depict a setting in which play serves not only adaptive purposes related to socialization pressures appropriate for the setting in which these children were to function, but also provides opportunities for learning that have yet to be fully or adequately considered in contemporary studies of play.

Implications of these contextual features of infant and toddler play as observed in this Italian community will be considered in the final section of this chapter.

RESPONSES TO PLAY BY ITALIAN EARLY CHILDHOOD EDUCATORS

The remaining task of this chapter is to consider the manner in which one group of Italian early childhood professionals are attempting to maximize the creative, intellectual, and social possibilities inherent in children's play while maintaining a vital continuity with Italian social norms and cultural values.

Reggio Emilia, a wealthy industrial town in northern Italy some distance from the small town previously described, has one of the most renowned examples of community-supported child care systems in the Western world (New 1991). The philosophy of education that characterizes this municipal early childhood program has offered early childhood professionals invaluable insights and inspirations regarding contemporary issues in child care and education. Increasing efforts are under way to describe in greater detail characteristics of the community-wide preschool program for American audiences (Gandini, Edwards, & Forman 1993).

One outstanding feature of the Reggio Emilia program is the manner in which the curriculum revolves around children's play activities. While there are many differences between this and the previously described community—cultural, economic, political, geographic differences—some aspects that support the valuing of children's play are reminiscent of the values and patterns of care previously described. Specifically, the two communities share in an emphasis on continuity and cooperation in the child's caregiving environment; the premium placed on adult-child and child-child social interactions; and the rights of adults and children to engage in playful activity.

The pedagogical approach that characterizes the Reggio Emilia preschools is similar to the Katz and Chard (1989) "project approach" to learning. Reggio Emilia teachers share a conviction regarding the value of child-initiated activities, yet are also actively involved in promoting, provoking, and facilitating children's pursuits of questions and explorations that engage children's minds.

The projects with which young children become engaged in Reggio Emilia are of three broadly defined types, each drawn in some way from children's play activities. One type of project might result from a serendipitous event such as a rainy day and a playground full of puddles. Overhearing children's comments regarding their reflections in the upside-down world of the puddle, teachers proceeded to co-construct, with the children, an elaborate curriculum around the physical properties of reflections as well as the notion of being "all upside-down." Children not only grew in their ability to imagine and represent visual imagery in the reverse; they also enjoyed playing with their understanding of language ("If everything was upside down, people would laugh when they were sad."). This project is a typical example of how teachers capitalize on children's playful explorations of their environment.

Another type of project is teacher-initiated, but is, nonetheless, also based on their observations of children at play. For example, infant, toddler, and preschool teachers had noted on many occasions children's delight in playing with their own self-images in the mirrored surfaces of the bathrooms, classrooms, and hallways. This project, eventually known as "the delight of seeing one's self," was continued off and on throughout the year; preschool children, for example, were encouraged to draw and redraw themselves and each other, describe their facial features into a tape recorder, and collaborate on projects involving their bodies—body language, body movement, conversations, and the brain.

All of the children's "work" on such projects is conducted in an atmosphere that is simultaneously playful and serious—playful in that children are free to explore their ideas by themselves and with each other, with no pressure or expectation that they will stay with a project for any predetermined length of time, nor that there is any set goal which they must obtain. The seriousness of such projects is reflected in the extent to which children's ideas, and their play, influence adult decisions. In fact, the third type of project is directly attributable to the seriousness with which the Reggio Emilia adults view children's play.

In one classroom recently, parents and teachers were concerned about the extent to which television cartoon programs featuring war-like drama and action heroes were being reflected in children's play. Rather than ban such play and the accompanying war toys, the teachers and parents discussed ways in which such play could be channeled into more appropriate directions. After much discussion and observations of children at play, the teachers slowly began bringing in materials to use in the creation of a setting for the drama—in this case, outer space. As a result of teacher questioning and carefully placed suggestions, the children began constructing a space ship. Soon, the toy figures were forgotten, as children moved to the computer to attempt the creation of a secret code that would transmit the concept of "friend" to an alien planet.

Work or play? There often appears to be no distinction in the minds of either the teachers or the children, as they collaborate on questions and avenues of interest. In each of the projects just described, the play of children is respected and expanded through opportunities to explore and interact with materials, objects, and each other. Teachers in Reggio Emilia consider the child's social and intellectual development as highly dependent on a collective social process that involves repeated encounters and exchanges with others. This theoretical perspective, which is somewhat consistent with Vygotsky's emphasis on the child's growing ability to understand the world through interactions with others (Bruner 1985; Wertsch 1985), emphasizes the importance of multiple points of view. Thus teachers capitalize on children's willingness to engage in discussions regarding their ideas, their perceptions, and their understanding of their experiences and the world around them. They also directly promote and facilitate such *discussione*. Teachers tape record children's conversations during play as well as at group meetings, and then play back the tape to large or small groups of children, followed by such comments as "What do you think about that? Do you still feel the same way about it? Does anyone else have any thoughts on the subject?" Such dialogue might center around a discussion regarding the source of a shadow, the differences between boys and girls, or the meaning of death.

Teachers observe, document, and engage children in conversation that reflects the seriousness with which children themselves view their play activities. In each case, the teachers promote more than a cultural routine; they also promote and challenge children's abilities to take multiple perspectives and to reflect on their own thinking as well. Another program characteristic that dramatically increases the likelihood of such conversations as well as the teachers' ability to respond to the needs of individual children is that of continuity and collaboration.

These features are fostered by the practice of keeping the same children and teachers (two per class) together over a period of three years, so that adults (parents and teachers) as well as children have the advantages of a stable and familiar social network. Such long-term relationships are reminiscent of the neighborhood play groups and extended family relationships previously observed in another Italian community.

Thus the context of children's play in the Reggio Emilia preschool program is similar in a number of respects to that observed in the other small town in central Italy described in this chapter. There is little distinction between play and the child's other activities; there is an emphasis throughout on social interactions—so much so that teachers go out of their way to foster encounters and conversations between adults as well as children; and there is the comfort of being a part of a group that functions as a community of adults and children, all of whom learn to know each other well. Finally, there is an attitude regarding play as an entitlement of children that fuels curriculum planning and directly challenges formal, academic instruction at the expense of play in early childhood programs.

CONCLUSION

Harkness and Super (1986) point out that the confusion regarding what the real definition of play is may be because play is a very different kind of phenomenon depending on the context in which it takes place. In the first Italian community described in this chapter, according to their mothers, children were "always" playing; when they were not eating or sleeping, there was virtually no distinction between their play and other activities. In Reggio Emilia, there is not the emphasis on structured, adult-guided play activities such as those found in many settings with young children in the United States. Yet teachers in Reggio Emilia are not uninvolved in children's play; instead, they actively search for avenues of entry and exploitation of children's play. Such diverse views of children's play activities, seen as dependent on culturally determined attitudes regarding children's development and adult roles in fostering that development (Edwards & Gandini 1989), suggest an evolution in the interpretation of Italian adult and child play relations. Yet consistencies between the two settings highlight the importance of traditional cultural values in a rapidly changing society.

It has been observed that through play one learns the rules of the culture and-the family (Bruner, Jolly, & Sylva 1976). Specifically, these two Italian communities share in an emphasis on continuity and cooperation in the child's caregiving environment; the premium placed on adult-child and child-child social interactions; and the rights of adults and children to debate within the framework of playful activity. The context of children's play in each of the two settings reinforced these values, while providing children with opportunities to contribute to their maintenance. As they began to demonstrate their own communicative competencies, infants and toddlers in the first community were included in multiple-partner discussions, characterized by overlapping conversations rather than the reciprocal turn-taking observed during middle-class American mother-infant exchanges. In both communities, children regularly participated in cooperative peer groups, and shared in the care of one another. In each, they observed, imitated, and eventually engaged in culturally prescribed *discussione*, thereby becoming acquainted with culturally appropriate forms of behavior (LeVine 1969; Lewis & Feiring 1981) as well as the "ethnography of conversation" (Hymes 1962). As children in both communities learned that they could not always control or predict their playful interactions with others, they also discovered that they were a part of a large community of people that extended well beyond the nuclear family, thereby broadening their secure base for a variety of playful explorations.

The research presented in this chapter raises several questions that deserve serious consideration in future studies of children's play. To what extent are toys necessary in promoting children's play, and under what circumstances? In what manner does the physical setting determine the extent and quality of play? How do children and adults distinguish between work and play? Is such a distinction necessary for the benefits of play to be realized? How might a child's participation in a multiage peer group promote or facilitate certain types of play? Is there a time when such mixed-age play groups are more or less optimal? How important is it that infants and toddlers have the type of one-on-one play that characterizes American middle-class parent-child dyads? And finally, to what extent should quality early childhood programs reflect children's natural play groups and settings? These, and other related questions, will not be asked nor answered until further study takes place in the context of children's play in natural settings. Indeed, the very isolation of play from its contextual setting, including its relationship to other behaviors, may be an artifact of American middle-class biases, where environmental features such as playgrounds and educational toys create the expectation that only under certain circumstances can play take place. Such artificial separation of play from other activities and settings of children may well hinder the development of a comprehensive theoretical understanding of play (Schwartzman 1978). Until such time, the proclamation that the "ethnography of childhood remains a genuine frontier" (Schwartz 1981) will serve as a challenge to researchers of play.

NOTES

1. Preparation of this chapter was supported in part by a Spencer postdoctoral fellowship awarded to the author by the National Academy of Education. The original research summarized in this chapter was made possible through the cooperation of the Istituto di Psicologia del Consiglio Nazionale delle Ricerche, Rome Italy; a Sinclair Kennedy Traveling Grant from Harvard University; and funds from the Population Council, the MacArthur Foundation, the Spencer Foundation, and Syracuse University. All statements made and opinions expressed are the sole responsibility of the author.

2. A pseudonym, to comply with the promise of anonymity.

REFERENCES

Bloch, M. (1989). Boys' and girls' play at home and in the community: A cultural-ecological framework. In M. Bloch & A. Pellegrini (Eds.), *The ecological context of children's play.* Norwood, NJ: Ablex.

Bloch, M. & Pelligrini, A. (Eds.) (1989). *The ecological context of children's play.* Norwood, NJ: Ablex.

Bredekamp, S., (Ed.) (1987). *Developmentally appropriate practice in early childhood programs serving children from birth through age eight.* Washington, D.C.: NAEYC.

Bronfenbrenner, U. (1979). *The ecology of human development.* Cambridge, MA: Harvard University Press.

Bruner, J. (1985). Vygotsky: A historical and conceptual perspective. In J. V. Wertsch (Ed.), *Culture, communication, and cognition: Vygotskian perspectives.* New York: Cambridge University Press.

Bruner, J., Jolly, A., & Sylva, K. (Eds.) (1976). *Play*. New York: Basic Books.

Corsaro, W. (1988). Routines in the peer culture of American and Italian nursery school children. *Sociology of Education, 61*, 1-14.

Corsaro, W. & Rizzo, T. (1988). *Discussione* and friendship: Socialization processes in the peer culture of Italian nursery school children. *American Sociological Review, 53*, 879-894.

Edwards, C. P. & Gandini, L. (1989). Teachers' expectations about the timing of developmental skills: A cross-cultural study. *Young Children, 44*(4), 15-19.

Erchak, G. (1980). The acquisition of cultural rules by Kpelle children. *Ethos, 8*, 40-48.

Gandini, L., Edwards, C., & Forman, G. (1993). *Education for all the children: The symbolic languages approach to early education in Reggio Emilia, Italy*. Norwood, NJ: Ablex.

Harkness, S. & Super, C. (1983). The cultural construction of child development: A framework for the socialization of affect. *Ethos, 11*:4, 18-23.

Harkness, S. & Super, C. M. (1986). The cultural structuring of children's play in a rural African community. In K. Blanchard (ed.), *The many faces of play*. Champaign, Illinois: Human Kinetics Publishing.

Harris, J. C. (1979). Beyond Huizinga: Relationships between play and culture. In A. T. Cheska (Ed.), *Play as context*. 1979 Proceedings of The Association for The Anthropological Study of Play. West Point, N.Y.: Leisure Press.

Hymes, D. (1962). The ethnography of speaking. In T. Glawin & W. C. Sturtevant (Eds.), *Anthropology and human behavior*. Washington, D.C.: Anthropological Society of Washington.

Hymes, D. (1974). *Foundations in sociolinguistics: An ethnographic approach*. Philadelphia, PA: University of Pennsylvania Press.

Johnson, J., Christie, J., & Yawkey, T. (1987). *Play and early childhood development*. Glenview, IL: Scott, Foresman.

Katz, L. & Chard, S. (1989). *Engaging children's minds: The project approach*. Norwood, NJ: Ablex.

Kelly-Byrne, D. (1989). *A child's play life: An ethnographic study.* New York: Teachers College, Columbia University.

Konner, M. (1976). Relations among infants and juveniles in comparative perspective. In M. Lewis and L. Rosenblum (Eds.), *Friendship and peer relations.* New York: Wiley.

LeVine, R. A. (1969). Culture, personality, and socialization: An evolutionary view. In D. A. Goslin (Ed.), *Handbook of socialization theory and research.* Chicago, IL: Rand McNally.

LeVine, R. A. (1974). Parental goals: A cross-cultural view. *Teachers College Record, 76,* 226-239.

Lewis, M. & Cherry, L. (1977). Social behavior and language acquisition. In M. Lewis & L. A. Rosenblum (Eds.), *Interaction, conversation, and development of language.* New York: Wiley & Sons.

Lewis, M. & Feiring, C. (1981). The child's social network: Social object, social functions, and their relationships. In M. Lewis & L. A. Rosenblum (Eds.), *The child and its family.* New York: Plenum Press.

McGillicuddy-DeLisi, A. (1982). Parental beliefs about developmental processes. *Human Development, 25,* 192-200.

Miller, P. M., New, R. S., & Richman, A. (1982). Social ecology of infant development in Italy and America. Paper presented at International Conference of Infant Studies, Austin, Texas.

Munroe, R. H. & Munroe, R. L. (1974). Household density and infant care in an East African society. In R. A. LeVine (Ed.), *Culture and personality.* Chicago: Aldine.

Munroe, R. H. & Munroe, R. L. (1980). Infant experience and childhood affect among the Logoli: A longitudinal study. *Ethos, 8:4,* 295-315.

New, R. (1984). *Italian mothers and infants: Patterns of care and social development.* Doctoral dissertation, Harvard University.

New, R. (1987). "Don't touch the baby!": Sibling relationships in an Italian sample. International Conference of Infancy Studies.

New, R. (1988). Parental goals and Italian infant care. In R. A. LeVine, P. Miller, & M. West (Eds.), *Parental Behavior in Diverse Societies.* New Directions for Child Development, no. 40. San Francisco: Jossey-Bass.

New, R. (1989). The family context of Italian infant care. *Early Child Development and Care, 50,* 99-108.

New, R. (1991). *Bello, buono, bravo: Italian early childhood.* New York: Guilford Press.

New, R. & Benigni, L. (1987). Italian fathers and infants: Cultural constraints on paternal behavior. In M. E. Lamb (Ed.), *The father's role: Cross-cultural perspectives.* Hillsdale, NJ: Erlbaum.

Norbeck, E. (1976). The study of play: Johan Huizinga and modern anthropology. In D. F. Lancy & B. A. Tindall (Eds.), *The anthropological study of play: Problems and prospects.* Proceedings of the First Annual Meeting of the Association for the Anthropological Study of Play. Cornwall, N.J.: Leisure Press.

Rogoff, B. (1981). Adults and peers as agents of socialization: A Highland Guatemalan profile. *Ethos, 9,* 18-36.

Samaroff, A. (1975). Transactional models in early social relations. *Human Development, 18,* 67-79.

Schieffelin, B. & Ochs, E. (1986). *Language socialization across cultures.* Cambridge: Cambridge University Press.

Schwartz, T. (1981). The acquisition of culture. *Ethos, 9:*1, 4-17.

Schwartzman, H. G. (1978). *Transformations: The anthropology of children's play.* New York: Plenum.

Schwartzman, H. G. & Barbera, L. (1976). Children's play in Africa and South America: A review of the ethnographic literature. In D. F. Lancy & B. A. Tindall (Eds.), *The anthropological study of play: Problems and prospects.* Proceedings of the First Annual Meeting of the Association for the Anthropological Study of Play. Cornwall, N.J.: Leisure Press.

Snow, C. (1985). Parent-child interaction and the development of communicative abilities. In R. L. Schiefelbusch (Ed.), *Communicative competencies: Acquisition and interaction.* Baltimore: University Park Press.

Spencer, M. B. (1990). Development of minority children: An introduction. *Child Development, 61,* 267-269.

Super, C. & Harkness, S. (1982). The infant's niche in rural Kenya and metropolitan America. In L. L. Adler (Ed.), *Cross-cultural research at issue.* New York: Academic Press.

Super, C. & Harkness, S. (1986). The developmental niche: A conceptualization at the interface of child and culture. *International Journal of Behavioral Development, 9,* 545-569.

Sutton-Smith, B. (197ℱ). Comment on my brother's keeper: Child and sibling caretaking, by T. S. Weisner & R. Gallimore. *Current Anthropology, 18,* 184-185.

Sutton-Smith, B. (1978). The dialectics of play. In S. Landry & W. Oban (Eds.), *Physical activity and human well-being.* Miami, FL: Symposia Specialists.

Sutton-Smith, B. & Roberts, J. M. (1981). Play, games, and sports. In H. C. Triandis & A. Heron (Eds.), *Developmental Psychology (Vol. 4): Handbook of cross-cultural psychology.* Boston: Allyn and Bacon, Inc.

Tannebaum, A. S. (1980). Organizational psychology. In H. C. Triandis & R. W. Brislin (Eds.), *Social Psychology (vol. 5): Handbook of cross-cultural psychology.* Boston: Allyn and Bacon, Inc.

Wenger, M. (1983). *Child-toddler social interaction in an East African community.* Doctoral dissertation, Harvard University.

Weisner, T. S. & Gallimore, R. (1977). My brother's keeper: Child and sibling caretaking. *Current Anthropology, 18,* 169-190.

Wertsch, J. V. (Ed.) (1985). *Culture, communication and cognition: Vygotskian perspectives.* Cambridge: Cambridge University Press.

West, M. J. (1979). Play in domestic kittens. In R. B. Cairns (Ed.), *The analysis of social interactions: Methods, issues, and illustrations.* Hillsdale, NJ: Erlbaum.

Whiting, B. (1980). Culture and social behavior: A model for the development of social behavior. *Ethos, 8,* 95-116.

Whiting, B. & Edwards, C. P. (1988). *Children of different worlds: The formation of social behavior.* Cambridge: Harvard University Press.

Whiting, B. & Whiting, J. (1971). Task assignment and personality: A consideration of the effect of herding in boys. In W. Lambert and R. Weisbrod (Eds.), *Comparative Perspective on Social Psychology.* Boston: Little, Brown & Co.

Whiting, B. & Whiting, J. (1975). *Children of six cultures: A psychocultural analysis.* Cambridge: Harvard University Press.

MARIANNE N. BLOCH
SUSAN M. ADLER

8

African Children's Play and the Emergence of the Sexual Division of Labor

INTRODUCTION

Research on children's play in diverse cultures around the world focuses attention on issues related to the validity of generalizing theories and results from one cultural/ethnic group, for example, Euro-American children, to others. It can also illuminate features of environments and play that children engage in worldwide that expand our concepts of how to do research, and, indeed, even our definitions of the construct or metaphors we use to examine "play" (e.g., Schwartzman 1978). Research can also help to illuminate issues related to ideological, political, or economic issues affecting children from different racial, class, cultural, or gendered groups.

In the past decade, studies of children's play that have specifically focused on and been conducted in Africa have examined play and its relation to gender and age differences in the activities children do, what they learn, and with whom (e.g., Bloch 1989; Harkness & Super 1985; Whiting & Edwards 1988; Wenger 1983). In addition, most recent authors have focused on play and nonplay activities in relation to a variety of ecological variables (e.g., Bloch 1989; Hampton 1989; Liddell 1988; Liddell & Kvalsvig 1991; Udwin & Schmukler 1981) and have made implicit or explicit comparisons of their data with those collected (by the authors or others) in American or other Western, industrialized contexts. While some studies have examined children's play in Africa in relation to play and environments in multiple other cultures (e.g., Munroe, Munroe, Michelson, Koel, Bolton, & Bolton 1983; Whiting & Edwards 1988), the majority of studies in the 1980s and early 1990s have been on children's play within a particular country/ethnic context in Africa, or have compared data from such contexts with studies done in one other group in the West. The majority of the above studies focused on children's play out of school; only recent studies by Udwin and Schmukler (1981), Hampton (1989) and Liddell, and colleagues (e.g., Liddell 1988; Liddell & Kvalsvig 1991) in South Africa have presented some results of children's play within school contexts. Several studies deviated from these general approaches and focused on children's play in relation to economic or political oppression in different East and South African contexts (e.g., Kilbride & Kilbride 1990, sections on child abuse; Reynolds 1989, on children's play in South African townships). A few studies specifically focusing on children's play in Africa also related play to hunger or malnutrition, an extremely important topic that is often overlooked in much of the Western or United States literature on play with its dominant focus on well-nourished children in controlled preschool settings. While some attention to these issues was given by the author in a 1989 publication (Bloch 1989), and by Hampton (1989), we are certain more literature in this area exists, and readers should be conscious of this omission in this chapter.

The majority of studies in Africa during the past several decades have focused on children's play as a way to describe environments and their relation to play as a form of development and learning, what Schwartzman (1978) called a structural-functional approach to the study of play. While the focus of this chapter also assumes a relationship between play, children's learning, and male/female differences in the labor they do (a structural-functionalist perspective), it does not assume that differences are functional in an equitable way for males and females, or for any African (or other) society. This latter perspective places this study more in a critical theoretical framework, where underlying patterns of behavior or ideologies are examined, especially in terms of the ways in which race, ethnic, class, or gender biases are reproduced in different societies.

GENDER, PLAY, WORK, AND EDUCATION IN AFRICA

The current chapter focuses on young children's play based upon a series of studies done in one context in West Africa, where the first author has conducted field research since the mid-1970s. Its particular focus is on the relationship between work and play, as well as the emergence of gender differences in children's play, "play-work," and work. This focus stems from literature related to play and work (see Bloch 1989; Harkness & Super 1986), gender differences in children's activities, and in the sexual division of labor, as well as a cultural-ecological model that forces one to examine the interrelationships between macro-level ideologies, economic, social, and political patterns and children's education (see Bloch 1989). This literature has focused our attention on the relationship between early childhood experiences in work and play in African contexts and children's opportunities for different experiences subsequent to the early childhood period, including schooling (e.g., Stromquist 1989) and different reproductive and productive activities in adulthood.

While there are many differences in the political, cultural, and socioecological contexts of African children, the majority of recent studies of African children's play have been consistent in describing the mixture of work and play that children as young as age two years engage in within, at least, rural environments—the primary setting for most children in Africa. Whiting and Edwards (1988) vividly portray the extent to which African children engage in "directed" activities (work) vs. "undirected" activities, which include play. Both Whiting & Edwards (1988) and Munroe and Munroe (1984) and Munroe, et al. (1983) quantify the extent to which children, at least from age five on, engage in more work than play in Africa than in many other societies. In addition, middle-class Euro-American groups that were studied in both of these research efforts (Whiting & Edwards 1988;

Munroe et al. 1983) engaged in significantly more play than their African same-age counterparts. Harkness and Super's (1986) research in Kenya among the Kipsigis showed specifically that parents' assumptions about both boys' and girls' ability to assume greater responsibility changes during the "five-to-seven shift," but that even with such a shift, girls were expected to do, and did, more work than boys.

The cultural-ecological context in which these age and gender-related differences occur have been discussed by these authors and have been related to differences in (1) cultural and parental beliefs about the value of work vs. play (Whiting & Edwards 1988); (2) workload requirements in different seasons and in different cultural or economic contexts (e.g., agricultural, pastoral-nomadic, hunter-gatherer, or modern= technological), where Whiting and Edwards (1988), for example, describe African societies as training oriented, while American middle-class Euro-American community socialization was characterized as sociable; (3) perceptions of responsibility, expectations (e.g., Harkness & Super 1986) or goals; and (4) social residence and organizational system (e.g., polygamous vs. monogamous, sibling caretaker sociocultural patterns vs. nonsibling caretaking pattern; clustered vs. sparsely settled (e.g., Whiting & Edwards 1988).

The Emergence of the Sexual Division of Labor

Many ethnographic accounts as well as recent empirical studies document the emergence of and/or differences in boys' and girls' play and work during their preadolescent years. Negussie (1989), for example, suggests that during the first years of life Ethiopian children play in the surroundings of their houses, constructing toys with available local materials. Negussie describes one person's memory of boys' and girls' work and play as they learn the work of older peers and adults:

A highly educated, middle-aged man described his first informal learning period as being one, in which he followed his father in his work. Among the first tasks was the herding of goats, in the close surroundings of the house. Having a stick instead of a spear gave him a feeling of having a weapon to defend his small herd. He learned his behavior from watching the older boys when they went and returned with the cattle-herds. By and by he then got the chance to follow some older herders to the grazing areas outside the plantations. Secondly, the father constructed small tools for the son, such as a small hoe, and then instructed him to imitate the father when working. . . . Girls follow their mothers in a similar way, learning domestic chores, such as fetching water from the water-hole in a small clay-pot, carried in the same way adult women do. Girls also start to watch their smaller siblings at a very early age. . . . Dietary knowledge, traditional health customs, and traditional pharmacological competence are taught at the same time. The evidence of poisonous plants is taught to children at a very early age. (Negussie 1989, p. 12)

Leacock (1976, p. 45) describes play as "consciously patterned ways in which children relate to, and experiment with, their social and physical environment and their own abilities." She also suggests that "In pre-industrial society, as children grew to adulthood, play merged with work, and formal instruction supplemented what children were already learning through direct observation and experimentation." As industrialization, modernization, and formal education increase in African countries as they have elsewhere, Leacock's 1976 article on children's play in Africa suggested, also, that there would be sharper distinctions between play and work than in the past, and that learning through observing, experimenting, and through supplemental instruction from adults would change as the dominant ways in which younger children learn and develop knowledge related to their life and culture in Africa.

Lancy (1975, 1977, 1980) interviewed Kpelle villagers in Sierra Leone to determine their own or emic definitions and descriptions of work and play during childhood. This process resulted in eight categories of play, the first five of which Lancy suggests Kpelle children do: (1) *Nee-pele* or make-believe; (2) *Sua-Kpe-pele*, or hunting play; (3) *Pelle-seng* or toys; (4) *Pele-Kee* or games; (5) Polo or storytelling; (6) *Mana-Pele* or dancing; or (7) musical instrument play; and (8) *Kppa-kolo-pele* or adult play. In an effort to understand the relationship between play and work, Lancy (1977, p. 87) stated:

I didn't find that play has no relationship to work. They are, to use a favorite anthropological term, "integrated" . . . make-believe play seems to be one step in an alternatively collapsing and expanding process. A child of three spends hours observing a blacksmith at work. A child of four brings his stick down on a rock repeatedly and says he is a blacksmith. A child of eight weaves with his friends an elaborate reconstruction of the blacksmith's craft, all in make-believe. The child of ten is a blacksmith's helper in reality; he fetches wood for the forge and no more. At twelve he begins learning the actual skills of smithing, adding a new one every few months or so. At eighteen he is a full-fledged blacksmith with his own forge. Parallel patterns can be observed for virtually every class of work. . . . In hunting play, the child gradually moves from play to serious hunting but again the transition is far from direct. He has played at trapping for a number of years. But when he learns to trap, his father or older brother will assist and guide him in the slow and complex art of making dozens of different traps, in recognizing the signs of the 40 plus animal species, which are trapped and hunted, and then in combining these two skills into effective trapping.

Over and over, no matter which document describing play or work in the African context, one finds rich descriptions of young children's play, and a subset of play that appears to be functionally related, according to the individual authors, to adolescent or adult work patterns (e.g., see Hampton 1989; Shostak 1980; Wenger 1983). Throughout the descriptions, girls' and boys' play evolves as separate types; for example, the *Luba*, *Sanga*, and *Yeke*, girls play with dolls, not boys, although boys may help girls gather materials needed to create them. Boys construct or replicate "modern" objects of life—cars and trucks, military personnel, weapons and vehicles.

But the definitions of work and play are also important. First, definitions of play forms and activities are debatable depending upon perspective and source. For example, Lancy gains his definitions from his adolescent and adult sources, one of the few examples of using an emic rather than a Western researcher's definition for play. Shostak (1980) in *Nisa* describes, as do others, early sex play, where the majority of Western researchers examining African children's play would never cite or, perhaps, see such play. Many researchers on African children's play include verbal insults, singing, dancing, and music-making in their descriptions of play; these could be included in make-believe as often they involve a reconstruction of adult jok-ing, celebrations, etc., or not. Others include certain activities as play or work in adulthood; again, dancing by women in celebra-tions is considered by some as productive work that is required for family ritual maintenance, and thus productive labor, while others consider this adult female leisure or play. Finally, recent research by King (1982) elicits young American children's defi-nitions of play and work to prove that children's constructs are different from those of adults; in both of these studies, children's definitions of play included those activities that they engaged in on their own volition, regardless of whether they were defined by adults as play or work. Work was anything assigned or expected or structured into children's days by adults, even if the activity were what would normally be considered "free choice" or play.

These debates about the definition of play and work are one thorny research issue, while another issue is the extent to which researchers see play as integrated into work, or function-ally leading into work. One of the better discussions of this issue is cited by Schwartzman (1978) in *Chaga Childhood* by O. F. Raum, first published in 1940. Raum provides rich descriptions of girls' and boys' play as well as their work. For example:

> The child's first interests centre round the processes imme-diately preceding eating. . . . As soon as they can walk, chil-dren help in these activities. Firewood must be fetched, and carried for long distances. In the mornings the fire has often died down and a child is sent to a neighbour to ask for coals. The blowing of the embers into a bright flame must be done skillfully, and children delight in learning it. In the evenings processions of mothers with their children go to the irrigation canals to fetch water. The girls carry small calabashes, some still holding them gingerly with both hands, others balancing them gracefully on their head. The advantage of the miniature vessel used is that from an early age girls are able to perform all the necessary manipula-tions without help. They can fill it without fear of letting it slip. They can carry it home and pour the water into its receptacle (an earthenware pot) without knocking the one against the other.
>
> After having taken part in auxiliary work for some years, a girl receives "object lessons" in cooking from her

mother when she is six or seven. She is shown the essential steps in preparing a cooked dish: the quantity of water required and the amount of soda. . . . If the girl gets bored, her mother rouses her attention by means of certain tricks. She tells her, "I shall give you the spoon to lick!" or "Just come back for a minute to hold this brand so that I can see into the pot"; or, again, hoping to rouse her daughter's ambition: "You are no use at this job!"

At last a day arrives when her mother is either sick or desirous of going to the market and the girl has to show what she can do by herself. . . . Then the girl is left to perform the whole task on her own. . . . On coming home, the mother finds the baby playing peacefully because it has been fed. She asks her daughter if she left some over for her. Delighted with her mother's question, she replies: "Indeed I have, but I am afraid to let you eat it; it is so bad!" Her mother tastes it and reassures her: "Oh how very good! I couldn't have cooked it better myself!" But secretly she remembers all the mistakes made and on a later occasion warns her daughter against them. . . ." (Raum 1940-1967, p. 196-197.

Raum goes on beyond this cheerful indoctrination of young girls to the cooking process, to describe in great detail other activities of young girls and boys. After describing boys' staging of a fake court sitting, with chief and all, he looks more critically at the concept of imitative play. Is all pretense directly related to functional activities in later life?

From the sociological point of view, the copying of actions among people having the same status—as in the case of the spreading of a new fashion—must be clearly distinguished from "imitation" which cuts across boundaries of status, such as is seen in the native's craze for European clothes, the child's pretense of acting the role of an adult. While in the former case, the presence of "likemindedness" may be assumed, in the latter the mentality of the imitator differs profoundly from that of the imitated, and his performance has an altogether different function from the original. For instance, in playing at marriage, the children taking part have not seen the ceremonies performed. Much of the subject matter of "imitative" play is, in fact, relayed through the medium of speech only. Most children know but by hearsay of weddings and court meetings. If, therefore, the term "imitation" is to be retained, it should be qualified by some such term as "blind," for the children's performance resembles much more a reconstruction of certain happenings from a limited number of data. Furthermore, "imitative" play activities never achieve a complete reproduction of the example, nor are they intended to do so. They are clearly selective. Certain traits important or striking to the child, and to him alone, are chosen from the adult pattern and are remoulded in his hands. . . . The essential feature of "imitative" play is therefore that of make-believe, the tendency of the child to construct an imaginary adult society from the scraps he is allowed to know about it . . . the choice of subject and its development are a result of the child's independent and spontaneous action. . . . Imitative play is the particular response of the child to his adult social environment; in it he anticipates adult life. The term "anticipation" is the best to cover those aspects which make play appear to be imitative and preparatory, and those which show that it performs an independent function. (Raum 1940/1967, p. 255-257)

Raum, in some ways, thus describes, both the dependence and the independence of play with adult activities such as work, and at the same time provides the basis for much of our current orientation toward peer culture and play, resistance in play, and, especially, for the notion of the social construction of play and roles within play.

In order to illustrate these points better, specific examples from the first author's study of young two- to six-year-olds' play and work in Senegal are described below, with some additional perspectives on their relation to the development of gendered divisions in labor in adolescence and adulthood in African societies.

The description of the sociocultural context of the study, as well as some of the original purposes of the study will be described first in order to draw the reader into the setting. This section will be followed by illustrations of findings that relate to the questions of play and work and possible consequences of gender divisions in children's play and work. The final section will summarize remaining research questions and methodological issues raised by the study, and this specific report.

CHILDREN'S PLAY AND WORK IN A LEBOU VILLAGE IN SENEGAL: THE SOCIOCULTURAL CONTEXT

Imagine that you are beginning fieldwork in Senegal in 1973, when the first author, Marianne Bloch, began to do research on children's play in this country. Imagine that you faced issues related to research on the development of children's play, the relationship between play and other activities, and their collective relationship to the cultural-ecological context in which they are situated. Also imagine that you began to engage in some of these research questions in a country that was initially unfamiliar to you.

In envisioning decisions one makes as a researcher in the field, we hope that you will better understand some of the cultural and ecological features that were observed and coped with in cross-cultural field research. We also hope that this approach will provide more in-depth images of children's play and work in this context.

Children's Work and Play as They Were Observed[1]

From 1973-1976, and again in 1979, research was conducted on the relationship between women's work, child care and socialization, and children's development in one rural village in Senegal. This research has been published in a number of articles (see Bloch 1984, 1988, 1989; Bloch & O'Rourke 1982). In 1985, a study in another area of Senegal was focused on the relationship between women's participation in different kinds of agricultural activities, and its potential relationship to issues of child development and learning, particularly in terms of gender differences in children's participation in play, work, and the opportunity to participate successfully in formalized schooling. In 1988, and in 1990, Beth Blue Swadener and the first author investigated the introduction of early preschooling in Senegal (and the Gambia), and began to also investigate teachers' beliefs about play and work within the classroom environment. During this period, data were collected on factors related to girls' and boys' differential access to schooling during the preprimary and primary period (age three to eight years) in Senegal and the Gambia. These different types of experiences and issues will be integrated into a discussion in this chapter that focuses on young children's play and work in Senegal. The general questions posed in this essay are the following: (1) how can one describe children's play, in relation to other activities of early childhood?; (2) to what extent do different features of the cultural-ecological environment, including values, expectations, and beliefs about children and their activities, relate to the way children spend their time and with whom?; (3) what are some of the longer-term relationships, to the extent that one can judge from cross-sectional data, on patterns of child development and learning?

The Geographical and Social Context of Research:
Fieldwork in Senegal

Field research in another culture, ethnic group, or country requires extensive preparation. Ideally, one should have engaged in extensive language training, readings on the particular country, culture, and specific ethnic group, and have identified pertinent literature, at the least, that might have a direct relationship to the field research one wants to do. With few exceptions, the first author's beginning field research in Senegal violated each of these requirements. She arrived in Senegal with little prior research or reading on Senegalese culture, ethnic groups, history, economy or languages in 1973. While she was moderately fluent in French, the official language of Senegal, she had had no previous training in any of the local languages used including Wolof, the primary language of the dominant ethnic group (the Wolof) and of the Lebou (the ethnic background of the group studied in the earliest field research).

State department issued information had suggested Senegal was a small (in 1973, approximately 6,000,000 population; 1991 estimates are now nearly 8,000,000) coastal country off the coast of West Africa; that it was pretty; and that the climate was warm but moderate almost year round (in fact, the climate is wonderful, about 75 degrees Fahrenheit most of the year, except for the summer rainy season, when it is quite hot, typically over 90 degrees Fahrenheit and very humid). There were seven major different ethnic groups in the country: the Wolof, Lebou, Mandinke (see Whittemore & Beverly 1989). The majority lived in rural areas and engaged in agricultural work. With regard to childrearing, extended childcare environments were, theoretically, the norm. In short, this researcher entered the "field site" with such little information and knowledge that it is embarrassing to make an admission in print; in fact, she does admit this only to help future researchers avoid this type of "tourist" research error.[2]

Upon arriving in Senegal, particularly in the urban area of Dakar, a fairly cosmopolitan city of half a million people in 1973 (one million people in 1990 estimates), there were many new images. The city was large and laced with a mixture of beautiful, large hotels near the ocean, French and Senegalese tourist restaurants, supermarkets for the wealthy in government, etc., pockets of shacks where many of the Senegalese lived with their families, open air markets where the majority shopped, pumps where many retrieved daily water supplies, and open gutters filled with various wastewaters (laundry, bathing, sewage).

The first overwhelming image was a vision of French colonial influence laced with images of great poverty. While Senegal achieved independence from France in 1960, it was the capital of French West Africa before independence, and, in 1973 as today (1992), the colonial influence and presence of many French advisors in government, French and other European industry, was/is very visible. In short, the illusion that colonialism died with independence is just that. For the purposes of this paper, this has implications for, in particular, the colonial type of transmission of Western theories and research knowledge concerning child development, early education, and the importance of play for child development and education. This influence affected the way research theories were constructed, questions were asked, methods were determined, and results were interpreted, particularly at first; it also affected and affects others who have been the elite "researchers" on play in Africa.

One can say a bit by simply describing the per capita income, which in Senegal is approximately $100 per annum. With an average rural family consisting of at least one wife, as the Senegalese are largely Moslem and polygynous marriages are still very typical, and approximately seven children, one can estimate family (one wife, her husband, and their children) annual income of about $1,000. While in rural Senegal, one can live on such "income," there is little money for extras, which include at times adequate nutritious food for the entire family, medication or health care that is not, essentially, free, or education beyond the primary level.

Although Senegal is not considered to be the poorest of the third world nations in Africa, or elsewhere, it is still among the poorest countries worldwide by most social or economic indicators (e.g., see World Bank reports 1990). Those living in the cities, of which Dakar was the largest, are likely to have jobs with the government; the tourist industry; low-wage, low-skill jobs in other industries; or local market industries near the cities. The vast majority still live in rural areas and engage in subsistence (vegetable, millet) and cash-crop (peanuts, corn, rice) agriculture. Schools are more prevalent and accessible, (at the primary, secondary, and tertiary levels) in the cities, with fewer schools, even at the primary levels, available close to rural village settings. Preschools or daycare (crèches) are generally available as private enterprises for the wealthier, and in urban areas, with a small (1.5% of the population of children in 1990) but important publicly financed government preschool program.

A second overwhelming image that came from the first period in Senegal was the image of health care. As a "polio pioneer," the first author had been in the first generation of United States-born children to have been immunized against polio and to have had little contact while growing up with children afflicted with polio; similarly, we take for granted that diseases such as tuberculosis, smallpox, and leprosy are controllable and typically no longer seen in the United States. The immediate experience in Senegal with those afflicted visibly with polio, measles, leprosy, smallpox, river blindness, and malaria was sadness and disbelief that some countries of the world had so little access to immunizations or health care, when most people in the United States take such health care for granted.[3] As naivete decreased, knowledge of the privileges of power, wealth, and colonial influence increased. It became apparent that immunizations and medication that we take for granted at the time were not available to most,[4] and that the majority of children, in rural areas, had little access to formal schooling, particularly beyond the elementary level, to decent housing, especially in urban areas, to reasonable safe water, or, with too great frequency, a stable diet. The potential implications for children's play, of malnutrition, and of disease, which have been only superficially addressed in the author's research to date (see Bloch 1989) are nonetheless known.

Within this framework of poverty where many of the basic rights to health care, food, reasonable housing, and education are not provided to children, an appreciation and understanding of the beauty of Senegal, its family system, the cultural history, socialization, child development and learning grew. Indeed, after several projects in Senegal (1973-76, 1979, 1985, 1988, and 1990), the first author still has a fairly romantic vision of childhood in Senegal; however, this vision is now laced with a much more detailed understanding of the costs of poverty in terms of health care, stable and reasonably nutritious diets, and access to necessary goods and resources that stable adequate income can provide. It is to the story of young children's life, as this was observed during research in Senegal, and with particular regard to children's play and work, that we now turn.

Village Context

The majority of anthropological studies of child development begin by fairly detailed descriptions of the context of the study, the specific site, and the ethnic group. However, it is often overlooked that there are different theoretical underpinnings of those descriptions of context that result in descriptions that prioritize certain information over other information. In the present case, we have drawn from a cultural-ecological perspective expressed by Beatrice and John Whiting, their colleagues, and former students (including the first author) (see for example, Whiting 1980; Whiting & Edwards 1988, as well as the author's reports cited earlier). From this perspective, the notion of context is one that must include the history and economy of an area or group as well as the current maintenance systems including political, economic, and social organization that, it is posited, constrain, as well as provide, the opportunities for child development and learning. The notion of activity settings is similar to one expressed also by Wertsch (1985) in describing Vygotsky's sense of activity as well as the relationship between cultural and historical relationships and learning within various activity settings. From an essentially cultural-material theoretical perspective, the historical, social, political, religious, and economic (past and current) characteristics of an environment affect activities, ideologies, and outcomes for adults as well as children. While these ideas are hardly contestable, different researchers examine them in quite different ways (see Bloch & Pellegrini 1989; Schwartzman 1978).

The majority of cultural-ecological research on children's

play has been called "functionalist" by Schwartzman (1978), and has included empirical-analytic research assumptions and methods associated with these (Bloch 1991). More recently, a number of studies of children's play in different cultural contexts have included greater emphasis on interpretive or symbolic interactionist perspectives where adult and child meanings and beliefs in play, work, or other activities are examined by the researcher(s) as critical elements of their understanding and interpretation of play. To date, very few have used critical or other paradigmatic frameworks for such study (e.g., one exception is King 1982). By focusing on a detailed examination of children's play and work within the context of Senegal, in this work, we hope to use a critical lens to examine, indirectly, the relationship between play and gender-based divisions in subsequent work patterns as well as learning opportunities beyond early childhood.

PLAY AND WORK: THE EMERGENCE OF GENDER DIVISIONS IN LABOR AND SCHOOLING

Where, how, and with whom do children have opportunities to learn at particular cultural-historical periods, and in which ways do these settings provide unique opportunities for learning and development? It was toward these questions that the study of play and work in Senegal was directed.

Dene: The Village Context

The specific research discussed in this chapter was conducted within a village called Dene, of approximately 700 people in a rural agricultural setting about sixty miles east of Dakar, the capital city, or sixty miles east of the western coast of Senegal. Initially, the first author was taken to the village site by members of an International Young Men's Christian Association (YMCA) group that had initiated a youth employment project in the village. Knowing of the author's early childhood education background, they suggested that women in this particular village were interested in forming a daycare center, and wanted advice. With this opening opportunity, a Peace Corps short-course on speaking Wolof, and a tiny grant to help defray costs of an interpreter-research assistant, the author began work in this village to study early child development as well as factors related to the need for child care in a site where extended family child care was the cultural norm and practice (see Bloch 1988 for a specific report on this project).

The village had been established by a group of elders in the 1920s as these men and their families had split from a different village that had become too large. The majority of those living in the village were Lebou, a small ethnic group in Senegal, who were known generally as fishermen, and who typically resided on the coastal areas. This group had moved inland and become agriculturalists.

While there were communal work groups, in general, there were sharp distinctions between men's and women's work, with men engaging in more cash-crop agriculture with corn and peanut production, while women engaged in subsistence agricultural vegetable farming, with surplus vegetables and other food sold at the nearest roadway crossing. In the early 1970s, a European-funded agribusiness moved to within one mile of the village site, which we call Dene, and many men and women in the village had begun to engage in wage labor in the fields, or in production. The perceived need for a daycare program in the village was related to shifts in the numbers and ages of women available to supervise and care for young children, largely because of the introduction of the agribusiness eight-hour shift days, reducing flexibility in the location and duration of women's work away from children (see Bloch 1988). Indeed, while extended family child care has remained the norm in this village, changes in caretaking patterns had occurred. The absence of older daughters, the preferred alternative caretakers of mothers, due to the youth employment program initiated by the YMCA, coupled by mothers' participation in the neighboring agribusiness, as well as maternal participation in traditional rainy season agricultural and petty trade labor had resulted in mothers of young children feeling that a daycare program focusing on care of quite young children (age eighteen months to three years) would help. Interviews done with mothers that focused on the ages of children they hoped to place in a daycare center, if one were instituted, showed clearly that the children who had just been weaned (weaning typically took place between twelve and twenty-four months, with eighteen months the norm) as well as the children who were young (through age three years) were seen as being too young to, with ease, leave the family compound and/or village under the supervision of older children and relatives. In our interviews in 1975-76, the children who were age four or five years were seen as old enough to be left without day care or supervision, as they played with older siblings, and generally, were seen as old enough to take care of themselves within the confines of the village and within the normal supervision system that existed.[5]

The social organization of the village as well as the organization for child care was an important part of the social and cultural context in which women's work at home and away from home was conducted, and in which child care took place. Indeed, one study (Bloch 1984) suggested that the availability of child care that a mother felt comfortable with was a significant predictor of women's participation in traditional as well as wage agricultural labor.[6]

In this village of 700, families lived in a clustered settlement pattern where there were multiple circular and clustered "compounds" consisting of numerous households all related to the eldest male in the extended family of that compound. Residence patterns were organized around a patrilocal system of residence, where the eldest male had a household with his wife or wives, their older sons and their wives and families. The largest compounds had been formed by an older man in the village, who had multiple (older sons) by the time of the study, and they, in turn had their wives, sons, and their families living in the compound with them. Compound size ranged from about twenty people living together in two clustered residences to about 200 people living together in multiple clustered residences.

The Lebou in this village had settled in a traditional residence pattern within compounds based on the patrilocal organization briefly described above. It was also important, however, that the different compounds in the village all consisted of near and distant relatives along both the maternal and paternal lines. Preferred marriages took place within family lines, and endogamous, as well as exogamous marriages (outside the village), but still with relatives were the cultural norm. This was important for child care, as children were perceived to be able to move fairly freely around the village or at least between the compounds of the closest relatives (e.g., the maternal grandmother may have lived at the other end of the village) for play, work, and child care supervision.

Individual household composition as well as compound composition was important in our analyses (Bloch, 1989) under the hypothesis that the number of boys and girls of different ages and gender that a child might play with easily was expected to affect children's play. The number of boys and girls within a child's family ranged in size depending upon the specific stage of the family reproductive cycle. Some children that were observed during the 1973-1976 study, where three- to five-year-olds were studied, and during the 1979 study, where zero to six-year-old children were studied, were in families where they were one of seven children, while others were the first or second born in families that were in an earlier period of the family reproduction cycle. Nonetheless, because of the compound organization, the nearness of other large families, including many similar-age cousins, children had many others with whom to play. Within this context, we observed two- to six-year-old children who engaged in solitary as well as social play and social play with both same-age and mixed-age peer/sibling groups. The vast majority of children in peer group play were siblings or cousins. Girls were observed to engage in somewhat more mixed-age social play with children who were younger than they, while boys engaged in somewhat more mixed-age play with older children (Bloch, 1988, 1989).[7]

THE EMERGENCE OF THE GENDERED DIVISION OF LABOR THROUGH CHILDREN'S PLAY-WORK

While cross-cultural data generally support the conception that boys and girls engage in different activities—both play and work—during childhood, there are still numerous inconsistencies in reports on specific samples (e.g., see Whiting & Edwards 1988). In African literature, however, the emergence of early differences in children's assignment to different kinds of work tasks, by gender, is well documented, as are the gender differences in the division of work during adulthood (e.g., Whiting & Edwards 1988; Harkness & Super 1986). Explanations for the division of labor in Africa are controversial. Some maintain that the gender divisions in labor represent complementary work patterns that, in the African context, have been necessary for social and cultural survival and reproduction. Others critique this perspective as one that supports continued lack of recognition of the role of women's work in production or economic activities in Africa, and continues inequalities between men and women in terms of the types of activities that are expected to do, and the type of participation that girls/boys/women/men are able to engage in with a modernizing or changing economy. Consequences of the gender division of labor that do not seem to favor women include lowered access to or success in Westernized schooling, as well as lowered participation in economic development projects and activities that provide greater economic income or resources to individual participants (see Stromquist, 1988, for example, on these points). A variety of studies document the extent to which participation in household labor diminishes African girls' ability to enter, participate successfully, or achieve in school (graduate, go onto higher education, etc.) (Stromquist 1988). Other literature documents different ways in which girls' household responsibilities and expectations for their reproductive/productive labor negatively influences their ability to participate in or learn to participate in economic development projects, when they are open to women. While the emergence of the gender division in labor that leads to these inequitable consequences is understood, no studies in Africa have yet documented how this difference or division occurs. Do children observe their elders and simply imitate them? Are they reinforced for some types of work or play and not others that would lead eventually toward gender differences in children's work patterns? Do children help to construct their own play and work patterns? Is there any evidence of resistance to the divergence in work by gender that is so well-documented in the African and cross-cultural literature?

While no study has provided the answers to the above questions, literature seems to support that all of these processes occur in a complex and interactive fashion as children construct and apply their understandings of culturally appropriate behavior. Schwartzman (1978) and Raum (1940) contest, through examples, that children imitate precisely the behavior of their elders, and document scenarios when children play with their play as they construct their own version of their own behavior. The Senegalese studies conducted by the first author provide some evidence that can be used to describe children learning responsible work patterns through their play, and during "play-work" (see term in Bloch 1989). The following descriptions of Lebou children's play in the one village setting that we described above shows patterns of development of play and work during the two- to six-year-old period, divergence by gender, and some of the processes that are involved in the construction of gendered notions of play and work in this context.

Play, Work, and Play-Work in the Two- to Six-Year-Old Period

In the 1989 report by Bloch on two- to six-year-old children's activities, boys and girls appeared to engage in similar proportions of time in play, and both boys and girls engaged in similar proportions of thematic play or pretense play during the two- to four-year-old period (see Bloch 1989, pp. 139-141); however, by the five- to six-year-old period, girls were observed to engage in pretense play, while boys were not. In addition, boys and girls pretense play during the two- to four-year-old period was observed to be differently "directed" with different content or themes in play by gender (cooking, domestic cleaning, marketing, child care for girls more than boys while boys engaged in more thematic play related to cars/transportation and hunting activities than girls). While both boys and girls engaged in more responsible work during the five- to six-year-old period compared to the two- to four-year-old period, there were significant gender differences, with girls engaging in more responsible work than boys during both the two- to four- and the five- to six-year-old periods (Bloch 1989, p. 139). Finally, the 1989 analysis of Senegalese children's play and work showed that those children who engaged in more responsible work, engaged in less play ($r = -0.397$ between proportions of observations in play and those in responsible work).

Analyses of narrative prose records of children's activities that examined children's play and work patterns in greater descriptive detail suggested that girls were more likely to be asked to do work by their mothers or other female relatives, interrupted in their play to participate in momentary help with "women's work," and were more likely to self-initiate play-work, a category that Bloch described as combining "playing at learning the tasks for which they would soon take full responsibility." An example from this study (Bloch 1989, p. 139) illustrates this category more fully, with inserts added by the current authors to describe differences in the labels play, play-work, and responsible work:

> Binta (age six) has just returned from the village well with a small basin of water on her head <self-initiated or assigned "responsible work">. She pours some of it into the drinking water jar, and her mother says, take the rest and go wash

your clothes. She puts the basin down and fetches her clothes and soap <Assigned work by mother; not "play-work">. She starts to wash her clothes, singing while washing <singing can accompany "work" as the phrase "whistle while you work" suggests; this was considered work>. Then Demba (another six-year-old girl) comes and calls her to come play. Binta tells Demba she can't go now, that she's "learning" to wash the laundry. Demba comes over to Binta and starts to wash the laundry (several of Binta's cloth skirts) with her <this last discussion between the two girls, and particularly Demba's self-initiated participation in washing signaled "play-work">.

The emergence of gendered divisions in young Senegalese children's play, play-work, and work. As suggested above, the quantified proportions of observations in which children were observed in play and responsible work were observed to be somewhat different for boys and girls in this setting. Boys' and girls' themes in dramatic play varied along predictable lines with girls' play themes reproducing—in a fashion—the activities they saw older girls and women doing as their labor in the village: cooking, cleaning, marketing, and child care.[8] Small two- to four-year-old boys engaged in pretense that included some similar themes—cooking, child care, some agriculture, for example—but also included more pretense with vehicles or play construction. By five to six years, girls' play and play-work activities, where there was greater emphasis on playing at learning work, in the first author's opinion, continued; in addition, assigned or initiated activities that transformed the former "play/play-work" into nonplay or real work activities was also done. Boys, on the other hand, at five to six years, were no longer observed in pretend activities that had been observed earlier: carrying a baby on their back at age two years, helping others to cook with play materials, or even play with toy trucks that might be called pretense. They spent more time with other boys, frequently outside their village, exploring the countryside, climbing trees, swimming in nearby lakes, or playing sports games. After six years of age, even greater divergence in boys'-girls' activities were observed, with girls, by age seven, spending more and more time outside of school, helping with "women's work" activities, including agriculture, when possible; boys began to help more seriously with agricultural activities in family fields as well as small animal herding activities, work generally only assigned to seven-to twelve-year-old boys.

The construction of these gendered differences in work and play patterns is not obvious. While there were too few examples of each type of play, play-work, or work to suggest that this process was studied sufficiently to draw conclusions, examples culled from the narrative reports on children's activities help to define how some of children's play merged into labor, and how some children learned to do, or not to do work expected for the opposite sex.

While children engaged in many different types of play, including oral joking, dancing, playing with musical instruments, and car or vehicle play, the most obvious types provide a more direct way to ages at which some forms of work began, and aspects of the processes involved with boys' and girls' construction of different types of labor.

Learning to labor at two. At two years of age, little real work was expected of the Senegalese children, yet boys and girls were given small errands to do by adults, almost as a preliminary to more serious errands or work that would be assigned later. Young children carried things to different people, or, for example, a cup of water into the house. There were no apparent gender differences in these assignments at this early age, although there were some differences in "play-work." Boys, at two, were observed in "animal beating," which generally referred to playful herding of small animals such as goats and chickens; this was generally some form of imitation of older boys, perhaps embodying the constructive aspects mentioned earlier by Raum (1940-1970). Boys also participated in early tam-tam (drum) making, observing or imitating older boys' soccer games (all considered play), and, in three cases, child-care related play-work. Two times, two-year-old boys helped someone older to take care of a younger baby, while once, a two-year-old boy was observed to tie a baby on his back, as older girls and women did; in this case his mother intervened, and, said no, the activity was "for girls." At three, boys were observed in different games such as hide-and-seek, playing at harvesting in a field along with older boys, and playing with constructing a car. In addition, three-year-old boys cut branches (small twigs) with rocks, and played at cooking corn (imitating older children). One narrative shows a child's pretense at harvesting in his father's field. By four, boys were spending somewhat more time with older boys, but also engaged in some pretense with group of young two- to five-year-old girls and some young boys in pretend play with cooking outside the village. Children had leaves in small pots, and cooked evening meals. In another narrative, a young four-year-old boy helps to wash a pot with his older six-year-old sister. A four-year-old was assigned to feed ducks, considered an assigned task (work). Five- and six-year-olds were observed playing at constructing different transportation vehicles, playing at making and then doing hunting of small animals outside the village with self-made sling- shots, playing soccer (not just imitating) with some older boys, and some work activities consisting of carrying vegetables from fields, peeling onions (ordered by a fourteen-year-old sister), emptying large basins of water, and running errands, the most common of boy's work activities at this age. One boy was also observed being ordered, but refused the assignment, and ran away.

Girls' labor was progressive as the boys' initiation into labor was; however, their activities varied some from boys, and we saw more consistent compliance to assigned tasks than with the boys. At two years of age, little girls imitated older girls and women by carrying tiny cans of water on their heads from the vil- lage well to their house. Progressively, as they got older and more capable, they carried larger cans of water on their heads until, by age seven, they could carry real buckets of water. The stage of learning to carry water was considered self-initiated "play-work." Play-work at learning to wash clothes was described earlier while play-work at progressively learning stages of peeling parts of onions or other vegetables, or pounding grain for the evening meal took the form of both assigned experimentation with some observation and some instruction as in the earlier example, described in the passage in Raum (p. 154 of this chapter), or self-initiated play-work as in the example of the two young four- year-olds beginning to learn to wash clothes (also described ear- lier). In no case, were there observations of young girls trying boys' or men's activities, or being told that something was boys' work (men's work). Girls frequently work with small dolls on their backs at young ages, pretended to cook with fairly intricate natural food (sand, leaves, onion peels, etc.) in small metal pots fabricated by adults, or pretended to do laundry, sweep, or carry water from the well. Each play or play-work activity progres- sively, by age five to six, developed into more serious errands or assigned tasks in child care of younger babies, more serious help with cooking, doing some laundry, or running errands to other parts of the village or marketing. While some of these activities were left to be "seriously" done as expected tasks at even older ages (e.g., eight to fourteen years), the frequency of times that tasks embodied more work than either play or play-work by five to six years of age was noticeably different than that for boys.

Adult Belief Systems and
Social/Economic/Cultural Factors that
Support the Beginning Gender Division in Labor

Clearly, the majority of research that has assessed adult belief systems regarding children's work supports the notion that boys and girls are expected to do different types of work and from somewhat different ages. Harkness and Super's (1986) study is clearest in showing adult expectations for children to have different abilities beginning about the age of five. The research conducted in Senegal showed that mothers believed girls and boys should engage in different types of activities, and several examples document adult women negating boys' experimentation with "women's work" activities as early as two to three years old (see examples). In addition, adults believed that children needed to take on responsibilities from an early age (boys and girls) in this society, and many others where workload demands in agriculture and at home were great. Women's work in fields and in trading could not take place without a full support system of other younger girls at home to help cook, do laundry, and, especially, take care of young children when the mother was absent. While boys could do child care, girls were preferred child caretakers according to our interviews. Additional cultural-ecological data showed girls were more likely to stay close to their mothers, to other adult women, and in girl groups, while boys were more likely, by age four to six, to spend time away from home, and with same-age or older boy groups. The earlier studies in Senegal suggested that when children were near adult women, they were (not surprisingly) more likely to be assigned errands or other work, and probably pretended to imitate adult women's activities to a greater extent, too; boys, on the other hand, were less likely to be near, and more likely to be noncompliant when requests were made (Bloch 1988). When women were absent from the village due to wage labor, young girls were found to spend more time in play, and less in work, as compared to periods when their mothers were at home. Fathers, who were more likely to be absent from the village during the day, were more likely to be observed assigning tasks only if their sons accompanied them to their fields.

CONSEQUENCES AND FURTHER QUESTIONS

The reports on children's early "learning to labor" through play and play-work activities in Senegal support other reports in many rural African cultures (e.g., Leacock 1976; Hampton 1989; Harkness & Super 1986; Lancy 1980). They document the gradual increase in work assignments as well as expectations and needs of adults to have children actively participate in work at early ages. By the early elementary years of seven to twelve years, girls' and boys' leisure and labor activities and the people they are around, in the Senegalese case described as well as in many other sites, are clearly differentiated.

The social and self-initiated processes that contribute to this early divergence in activities are as yet not clearly understood, although the brief observations described in literature as well as in the Senegalese research support experimentation, observation, gradual support and instruction, negation (as in "that's for girls"), as well as some resistance. Some boys tried women's activities at early ages only to learn through example and direct instruction that these activities were not for them.

Are these cases of simple play and work? In some ways, yes; they seem natural and fairly pervasive throughout the literature, documenting early gender differences in African children's activities. Yet, these differences are those that are viewed as "complementary" work patterns by some theories of gender differentiation in labor patterns, while others consider them the precursors to important inequities in girls' ability to gain access to or continue in schooling beyond the primary level because of heavy household (child care, cooking, etc.) responsibilities (Stromquist 1988). Beliefs about which types of reproductive and productive activities boys and girls and men and women can engage in as adults also contribute heavily, according to many economic development researchers to gender-related differential access to opportunities for participation in later economic activities in modern agricultural or wage sectors of the

African economy. Questions remain as to the inevitability of these early differences in play, play-work, or work. Questions for research remain as to their relative contribution to later differential outcomes in schooling or job/resource access, in comparison with other factors (curriculum, teaching biases, different economic opportunities offered in adulthood). Questions remain as to the extent to which girls or boys resist these roles, and the consequences for those who might resist or learn cross-gender roles. Questions remain as to whether the views and values of western researchers, and ideologies about gender roles have validity or should be counted as important in the African context. These and other questions raised in earlier parts of this chapter related to researching the play and work of young children in different cultural contexts remain for further inquiry.

NOTES

1. This subtitle is very intentional after the broad overview written earlier concerned with issues of definition, etc. The definitions used by Bloch in the Senegalese studies evolved over time from the first study begun in 1974 to the last sets of studies, on somewhat different issues, in 1990. Acknowledgment to Beatrice and John Whiting for urging the use of prose narratives to describe children's activities in research from 1979 onward, which allowed for analysis and reanalysis of categories that could be used, and interpretations by others than the primary researcher.

2. Subsequent to the first three-year period in Senegal, some of these problems were rectified by an NIMH sponsored postdoctoral fellowship at the Laboratory for Human Development at Harvard University. There, the author gratefully acknowledges training in human development and anthropology by Beatrice Whiting and Robert LeVine, which helped to frame the future work of the author in Senegal and elsewhere.

3. Of course, the U.S. health care system offers such care to children of middle-class or more elite backgrounds, who pay for such care, while still not ensuring basic good prenatal care, immunizations, or postnatal care for far too many children.

4. While the U.N. and W.H.O. sponsored initiatives to immunize all children against normal childhood, deadly diseases, has been a particularly effective initiative in Senegal during the past decade, it is still very common for children to not be immunized, to not have immediate or long-term health care, and to have no easy access to clinics, medical help, or medication.

5. These perceptions came from mothers who were asked "If a day care center were developed, but did not have enough room for all young children in the village, which age groups are most important to include in a day care center, and why?" When mothers believed that more children could be in a daycare, they did include older four- to five-year-old children in their discussion and explicitly stated that four- to five-year-olds might use day care for preschool purposes, but did not need supervision or custodial care. The preference for younger children's custodial supervision as the first priority for parents is understandable, but the fact that parents perceived four- to five-year olds to be unneedy of this type of custodial supervision is also important, and fits within Lebou norms that children are old enough to care for themselves by this age, and can be easily supervised by other older children in their play throughout the village.

6. This particular study suggested that there were two important predictors of women's participation in agricultural activities (traditional and wage-labor). These were the extent of availability of childcare providers (older daughters, grandmothers, co-wives) and economic need of the family.

7. This finding related to same-age as well as mixed-age play in this group of Senegalese children is reported in greater detail in Bloch, 1988 for the 1973-76 study and in Bloch, 1989 for the 1979 study. The finding of same-age play, we believe, relates to the availability of similar age cousins in close proximity for play, as well as the cultural custom toward sex and age grouping of same-age children. Other studies of children's play groups have noted more mixed-age grouping of children, where the social density of children is less (see Konner 1975 on reports on the Kalahari Kung Hunter-gatherers, and Harkness & Super 1985 related to Kipsigis children's play and work).

8. Girls also imitated dancing by women during festivals, weddings, etc., as well as some agricultural work they saw men and women doing outside the village.

REFERENCES

This is a selective bibliography on recent research on African children and play. It goes beyond the references cited in the chapter for those interested in examining children's play research in Africa, but is limited to the ERIC and journal searches that the two authors conducted. Finally, it concentrates on research conducted since the late 1970s when Schwartzman and Barbera's (1977) and Schwartzman's (1978) reviews were conducted.

Agiobu-Kemmer, I. (1984). Cognitive and affective aspects of infant development. In H. V. Curran (Ed.), *Nigerian children: Developmental perspectives*. London: Routledge & Kegan Paul.

Bloch, M. N. (1984). Play materials: Considerations from a West African setting. *Childhood Education, 60*(5), 345-348.

Bloch, M. N. (1988). The effect of seasonal maternal employment on young Senegalese children's behavior. *Journal of Comparative Family Studies*, vol. xix(3), 397-417.

Bloch, M. N. (1989). Young boys' and girls' play at home and in the community: A cultural-ecological framework. In Bloch, M. N. and Pellegrini, A. D. *The ecological context of children's play*. Norwood, N.J.: Ablex Publishing Co.

Bloch, M. N. (1991). Critical science and the history of child development's influence on early education research. *Early Education and Development, 2*(2), 95-108.

Bloch, M. N., & O'Rourke, S. (1982). The nonsocial play of young Senegalese children: Sex differences and the effect of maternal employment. In J. Loy (Ed.), *Paradoxes of play*. West Point, New York: Leisure Press.

Dickerscheid, J. D., Schwartz, P. M., Noir, S., & El-Taliawy, M. S. T. (1988). Gender concept development of preschool-aged children in the United States and Egypt. *Sex Roles, 18*(11-12), 669-677.

Dixon, S. D., LeVine, R. A., Richman, A., & Brazelton, T. B. (1984). Mother-child interaction around a teaching task: An African-American comparison. *Child Development, 55*, 1252-1264.

Eastman, C. M. (1986). Nyimbo Za Watoto: The Swahili child's world view. *Ethos, 14*(2), 144-173.

Hampton, J. (1989). Play and development in rural Zimbabwean children. *Early Child Development and Care, 47*, 1-61.

Harkness, S. & Super, C. (1985). The cultural context of gender segregation in children's peer groups. *Child Development, 56*, 216-224.

Harkness, S. & Super, C. M. (1986). The cultural structuring of children's play in a rural African community. In Blanchard, K. (Ed.), *The many faces of play*. Champaign, Illinois: Human Kinetics Publishing, Inc.

Heath, S. B. (1983). *Ways with words*. New York: Cambridge University Press.

Hennenberg, M., Warton, C. M. R., & Hollingshead, E. (1987). Physical growth and motor performance of socially disadvantaged children in the Western Cape Province. *American Journal of Physical Anthropology, 78*(2), 239-240.

Hinckley, P. (1985). "Let me dance before you": The educative role of performance in a West African children's masquerade, art, social change, third world education. Unpublished Ph.D. dissertation. Boston University. (publication no.: AAC8601351)

Kilbride, P. L. & Kilbride, J. C. (1990). *Changing family life in East Africa.* University Park, Pa.: The Pennsylvania State University Press.

King, J. (1983). The effects of nursery education as measured in junior primary school children. Unpublished manuscript, University of Pretoria, South Africa. (Abstract Only; Eric publication no.: AAC0554298)

King, N. (1982). Work and play in the classroom. *Social Education, 46*(2), 110-113.

Lancy, D. (1975). Play in the enculturation of children: A case study from West Africa. Unpublished Ph.D. dissertation. University of Pittsburgh.

Lancy, D. (1977). The play behavior of Kpelle children during rapid cultural change. In D. F. Lancy and B. A. Tindall (Eds.), *The anthropological study of play: Problems and prospects.* West Point, New York: Leisure Press.

Lancy, D. (1980). Work and play: The Kpelle case. In Schwartzman, H. B. *Play and culture.* Cornwall, New York: Leisure Press.

Leacock, E. (1976). At play in African villages. In J. S. Bruner, A. Jolly, & K. Sylva (Eds.), *Play—Its role in development and evolution.* New York: Basic Books.

LeVine, R. A. & White, M. I. (1986). *Human conditions: The cultural basis of educational development.* New York: Routledge & Kegan Paul.

Liddell, C. (1988). The social interaction and activity patterns of children from two San groups living as refugees on a Namibian military base. *Journal of Cross-Cultural Psychology, 19*(3), 341-360.

Liddell, C. & Kruger, P. (1987). Patterns of activity and social behavior in a South African township nursery: Some effects of crowding. *Merrill-Palmer Quarterly, 33*(2), 206-228.

Liddell, C. & Kvalsvig, J. (1991). Urbanicity as a predictor of children's social behaviour and activity patterns: Black South African children in the year before school. Unpublished manuscript, under review for publication.

Liddell, C., Kvalsvig, J., Strydom, N., Qotyana, P., & Shabalala, A. (manuscript in review). An observational study of five-year-old Black South African children in the year before school. *International Journal of Behavioral Development.*

Morelli, G. A. (1986). *Social development of 1, 2, and 3 year old Efe and Lese children within the Ituri forest of Northeastern Zaire: The relation amongst culture, setting, and development.* Unpublished Ph.D. dissertation. University of Massachusetts-Amherst.

Munroe, R. H. & Munroe, R. L. (1984a). Infant experiences and childhood cognition: A longitudinal study among the Logoli of Kenya. *Ethos, 12,* 291-306.

Munroe, R. H., & Munroe, R. L. (1984b). Children's work in four cultures: Determinants and consequences. *American Anthropologist, 86,* 369-379.

Munroe, R. H., Munroe, R. L., Michelson, C., Koel, A., Bolton, R., & Bolton, C. (1983). Time allocation in four societies. *Ethnology, 22*(4), 255-270.

Negussie, B. (1989). Health, nutrition and informal education of preschool children in South-West Ethiopia. Paper presented at the International Conference on Early Education and Development, Hong Kong.

Raum, O. F. (1940/1967). *Chaga childhood.* London: Oxford University Press.

Reynolds, P. (1989). *Childhood in crossroads.* Cape Town: David Philip.

Richter, L. M., Grieve, K. WE., & Austin, D. (1988). Scaffolding by Bantu mothers during object play with their infants. *Early Child Development and Care, 34,* 63-75.

Schwartzman, H. B. (1978). *Transformations: The anthropology of children's play.* New York: Plenum Press.

Schwartzman, H. (1986). The sociocultural context of play. In A. W. Gottfried and C. C. Brown (Eds.), *Play Interactions: The contributions of play materials and parental involvement to children's development.* Proceedings of the eleventh Johnson and Johnson pediatric round table. Lexington, Mass: Lexington Books.

Schwartzman, H. B. & Barbera, L. (1977). Children's play in Africa and South America: A review of the ethnographic literature. In D. F. Lancy and B. A. Tindall (Eds.), *The anthropological study of play: Problems and prospects.* Cornwall, New York: Leisure Press (pp. 11-21).

Shostak, M. (1980). *Nisa.* Cambridge, Mass.: Harvard University Press.

Sigman, M., Neumann, C., Carter, E., Cattles, D. J., D'Souza, S., & Bwibo, N. (1988). Home interactions and the development of Embu toddlers in Kenya. *Child Development, 59,* 1251-1261.

Stromquist, N. P. (1989). Determinants of educational participation and achievement of women in the third world: A review of the evidence and a theoretical critique. *Review of Educational Research, 59*(2), 143-183.

Strydom, L. M. (April, 1985). Development of communication between African mothers and their infants in the first year of life. Paper presented at the Biennial Meeting of the Society for Research in Child Development, Toronto, Ontario, Canada.

Super, C. M. & Harkness, S. (1980). *Anthropological perspectives on child development.* San Francisco: Jossey-Bass.

Turner, E. & Blodgett, W. (1988). The carnivalization of initiation in Zambia. *Play and Culture, 1,* 191-204.

Udwin, O. & Shmukler, D. (1981). The influence of sociocultural, economic, and home background factors on children's ability to engage in imaginative play. *Developmental Psychology, 17*(1), 66-72.

Wenger, M. (1983). Gender role socialization in an East African community: Social interaction between two- and three-year-olds and older children in social ecological perspective. Unpublished Ph.D. dissertation. Harvard University.

Whiting, B. B. (1980). Culture and social behavior: A model for the development of social behavior. *Ethos, 8*(2), 95-116.

Whiting, B. B. & Edwards, C. P. (1988). *Children of different worlds.* Cambridge: Harvard University Press.

Whittemore, R. D. (1988). Child caregiving and socialization to the Mandinka way: Toward an ethnography of childhood. Unpublished Ph.D. dissertation. University of California, Los Angeles.

Whittemore, R. D. & Beverley, E. (1989). Trust in the Mandinka way: The cultural context of sibling care. In P. Zukow, *Sibling interaction across cultures.* New York: Springer-Verlag.

KATHLEEN BENNETT deMARRAIS
PATRICIA A. NELSON
JILL H. BAKER

9

Meaning in Mud:
Yup'ik Eskimo Girls at Play*

The afternoon sun warms the muddy banks of the Kuskok-wim River as five young Yup'ik Eskimo girls sit quietly talking and working their dull, flat knives into the mud in front of them. They are carefully preparing smooth mud palettes to be used for telling stories. This spot on the riverbank has been a favorite story knifing place of the girls for years. It is well away from the foot and bicycle traffic of the boardwalks that connect the houses to the church, school, post office, grocery store, and other fre-quently visited buildings in the center of the village. After their palettes are ready, the girls begin their storytelling. Each story-teller illustrates her tale by drawing symbols in the mud, which are erased and replaced with new symbols as the story unfolds. When one storyteller finishes, another begins, until they tire of the play or it is time to go home for dinner.

This scene used to be common in many of the Eskimo vil-lages in southwestern Alaska. The activity, known as storyknifing, was a daily activity in good weather in the lives of girls (ages six to twelve). Now, storyknifing has been replaced by more contemporary forms of play, as well as television and videotaped films. Women who are now in their thirties and forties talk fondly of spending afternoon and evening hours storyknifing with friends when they were children. In many villages today storyknifing is alive only in the memories of these women. In other villages one can find an occasional group of young girls who still enjoys this traditional form of storytelling.

In this article we describe storyknifing as practiced by a small group of young girls in one Yup'ik Eskimo village on the Kuskokwim River. Following a discussion of our theoretical perspectives, previous literature, and research methods, we examine the process of storyknifing in the lives of these young girls. We describe the utensils they use, the places they select for the storytelling, and the types of stories they tell. We supplement this discussion with findings from our interviews with Yup'ik women from other villages who talked with us about their childhood storyknifing experiences. We conclude with a discussion of the role storyknifing has played in Yup'ik Eskimo culture. We found that storyknifing is an activity that continues to provide a forum for young girls to learn cultural knowledge about kinship patterns, gender roles, and community norms and values. It is also a way in which children learn and practice cognitive skills necessary in the communities in which they live.

THEORETICAL PERSPECTIVES

This study has been informed by several different theoretical frameworks. When we began the study we were intrigued with the work of Au and Jordan (1981) at the Kamehameha Early Education Program (KEEP) in Honolulu. Jordan had studied the "talk story" of the native Hawaiians who constructed stories cooperatively in daily play. This talk story participation structure was used then as a basis for reading instruction in the KEEP program. Anthropologists of education (Au and Jordan 1981; Mohatt and Erickson 1981; Van Ness 1981; Vogt 1985) have studied participant structures in social interaction within various cultural contexts and have proposed that for children from different cultural backgrounds to be successful in schools, classroom instruction must be congruent with children's home cultures. Erickson (1984) argues that

It may be that culturally congruent instruction depoliticizes cultural difference in the classroom, and that such depoliticization has important positive influences on the teacher-student relationship. Such a situation in the classroom might prevent the emergence of student resistance.

Our initial intention was to study the interaction structures of storyknifing to better understand communication patterns among Yup'ik Eskimos. We thought that our work could inform teachers who work with Yup'ik Eskimo children, but now find that with so few children engaged in the activity, this strategy may no longer be appropriate. Perhaps storyknifing is an activity that Yup'ik parents and grandparents could teach in schools as part of a cultural heritage curriculum.

A second perspective that informed our work is the work of those scholars who have studied children's cognition within sociocultural contexts. Vygotsky (1978) explained that external dialogues or interactions with people around us are necessary to develop inner speech and awareness of one's own thought processes. He recognized the importance of the individual's cultural context:

> From the very first days of the child's development his/her activities acquire a meaning of their own in a system of social behavior and, being directed towards a definite purpose, are refracted through the prism of the child's environment. The path from object to child and from child to object passes through another person. This complex human structure is the project of a developmental process deeply rooted in the links between individual and social history.

The work of Scribner and Cole (1981), Lave (1977, 1988), Rogoff and Lave (1984), and others suggest that to understand cognition it is essential to examine specific social and cultural contexts in which cognition takes place; context is an integral aspect of cognitive events. Tharp and Gallimore (1988) explore the process by which children develop cognition and communication skills within the interactions of their daily lives:

> Long before they enter school, children are learning higher-order cognitive and linguistic skills. Their teaching takes

place in the everyday interactions of domestic life. Within these goal-directed activities, opportunities are available for more capable members of the household to assist and regulate child performances. Through these mundane interactions, children learn the accumulated wisdom and the cognitive and communicative tools of their culture. They begin to develop functional cognitive systems; they begin to generalize their new skills to new problems and to novel aspects of familiar situations; they learn how to communicate and think.

Cognition studies in cultural contexts have been influential in the research presented here. We were interested in storyknifing as one of the everyday activities in the lives of Eskimo children that helped them to develop cultural, communicative, and cognitive skills. In our research, we found that storyknifing provided a forum for children to learn and reinforced the cognitive skills of observation, sequencing, classification, making inferences and predictions, problem solving, logical reasoning, and developing spatial relationships and memory skills. In addition, the girls developed their own symbol system, which they used as a way to "write" their stories.

A final theoretical lens that has shaped our thinking here is that of feminists. Because much of the work of the human sciences has concentrated on the lives of males, feminist researchers have used gender as a central analytic concept to deepen our understanding of women. Rosaldo reminds us that "sexist traditions have, of course, made our records uneven. Now more than ever we see just how little is known about women" (Rosaldo 1980).

The omission of women from scientific studies is almost universally ignored when scientists draw conclusions from their findings and generalize what they have learned from the study of men to lives of women. If and when scientists turn to the study of women, they typically look for ways in which women conform to or diverge from patterns found in the study of men. With the Western tradition of dividing human nature into dual but parallel streams, attributes traditionally associated with the masculine are valued, studied, and articulated, while those associated with the feminine tend to be ignored.

It is clear from the lack of research on storyknifing in Yup'ik Eskimo culture, an activity that is gender specific to females, that it has been overlooked as an object of anthropological study. Although storyknifing was a popular activity in traditional villages throughout the Yup'ik regions, there is little mention of it in anthropological literature. Ager (1971,1975,1980) relied on recollections of high school- and college-age women for her description of childhood storyknifing activities. In an earlier study, Oswalt (1964) described storyknifing in the Napaskiak area on the Kuskokwim River. He collected a series of stories as part of a larger ethnographic study of Yup'ik girls; at that time their stories were told to one another solely in Yup'ik. The stories, rather than analysis of the storyknifing process, were the objects of Oswalt's research. No studies to date have chronicled the storyknifing activities as they occur in the daily lives of Yup'ik girls. We were able to study the storyknifing activities of one small group of young girls as they played in their village along the Kuskokwim River. We have attempted to capture here what it has been like to participate in storyknifing in Yup'ik Eskimo villages in recent years.

METHODOLOGY

This research is the result of a project with three distinct phases. The first phase involved data collection during the 1986-87 academic year, when Bennett deMarrais lived in the Kuskokwim area and worked directly with Yup'ik women attending a University of Alaska, Fairbanks, field-based teacher education program. Her work took her to many Yup'ik villages in southwestern Alaska from the Kuskokwim River delta to the Bering Sea and north to the Yukon River area. During this time, she talked informally with women in many different villages about the use of storyknifing in those villages. This phase helped us to identify villages in which storyknifing was still in use by young girls and also those villages where storyknifing had been a common play activity but was no longer used. We learned about traditional storyknifing utensils and the types of stories told, but did not learn enough about specific symbols or the actual way in which the play progressed. We believed that we would have to actually observe the activity in progress to gain this knowledge. Readers must remember here that the cold climate in southwestern

Alaska limits time in which children can actually play in the mud, and thus limits access to viewing this activity.

The second phase of the project began in the summer of 1987, when we had gained entry into an Eskimo village where we spent one month living with an extended Yup'ik family. Both Bennett deMarrais and Nelson became close friends of this family through our university work and were invited to share in the daily life of the family for a portion of the summer, a time when we were most likely to see storyknifing activity in the village. In addition to accompanying the girls as they played, we also helped with family chores and participated in social activities. This village, similar in size to other Yup'ik villages in the region, had a population of approximately 250. The village center consisted of a post office, a general store, a health center, a laundry, and an airstrip.[1]

During this second phase, we visited several other villages in the vicinity (Achiachak, Bethel, Kipnuk, Scammon Bay) to look for storyknifing activity, but were unable to find any children engaged in storyknifing. We visited with many women who reported that storyknifing was no longer a part of the play activities of the children in those villages. We also talked with several women who demonstrated some of the storyknifing figures they remembered from their childhood play (see symbol drawing by mid-life women in figures 9.1, 9.2, 9.3, and 9.4).

In the final phase of the project, we continued to study storyknifing during the 1987-88 academic year also through interviews with ten Yup'ik Eskimo college students at the University of Alaska, Fairbanks. These audiotaped interviews with students were transcribed and added to our database to help triangulate the data we had collected previously. The students, who volunteered to be part of the study, talked about their storyknifing play in the southwestern Alaska villages of Quinhagak, Kipnuk, Bethel, Kwethluk, Scammon Bay, and Mekoryuk.

During the actual participant observation portion of the study, we were able to observe a group of children storyknifing, the primary participants included five girls between the ages of nine and twelve. Two of these were daughters of the family who had invited us to stay with them. The others were neighbors and cousins of the girls. These children were bilingual (English and Yup'ik) but used English as the primary language in their play together. The questions that guided our research throughout each phase of the study were the following:

FIGURE 9.1
Storyknife Symbols

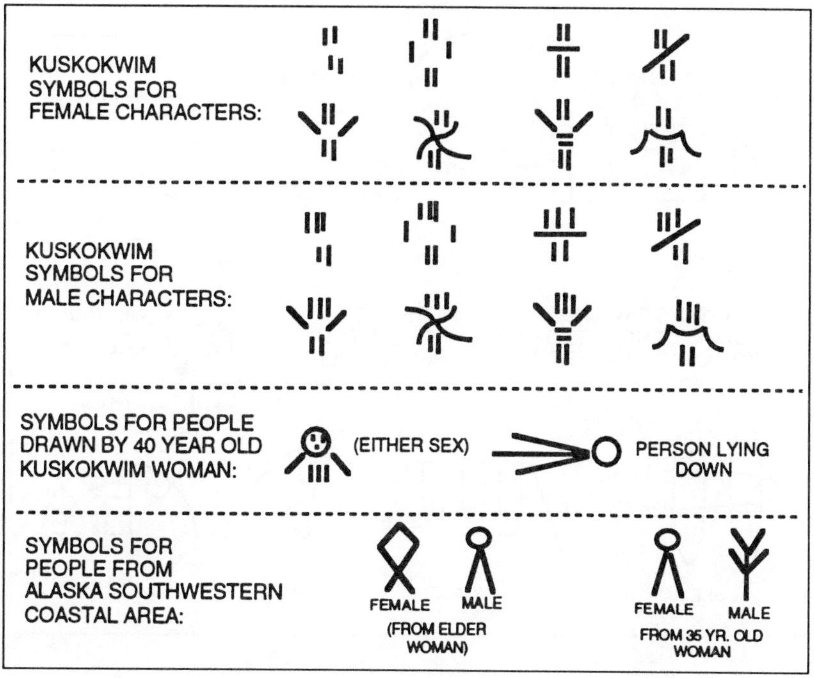

1. When and how does storyknifing occur in the community?
2. Who are the participants?
3. What are the types and content of the stories told?
4. What themes and/or values are expressed in the stories?
5. What symbols are used in the storyknife illustrations?
6. What are the communicative styles of the storytelling?
7. How has storyknifing changed with the increased introduction of Western culture into this area?

Primary data collection methods were participant observation and ethnographic interviewing (Goetz and LeCompte 1984; Spradley 1979, 1980). We gathered an extensive amount of data during this period in the form of field notes, informal interviews with children and adults, photographs, and audio- and videotapes. We used a battery-operated laptop computer to expand our field notes during the evenings. This proved to be extremely valuable because we were able to enter on the stories that were told by the girls during

FIGURE 9.2
Storyknife Symbols

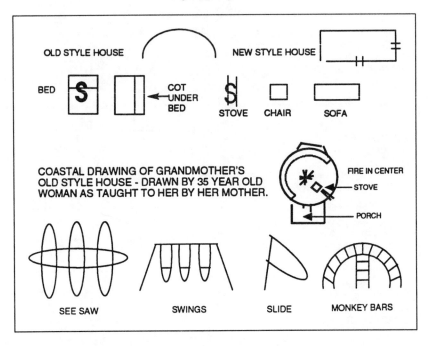

the day, and as we did so, the children assisted us by reading and correcting any errors we made in the notes. This was one way we were able to confirm with the children that the data (particularly the story transcripts) were accurate. We also had the children check all of the storyknife symbols we collected in our field notes to confirm their accuracy.[2] Another research strategy we used in the field was setting aside time to talk with one another on audiotape about our research process. We limited our videotaping to three two-hour sessions of actual storyknifing activity. Although we felt that videotape was essential for capturing a representative sample of the process of storyknifing, we tried to limit our use of videotape so as not to intrude extensively on our participants' lives.

DESCRIPTION OF THE STORYKNIFING ACTIVITY

A Typical Evening in the Village

It is approximately seven o'clock in the evening, and we have just finished a dinner of duck, rice, and salad. We all made a

FIGURE 9.3
Kuskokwim Storyknife Symbols

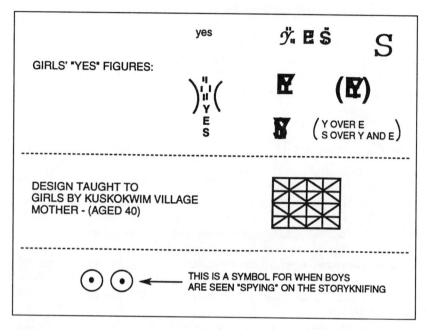

FIGURE 9.4
Kuskokwim Storyknife Symbols

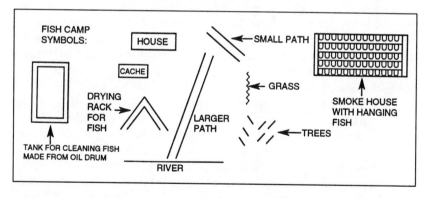

rather large dent in the huge bowl of agutag, an Eskimo favorite, which consists of a variety of wild berries, sugar, and something to hold it together—usually a mixture of instant mashed potatoes and Crisco. The adults continue to sit around the small circular table in the kitchen talking and drinking tea. The talk is a mixture of Yup'ik and English. John and Elizabeth (aged seventy-three and seventy-two) are the owners and elders of this home and have graciously included us in their lives as friends of their daughter, Margaret, and son-in-law, David, and their children (Katherine, Sharon, and Kenny). Although the elders speak very little English, they seem to understand quite a bit, and we are able to communicate comfortably. We are not Yup'ik speakers, so we must rely on Margaret and David and their children for translations.

As the children finish their dinner, they go into the living room to watch television with their cousins and friends from neighboring houses. The increasing number of young girls gathering in the living room makes it apparent that the activities are about to change. This is confirmed by Molly, a ten-year-old cousin, who comes into the kitchen waving her storyknife at us. This is her silent signal that the girls are about to go off to storyknife. Katherine and Sharon reach up to grab their storyknives from the ledge above the door. This is their secret hiding place. Their knives have been made by cutting and filing pieces of metal banding used to secure building materials that are barged into the village. Pieces of these bands can be found easily around the village.

The girls file out the door, walking through the tundra grass to a long boardwalk that leads to one of their favorite storyknifing spots on the bank of the river. These boardwalks are built throughout the village because of the constant summer rain and mud. It is very difficult to walk on a slippery tundra mud without falling. The children, who inevitably become covered with mud, have a practice of having one set of clothing for inside the house and another for outside. After a few falls in the mud, we quickly learned the value of this practice.

When we arrive at the storyknive "place" on the riverbank near Molly's house, the girls immediately take their places and begin to work the mud with their knives. Looking around the small circle of children, we notice that there are five girls: Sharon (eleven), Katherine (ten), Molly (ten), Bridget (twelve), and Pauline (nine). Each has a storyknife, either a metal butter knife from the kitchen or one made from the metal banding. They are all busy preparing their places for the next phase of actual storytelling. Two of the "tagalongs," or younger children, sit behind, but close to, their siblings to watch the activity and learn how to storyknife. This evening, Bridget's sister, Anastasia, and Kenny, who are both five years old, are present. Although the activity is gender specific to girls, it is acceptable for younger brothers to watch, especially if an older sister is responsible for child care. According to all the people we talked to about storyknifing, Eskimo boys never engage in the storyknifing activities.

We watch as the girls deepen the border around their places, dig deep, narrow holes next to their places, and use soft, wet mud from these holes to spread across their storyknife places. The girls spit on their places to moisten the mud. This is commonly done throughout the storyknifing activity. After about ten minutes, the places are of the consistency preferred by each of the girls. Katherine prefers hers to be very soft, so she sometimes leaves the circle to find softer mud closer to the river. These differences in preference are discussed by the girls. Katherine pokes her knife into the places of other girls to test their consistency. Overall, the storyknife places have the consistency of thick, creamy chocolate icing.

The next phase of the activity begins with a bid for a story, such as "Who has a story?" or "Do you remember when" or "One time I had a dream." One of the girls begins to relate the story that is illustrated on the storyknife place. As she talks, the other girls listen attentively while continuing to stroke their storyknife places with their knives. Occasionally, the excess mud gets scraped onto their shoes. If the girls are really involved in the story, they may imitate the storyknifer's drawing on their own place. After a particularly scary story told by Bridget, Sharon remarked, "I was copying you when all the people were getting killed." At the end of a story, the teller makes a statement such as "That's all I know" to indicate that she is finished. Bridget finished telling her very scary dream with the statement "It was crazy!"

The girls take turns telling stories and drawing illustrations with their storyknives. There is no set pattern for turn taking. Following the completion of one story, another girl begins, usually with something that relates to the last story. For example, following Bridget's scary dream, Sharon recalled that she remembered a dream she once had, and then proceeded to tell that story. The older, more experienced storyknifers dominate the storytelling.

The storyknifing sessions usually last for two or three hours. This evening, when the girls had finished telling stories, they drew some designs on their places and played guessing games with one another. There seemed to be mutual consent as to when it was time to stop the storyknifing activity for the evening. After a lull in the talk, Bridget wrote the word "yes" on her storyknife place. Each of the other girls followed her lead and did the same. The "yes" is the ritualistic way the storyknifing sessions end for this group of girls. It was interesting that each girl's "yes" was stylized and very different from the others' (see figure 9.3). Then the girls got up from their places and went off as a group, talking and laughing, to the monkey bars. Sometimes the girls would stay at the activity until the curfew bell was sounded at ten o'clock. The long days of the Alaskan summer provide many hours of daylight to enjoy storyknifing.

Storyknives

Historically, storyknives were made of ivory, wood, or reindeer antlers, usually by the fathers and grandfathers of the young girls. In addition to the storyknives made from metal banding described previously, girls also use their family's kitchen knife or butter knife. The following quotations from interviews with college students provide rich descriptions of the storyknives they used as children:

> The storyknives we mainly used were like bailing wire from construction places. Sometimes we used to go down where they were building houses and stuff. So we would take it out from those woods [building supplies] and those woods would start falling and the old women would chase us. We used to do that all the time. Then when we would get the bailing wire out, we'd cut them in pieces. When we'd have a whole bunch, we'd to go to the place where there is cement and we'd scrape them to our desired shape. Like some of them were shaped like that with rounded edges. Some of them were pointed like that. And my favorite, oh, that was the best, where they were banded together already or sometimes we tried to be cool and have different shapes and have both shapes—one side rounded and one side pointed—two-sided. My sister had a whole collection of storyknives. She never did let us use them so most of the times we were stuck with our own. Other times we'd take mom's butter knives, but I guess she wouldn't let us take them. Then other times, when there was nothing around, I took a spoon, one of my mom's wooden spoons and pounded it with a

hammer. Or sometimes, when you're just sitting around, you'd just take a piece of wood.

I don't have my old ones. We used to use those, you know, metal bands they strap boxes and crates with. We used to do storyknifing with those metal bands. We never used to really like the wide ones. They were too wide, you know, but there were some that were too flimsy, that you can't really hold onto them. But there were some that were just the right size, the right width and we'd get those bands and we'd break them in half, you know, just keep bending them back until it breaks off, then we'd get, what you call, wire cutters and like we'd have a piece of band like this, then we'd cut a piece off like this with the wire cutter and then we'd have another, so it would be like this. Then we'd get a file, and then file these parts, you know, roundish like so they won't be too sharp and file those ends and sometimes we'd have round shapes like this and sometimes we'd have sort of pointy shapes. And my grandpa used to make a whole bunch for us too, and then, later as we got older, you know, we could use the wire cutters and file, so we'd make our own, and sometimes we try to have the most storyknives than anyone else—try to find wire bands and make a whole bunch and oh, sometime we'd use our butter knife and sometimes she'd give up some of her old ones, or if she doesn't have any she'd give us a butter knife and say, you know, "Make sure you bring it in now." We'd say, "We will" and we'd go out and start storyknifing and we'd lose them outside and then we'd try to ask her again later for another butter knife and she won't give them to us and she'd say, "You're losing all my butter knives."

My dad made me a wooden storyknife, but it didn't work as good because it wasn't flexible enough and scratched the mud or scraped it off and so I never did use that. Silverware that didn't have grooves in it were better, more smoother, that were bendable. Some butter knives have grooves in them, but the ones that didn't worked better and they were wider. A friend of mine had a real good one that was really wide, was a big butter knife with a wide blade. It was the only one in Alaska.

Ivory storyknives were more common with the previous generation. The women college students we interviewed remembered that their mothers and grandmothers had ivory storyknives, usually carved for them by fathers and grandfathers. These storyknives were reserved for wintertime storykniving in the snow, as explained by one of the college students.

> Well I never storyknifed in the snow. My mom used to though. I guess if they storyknifed in the snow, they used to use knives and she has a whole bunch of those, and she has, I think, one that she used to use and be storyknifing in the snow with ivory.

In this village there are several sites used for the storyknifing activity. The favorite place is under the old, blue Bureau of Indian Affairs (BIA) school building. The girls refer to this place as the "blue school." It has been a favorite place for three generations. Molly's mother, Leota, who is also Margaret's sister, told us that the blue school was one of their favorite places for storyknifing when they were young girls. The girls crawl under the school through an opening near one end about two feet high, which has been worn down over time from children going in and out. Just inside this opening, there is a circle of storyknife "places" that remain from previous sessions there. The girls explained to us that this is a good place because they can hide from the boys who, when the girls are playing in more open places, like to ride their bikes through the activity. It is also a site that stays relatively dry during the rainy summer season and still maintains enough moisture in the mud to be of the appropriate consistency for the activity. A college student from this village also described the blue school as one of her storyknifing places:

> We had special, our own little special places. It would be like, probably under the school, if we were at school. Or it would be by somebody's house where the dirt was really good.

Another favorite among the girls is the place on the edge of the village by the riverbank. It is out of the way of both bike and pedestrian traffic, has a good quantity of suitable mud, and also provides a lovely view of the river. The storyknifing places on this site are well worn and appear to have been there for many years.

Leota told us that in the spring she and Margaret used to walk across the river on the ice, just prior to breakup time, to storyknife. Again, this was a place that was out of the way of the village traffic and therefore afforded some privacy. The girls mentioned several other storyknifing places, but during our stay in the village, these were not used by the children. They tended to use the same two places repeatedly.

Although we have found storyknifing to be primarily a summertime activity, there is some indication that it used to be more common throughout the year. A college student from a Bering seacoast village explained that she and her friends used to carry snow to their porches in the winter and spend hours storyknifing. Other interviewees told us of taking mud on boards into their houses for winter storyknifing.

Storyknifing Symbols

Storyknifers in our study used a variety of symbols in their play (see figure 9.1, p. 185). Although there were basic elements necessary for each symbol, there was also room for each girl to create her own individualized style. For example, the figure drawn for females had two top vertical lines, two bottom vertical lines, and some type of separating lines. However, we collected eight variations of the female figure drawn by the girls. The male counterpart matched the female. The male figure had three vertical lines on top and two on the bottom, with a separating line in the middle. When we asked how the girls determine what symbols to use for the male and female figures, Sharon explained that they draw whichever figure is "easiest and fastest."

Differences in the symbols can be seen from one village to another and also from generation to generation within the same village. For example, the male and female figures drawn by one of the women elders in a coastal village were very different from those drawn by the girls we observed. In the same village, Molly's mother, Leota, drew a unisex figure and indicated that when she was storyknifing as a young girl they did not differentiate according to sex.

Symbols change with the changing culture and Westernization of the villages. Symbols for old-style houses are rounded; newer houses are drawn as rectangles. On one occasion, when one of the girls was attempting to draw a new-style house with two stories, another remarked, "Two floors. You're in trouble."

Symbols for monkey bars, swings, slides, and seesaws, which are common in the storyknifing we observed, of course, were not drawn before such articles were introduced into the culture with the building of schools and playgrounds in the villages.

The use of the symbol or the word "yes" to signify the end of a storyknifing session was not used by the women in Margaret and Leota's generation. When they finished telling their stories, they agreed orally to stop the play. We found no suitable explanation for why this group of girls used "yes" to mark the end of the session. One possible explanation could rest in the difference in the use of the language.

Storyknifing used to be totally in Yup'ik, and because Yup'ik is primarily a spoken, rather than a written, language, a written word (such as "yes") would not have been used in the play. The storyknifing we observed was entirely in English, as the girls involved in the play were fluent English speakers and were not as fluent in speaking Yup'ik. It is quite possible that because the English-speaking world relies so much on the printed word, the girls incorporated English words into their storyknifing.

Phases of the Storyknifing Activity

We have identified three major phases involved in the storyknifing activity. The first is what we refer to as "getting ready." This includes the following activities: (1) A group of girls gather and make a decision to go yaaruik-ing, the Yup'ik word for storyknifing. Our observations revealed that this may be a decision made when the girls are already together at someone's house or while playing on the monkey bars in the center of the village, or it may entail one of the girls calling the others on the phone to arrange for such a gathering. It is a cooperative decision in that all girls agree to go storyknifing. They also agree on where to go to do the storyknifing. (2) Each of the girls then gets her storyknife, and as a group they proceed to the designated storyknifing place. (3) The girls sit down in front of their places and begin to prepare the mud by scraping, spitting, adding wet mud, digging a hole next to their place for additional wet mud, scraping the borders around their place, and so on. The girls usually take the same place each time. Sometimes, if the weather has been particularly rainy, the girls will find boards to sit on as part of this initial "getting ready" phase. This phase was described by one of our college students in an interview.

Well, we'd get our storyknives and we'd find a clear spot and if it was messy we'd clear up some wood chippings or grass and stuff and smooth it out, and we'd usually like to go over it with smooth mud or clayish mud-like and, you know, with the side [of the storyknife] and then with the flat part we'd smooth it out, and sometimes if it wasn't moist enough, we'd spit on there. If we wanted it moister, we'd spit on there and sometimes, you know, after you dry it, after you do something on it [draw], smooth it out again if you're gonna tell another story, or are waiting for someone to tell a story and we'd dig a hole in the mud here, a little hole by our storyknifing place and we'd add more on top and put more mud on top and erase it off again and we'd get logs or a piece of can and we'd sit down there. Well, I guess whoever had a story ready to tell then, or you know, someone who really wanted to tell a story, they'd tell a story.

The second phase of the storyknifing activity is the actual storytelling phase. This commences with a call for a story in the form of a statement, such as "Who has a story?" or a bid for a turn in the form of a statement, such as "I remember when." A story begins in this way. While one girl talks and illustrates her story, the others listen attentively. They may continue to work the mud at their places. After one girl completes a story, another begins.

The final "wrapping up" phase of the storyknifing session begins when there is a lull in the talk. This is usually after a couple hours of storytelling. One of the girls writes "yes" on her place, and the others follow suit. This signals the end of the storyknifing play, and the girls generally get up and go off to their homes or to another activity.

Types of Stories

Ager (1980) described three different types of knifestories: traditional, everyday happening, and introduced. Traditional stories are folktales or stories that usually contain a moral. Everyday happenings are biographical or autobiographical accounts of either real events in the girls lives or events that could be real. Introduced stories are non-Eskimo in origin and are likely to be learned in school. Ager reports that these introduced stories played a minor role in the storyknifing activity of her informants

(Ager 1980). The stories we observed fit into those same categories. In addition to Ager's categories, we have added an additional type, which we refer to as "games and designs." We discuss and provide examples of each of these types of stories using data from our observations.

Traditional folktales. We observed several Eskimo folktales told by the girls during the storyknifing activity. These had been learned from a book of folktales (English version) given to Sahron and Katherine by their mother and read in English. This was one way in which their mother ensured that the girls became familiar with the traditional tales. We were told by both Margaret and Leota that they consider the maintenance of the Yup'ik language and culture to be extremely important. They encouraged this through the telling of traditional stories (usually in English because the children were not as fluent in Yup'ik) as well as the demonstrating of storyknifing stories and games. Leota explained that she was very pleased that Yup'ik language classes would be taught in the school for the first time during the 1987-88 school year.

The girl told the folktale entitled "Raven and the Mink" on several occasions. In this story, the raven scared his wife, the mink, by hiding and pretending to be someone else who demanded to have the food she had prepared. The following is a direct transcription from videotape:

SHARON: Once upon a time there was this mink

KATHERINE: Always once upon a time

SHARON: And the raven and they were married and a long time ago the houses used to be like this and there'd be a fireplace in the middle and a hole at the top and over here would be a tunnel to go outside. One day the um mink and the raven were inside the house and the raven told the mink to make some agutaq cause he was gonna go out and hunt so he went out because he told her to make the agutaq cause he might be hungry, so he went out and after he went she heard a voice down the opening and said and the voice said "Mink gimme some agutaq else I'll eat you" so she gave half the agutaq to that voice. Then he said again "Voice [Mink], gimme some agutaq else I'll eat you." So she gave all the agutaq and he ate it and when her husband came home, he asked where the agutaq was and she told him the voice came and took all the agutaq and the next day he went to get firewood and he told the mink to make agutaq again so he could have it when he came back and then after he left she heard that voice again from down in the tunnel and it said: "Mink, gimme some agutaq else I'll eat you." So she gave more of the agutaq, half the agutaq, then she, there was a voice: "Gimme some agutaq else I'll eat you," so she tossed the agutaq in and when her husband came home she told him that the voice came again and she was scared and that night, the next day she had the fire lit and it was going out a little bit and there was smoke a little bit in the hole and he was going out to go hunting and shoot birds and he told her to make agutaq again and he went out. When the voice came again from down in the tunnel, the voice said "Mink, gimme some agutaq else I'll eat you." So she threw half the agutaq into the hole and the voice came again, "Mink, gimme some agutaq else I'll eat you." So she took a piece of the wood and threw it into the hole opening and the voice went away and when her husband came back and here's the raven's beak (referring to drawing), and he has his hand over his eye and she told to look in his eye and she saw a piece of charred wood in his eye and she took it out and she was upset that she [he] was scaring her and um, making, teasing her and making her scared and, but she forgave him later on in their marriage but they never had any children after that incident.

It was interesting that the ending, although basically consistent in content, varied in the amount of elaboration provided. For example, the following are two variations of ending for the story taken from the transcriptions:

> So she took a piece of the wood and threw it into the hole opening and the voice went away and when her husband came back and here's the raven's beak (drawing it) and he has his hand over his eye and she told to look in his eye and she saw a piece of charred wood in his eye and she took it out and she was upset that she [he] was scaring her and um, making, teasing her and making her scared

and, but she forgave him later on in their marriage but they never had any children after that incident.

. . . and she looked in his eye. There was a piece of charred wood in his eye. She took it out and she was really furious with him cause he had been unfaithful to her and she was scared of that voice and after that incident they never had any children. That's all. That's all I know.

Although both versions relate the same basic storyline, the second introduces the notion of the husband's unfaithfulness. There are variations in the stories as different storytellers elaborate on the basic traditional folktales.

Everyday happenings. These stories are retellings of the daily adventures in the lives of the girls. For example, one day we accompanied a group of about ten children to a beach by the river, which they referred to as "Hawaii" because of its sandy beach, unusual for the area. To get there we walked down a path from the south end of the village, through some bushes, and out onto the beach. The children spent over an hour digging in the sand and making sand sculptures. That evening, during the storyknifing activity, one of the girls told and illustrated the story of "going to Hawaii." Her drawing detailed the paths, trees, the river, the beach, participants, and the fish camp seen on the way home (see figure 9.4).

This story was typical of stories that relate the day's events. Stories such as this are introduced by phrases such as "Remember the time." This type of story includes such things as going to fish camp, going berry picking, happenings at school during the school year, and other daily occurrences in the girls' lives.

On several occasions the girls used dreams as the basis for their storyknifing tales. The dreams tended to be rather violent, as is illustrated in "Bridget's Dream" below. As she tells about her dream, Bridget draws very quickly, so that much of the story related below is punctuated by her drawings. Her storytelling style is rapid and rhythmic.

BRIDGET: I had a dream like this. The river, that house. Molly (getting her attention) remember that dream, I told you that house, right there, you know the people, I swear to Christ, in the house and I went in and I saw a couch, the stove, the house was like this, the couch, the stove was right there, then I didn't see anything else but there was a little table over there and when I went in there was nobody and I saw some dead people.

KATHERINE: Um, hm, in the house and I saw a pot, here was the stove, the pot and I saw heads and hearts and guts and everything and then when I looked back at that couch there was a man and I ran out, was scared, then I swam across . . . then when I told everybody, you know, at [name of town] they swam across, "Let's go see this man and kill him" higher tone of voice to indicate someone else talking and then when they didn't come back out, they were dead. Well, now the people were, the house was almost full and then you know like this and I went to go get a knife from my house and then you know there was this house, the roof, the people were dead . . . and the couch, he was sitting there, he was eating, I forgot to tell this that he was eating the guts and heads and everything and I went in, I killed, they were dead and I went, I stabbed the people with a knife and when I went right here, the table, the people were here and then I went, I stabbed some of the people and then I finally killed that person. Then I woke up. It was crazy!

KATHERINE: Umgh! It was like real life.

OTHERS: Oooooh!

SHARON: I was copying you when all the people. . . .

SHARON: One time I had a dream . . . (begins to relate hers).

The use of this type of scary story was also reported by our college students.

Well, actually, the kind of stories I remember were sort of scary, I guess. Like there was this one story about the little girls who used the storyknife in the evening. She was all by herself. It was too dark and some kind of ghost grabbed her hand right from her storyknife and was trying to pull here. A friend of mine was telling that one and it was sort of like in the evening and she ran home.

The stories they used to tell long ago are sort of like teaching us lessons of some sort, like not to stay out too late, or you know, never do this or do that, you know, like if you're hunting or berry picking, or if you are alone, like they sort of teach us something. And other stories we make 'em up, you know, just make up our own stories as we go along, or try to think of scary stories or scare the people that are with us, you know, storyknifing, or funny stories, just make up our own, I guess.

Introduced stories. These stories involved tales from the media, either from videotaped movies or from television shows. The stories we observed included one based on cartoons, such as the "Gummy Bears," and one based on the movie, *Children of the Corn,* by Stephen King. These stories involved movies or television shows that were familiar to all of the girls in the group.

Games and designs. A number of games were used in the storyknifing activities. One game frequently played by the girls and mentioned by college student interviewees and adult women in other regional villages was called "Guess Whose House This Is?" This game was also reported by Ager (1971, 1975, 1979-1980). The game begins with one girl drawing a blueprint-type diagram of a house with all of the furniture (see figure 9.2, p. 000), and the other participants guess who the house belongs to based on the arrangement of furnishings. After a girl successfully guesses who the house belongs to, it is her turn to draw the next diagram. In an interview, a college student described this same game as she had played it as a child with her village friends.

From what I could remember, you know, kids my age, back then, we storyknifed when we like played, when we were trying to play like we called it "guess-guess whose house." And we'd make up this like a bow-like thing and make rooms and divide the box up into little sections. I mean like describe the house. And that's why we called it guess-guess whose house.

But if it's a story about guessing games, like "whose house," they [the other girls] would take turns. You try to pick a house that nobody knows in the village, that nobody ever visits and you've been there and then you draw the house and that person tries to guess it.

Another game involved guessing what a word is that has been drawn in design form. For example, on one occasion a girl drew the word "HELLO" with one letter directly over another; the others then had to guess the word.

Although we observed only one design activity, this type of storyknifing activity was reported by Margaret, Leota, and other Yup'ik women. We watched the girls practice drawing a particular geometric design during one session (see figure 9.3, p. 187). When asked where they learned the design, we were told that Molly's mother had taught it to them. When we asked Leota about it, she explained that she had learned different designs by watching her mother when she made the borders for parkas. She practiced these designs in her storyknifing play and taught one of these designs to the girls while they were storyknifing this past summer. Other women have confirmed this practice of using storyknifing as a means to practice and create designs that could be used later in the sewing of garments.

Yup'ik Women's Ways of Knowing

What are the ways of knowing that Yup'ik girls and women learn through their participation in storyknifing? How does storyknifing fit into the process of enculturation? The traditional Eskimo culture relies on an oral tradition. People learn primarily through listening to and observing the activities of others. Stories, rather than explanations, are paramount in the enculturation process. Stories told in storyknifing help reinforce cultural traditions, values, and skills. There is little question that the storyknifing activity for those women who are presently the mothers and grandmothers in the village affected the way they came to know themselves and their worlds and is still ingrained in their actions today. This is evident in the way in which Margaret and Leota illustrate daily conversations in storyknife fashion, with their fingers on the table or in the mud as they speak. Grandmother Elizabeth's story told to a small group of women during a leisurely steam bath, about the way her husband built their fish camp on a series of hills, is very much like the stories the girls tell in their storyknifing sessions. She described, rhythmically using her hands in storyknife motions, how she must walk up to get to the cutting table and get up to get to the drying rack and up to get to the smokehouse and up to get to the house. At the end of her story she laughed and said that her husband "must be a little mouse" for building the fish camp like this. It is not difficult to envision Sharon or Bridget telling and illustrating such a story on their mud palettes.

Historically, in Eskimo society, boys were enculturated into the group by listening to stories and participating in men's activities. The traditional center for these activities was the men's community house, or the *qasgiq*. With the Westernization of the culture, men and boys no longer use these community houses. There is no longer a male analog to storyknifing for the boys. Although this article does not attempt to address the ways that boys learn their world, it is interesting to note that, despite the tremendous changes brought about by Western influences, women and girls in some villages maintain, and even encourage, this traditional activity of storyknifing through which they learn about themselves and their worlds.

In the following discussion, we will describe the categories of cultural cognitive knowledge that are found in the storyknifing activities we observed. Although they overlap somewhat, these categories will provide more specific means to understand storyknifing as a way of knowing for these Yup'ik girls.

Cultural Knowledge

Kinship patterns. Present-day storyknifing continues to teach young girls about the kinship patterns within the village. Eskimo culture is one of connected relationships, and the sense of family is still very strong in the villages. The actual stories contain much useful information about family and village relationships. Explanations of family histories are also prevalent in the stories that the children tell. For example, in their stories of everyday events, the girls tell about the people they saw during the day and where they fit into the kinship system. Often, one girl will have information that corrects or supports another's account. The stories may explain why a member of the community is known by a particular nickname, to which family a woman belonged before her marriage, or how certain people are related to others. The stories are a means by which the girls can work together to construct the kinship system of the community.

Historically, Eskimo culture has relied on cooperation among its members to survive in a subsistence lifestyle under extreme environmental conditions. Through closely knit kinship systems, Yup'ik communities are able to maintain this cooperation. The storyknifing activity serves as a means for the girls to practice group cooperation and consensus. They are the cornerstones of the activity. The girls decide together when to begin and end the activity. They encourage one another to take turns telling stories. There is a sense of group solidarity in the behavior of the girls, as well as the content of the stories.

Gender roles. Male and female roles are of primary focus in the content of the stories. In the traditional folktales told by the girls, men did the hunting and fishing, and women performed the duties involved in food preparation and childrearing. Women in the folktales, although traditional in their roles, were also portrayed as powerful people. This is evidenced in the story "Raven and the Mink."

The stories told of everyday events provide the girls with a means to explore the ways in which these roles are changing in the village setting. For example, the girls' everyday stories included activities of men and women that were not necessarily along traditional lines. Women today hold jobs and go to college. Men help prepare fish and go berry picking.

In actual storyknifing sessions, the girls display to one another ways in which they are handling the responsibilities of child care in the nurturing behavior they display with younger brothers and sisters, the "tagalongs." We often observed the girls caring for and comforting younger brothers and sisters. The responsibility for the family unit is extremely important and reinforced through the play activities of girls.

Oral tradition. The oral tradition is being continued and practiced in this activity. Girls retell some of the traditional folktales as well as create stories and games of their own. They learn to perform for others in a setting that is comfortable and nonthreatening. This performance allows for individual recognition from their peers. Although Sharon explained that the girls were "all about the same" in their storyknifing skills, we observed that some girls told particular stories better than others and were called on to do so by the group. The older girls tended to tell more of the stories, thus teaching the younger girls by example.

Practicing subsistence skills. In this culture of subsistence living and scarce resources, storyknifing in the past provided a means by which girls could practice the skills of the adult women without wasting valuable items. For example, drawing a parka border design in a storyknifing session allowed the girls to practice what they had observed their mothers cutting out of skin. Today, there is less evidence of practicing the sewing skills needed in later life, but there continues to be discussion in the knifestories about how to pick berries and also how to cut, dry, and smoke fish—skills that remain relevant to village life.

Community norms and values. Many of the earlier folktales and "scary" stories told through the storyknifing process were means to teach the norms and values of the community. The consequences of inappropriate behavior were incorporated into these stories. For example, some of the stories mentioned earlier described the consequences for children who stay out after dark or for husbands who were unfaithful to their wives. The women in this village continue to teach the traditional folktales to their children to reinforce the Yup'ik values.

In addition to serving the purposes of transmitting the norms and values of the community, the scary or violent stories told by the girls seem to serve as a means for dealing with the more violent aspects of their daily lives. In our living and working with the Yup'ik people, we gained a sense of some of the violence that touches their daily lives in actual life situation and through the Western media that has been introduced to village life in recent years. Violent themes were evident in the stories told by the young girls. "Bridget's Dream," which graphically describes murder, and a retelling of a horror film, *Children of the Corn*, are typical examples of these themes. In a culture that is undergoing tremendous change, storyknifing provides a forum for discussing frightening experiences. It offers to the girls a therapeutic palette on which their experiences can be described and then quickly wiped away. In the most violent portions of their stories, the girls would stab the mud to punctuate their words, then effectively smooth the mud palette into its original condition. Fantasies and fears can be expressed, shared with close friends, and then wiped away.

Cognitive knowledge. Storyknifing provides a forum for learning or reinforcing many cognitive skills. Observation, spatial relationships, sequencing, classification, making inferences and predictions, problem solving, logical reasoning, and memory skills were repeatedly evident in the activity. For example, the game called "Guess Whose House" requires that the children draw very detailed blueprint-type diagrams to complete this type of activity, careful observation of the interior of houses in the village is required. The girls must know the exact placement of all the furniture in the house they are representing. The symbols for the furniture must be drawn correctly according to their placement in the house, requiring skills in observation and spatial relationships. Symbols for the household items and for people are classified according to type. The skill of sequencing is of primary importance in stories in which the girls relate their daily activities. These are told in the exact order in which they occurred.

Careful observation of natural phenomena and daily events are required to produce storyknife stories. The environment was the focus of many of the stories. For example, vegetation, the weather, the river, local animals, etc., were all integral parts of daily life stories. This awareness and exploration of the natural environment provides a means for girls to share and construct knowledge about their worlds.

Young children (about six years old and younger), commonly referred to as "tagalongs," learn the sound-symbol relationship. They observe the girls telling stories and drawing symbols to represent their spoken language. An essential skill in a literate society, storyknifing may serve to prepare these young children for the world of schooling through the reinforcement of sound-symbol relationships and other cognitive processes.

CONCLUSIONS

Despite the tremendous Western influences in this small village in southwestern Alaska, storyknifing continues to serve as a means by which these young girls come to know their culture and themselves. This environment, which supports and encourages Yup'ik storyknifing, provides for its children a very rich base of experiences vital to the development of cultural and cognitive knowledge as well as language skills. Yup'ik girls learn ways to work cooperatively with others to find their own voices.

Past generations in more traditional Yup'ik Eskimo society used the activity of storyknifing to transmit culture from the elders to the children. Through this activity, which provided hours of entertainment for the young girls, many of the core values, folklore, and behaviors of the community were practiced and reinforced. Now, with the Westernization of the culture, in many villages storyknifing is no longer part of the daily lives of the children. In response to our questions as to whether storyknifing could still be seen in the Yup'ik villages, interviewees, all from different villages, responded:

> Well, I don't really see much [children storyknifing in the village today]. My cousins, they try to storyknife, you know, they don't, and I'm sure they don't know much of the old stories because I never see anyone, you know, we never tell them. I don't know that many old stories, you know. There is no one around telling some of the old stories they used to tell, so they just sort of make up their own, or just storyknife just to be storyknifing, I suppose. Not as much as when we were younger, I guess. Nowadays they like to watch TV or they'd be embarrassed to do that.

> I don't see them doing it, no. Not anymore.

> Well, it seems like kids now don't play out as much as we used to, because, you know, they watch a lot of TV and videos. It was great! We played out a lot. Sometimes I feel sorry for these kids who just don't get out to play as often as I did when I was growing up.

From our own observations, and according to our participants, it seems that technology, in the form of television and videotape players, is contributing to the elimination of this type of play activity in Yup'ik villages. However, as we discussed earlier, the stories children see on television and videotapes, in this particular village, actually provide the girls with new material for use in their storyknife play.

The women in this village were very concerned that some of the traditional lifestyle was being lost. They were pleased that a bilingual program was to be started in the school to help teach and reinforce the Yup'ik language. They were actively involved in teaching the girls traditional Yup'ik behaviors in their daily lives by demonstrating subsistence skills, telling stories, and participating in the storyknife activities of the girls. For the parents, storyknifing provides an important link to a more traditional native

Alaskan society. For the girls, it provides a forum for exploring and constructing meaning in a culture that is undergoing tremendous and rapid change.

ACKNOWLEDGMENTS

An earlier draft of this article was presented at the Annual Meeting of the American Anthropological Association, Phoenix, Arizona, November 1988. The research reported here was supported by a grant from the Alaska Humanities Forum. We gratefully acknowledge that support. We also thank the Yup'ik families who invited us into their lives.

NOTES

*Reproduced by permission of the American Anthropological Association from *Anthropology & Education Quarterly* 23:2, June 1992. Not for sale or further reproduction.

1. Travel among villages in southwest Alaska is limited to air and river. Each village has a small airstrip for bush plane traffic, which villages depend on for mail and supplies from the regional center. River travel is limited to summer, after the breakup, when boats can freely navigate, and winter, when the ice is strong enough for wheeled vehicles and snow machines.

2. See Ager's (1971) study for symbols used in various Kuskokwim villages.

REFERENCES

Ager, L. P. (1971). *The Eskimo story complex of southwestern Alaska*. Masters thesis, University of Alaska, Fairbanks.

Ager, L. P. (1975). Alaskan Eskimo children's games and their relationship to cultural values and role structure in a Nelson Island community. Unpublished Ph.D. dissertation, Ohio State University.

Ager, L. P. (1979-80). Illustrated oral literature from southwestern Alaska. *Arts and Culture of the North* IV(1), 199-202.

Ager, L. P. (1980). Illustrated oral literature from southwestern Alaska. *Arts and Culture of the North* IV(2), 225-227.

Au, K. & Jordan, C. (1981). Teaching reading to Hawaiian children: Finding a culturally appropriate solution. In H. T. Trueba, G. P.

Guthrie, and K. H. Au (Eds.), *Culture and the Bilingual Classroom*, pp. 139-152. Rowley, MA: Newbury House.

Belenky, M. F., Clinchy, B. M., Goldberger, N. R., & Tarule, J. M. (1986). *Women's ways of knowing*. NY: Basic Books.

Erickson, F. (1984). School literacy, reasoning and civility: An anthropologist's perspective. *Harvard Educational Review, 54*(4), 525-546.

Goetz, J. P. & LeCompte, M. D. (1984). *Ethnography and qualitative design in educational research*. Orlando, FL: Academic Press.

Lave, J. (1977). Cognitive consequences of traditional apprenticeship training in West Africa. *Anthropology and Education Quarterly, 8*(3), 177-180.

Lave, J. (1988). *Cognition in practice: Mind, mathematics and culture in everyday life*. Cambridge, MA: Cambridge University Press.

Mohatt, G. V. & Erickson, F. (1981). Cultural differences in teaching styles in an Odawa school: A sociolinguistic approach. In H. T. Trueba, G. P. Guthrie, and K. H. Au (Eds.), *Culture and the bilingual classroom*, pp. 105-119. Rowle, MA: Newbury House.

Oswalt, W. (1964). Traditional storyknife tales of Yuk girls. *Proceedings of the American Philosophical Society*, vol. *108*(4).

Rogoff, B. & Lave, J. (Eds.) (1984). *Everyday cognition: Its development in social context*. Cambridge, MA: Harvard University Press.

Rosaldo, M. Z. (1980). The use and abuse of anthropology: Reflections on feminism and cross-cultural understanding. *Signs: Journal of Women in Culture and Society, 5*(3), 389-417.

Scribner, S. & Cole, M. (1981). *The psychology of literacy*. Cambridge, MA: Cambridge University Press.

Spradley, J. P. (1979). *The ethnographic interview*. New York: Holt, Rinehart & Winston.

Spradley, J. P. (1980). *Participant observation*. New York: Holt, Rinehart & Winston.

Tharp, R. G. & Gallimore, R. (1988). *Rousing minds to life: Teaching, learning and schooling in social context*. Cambridge, MA: Cambridge University Press.

Van Ness, H. (1981). Social control and social organization in an Alaskan Athabaskan classroom: A microethnography of "getting ready" for reading. In H. T. Trueba, G. P. Guthrie, and K. H. Aud (Eds.), *Culture and the Bilingual Classroom*, pp. 120-138. Rowley, MA: Newbury House.

Vogt, L. A. (1985). Rectifying the school performance of Hawaiian and Navajo students. Paper presented at the Annual Meeting of the American Anthropological Association, Washington, D.C.

Vygotsky, L. S. (1978). *Mind in society: The development of higher psychological processes*. M. Cole, V. John-Steiner, S. Scribner, & E. Souberman (Eds.). Cambridge, MA: Harvard University Press.

CELESTE LASATER
JAMES E. JOHNSON

10

Culture, Play, and Early
Childhood Education

One might rightfully suppose that the desire for young children to grow up to become competent members of adult society is a cultural universal. Wanting children to do well academically is also no doubt near universal and prevalent across cultures with formal educational systems. In this country, children's play is widely regarded as a chief vehicle on the road towards academic success and competence within society. During the early years, other approaches to achieve academic success, such as direct teaching, are criticized as being developmentally inappropriate for young children (Bredekamp 1987; Smilansky & Shefatya 1991). Thus, play looms large in importance in the minds of Western early childhood educators as a medium for learning and for preparing for academic success. Moreover, children's play is cherished for other reasons as well, including literacy attainments, the development of internal controls and emotional mastery, and the fostering of social competence and peer group integration (Christie 1991; Howes 1992; Johnson, Christie & Yawkey 1987).

The field of early childhood education (ECE) is fermenting with exciting potentials and worrisome controversial problems and dilemmas. Even while many within the profession, both rank and file and top echelon, are jumping on the National Association for the Education of Young Children's (NAEYC) Developmentally Appropriate Practices (DAP) bandwagon, for instance (in effect creating an incipient orthodoxy), others are waving caution flags warning that premature closure on most critical and complex questions concerning best practices in curriculum, evaluation, and teaching could prove to be extremely pernicious to the profession's integrity (Kessler 1991; Kostelnik 1992). Subscribing in principle to the ideals of individualization, family-focus, and diversity-infusion into practices and policies, critics bemoan the lack of serious analysis and incorporation of matters relating to special education (Carta, Schwartz, Atwater & McConnell 1991) and cultural variation (Jipson 1991) in the formulation of NAEYC's DAP and other such position statements (see ACEI, 1988 in Isenberg & Quisenberry, for example). This neglect reduces the value of the original endeavors.

Few would dispute that the season is ripe for professionals to roll up their sleeves and to begin to devote their energies to rectifying sins of omission and sins of commission in these original definitions and articulations of best practices in early childhood education. The passage of special education legislation (e.g., PL 99-457, Individuals with Disabilities Education Act, 1991, etc.) has set into motion a surge of interest in inclusive education at the same time that shifting demographics and societal trends have made it ever more imperative to respond to the needs of diverse minority groups in our pluralistic nation. Poverty is affecting young children, especially in urban and rural areas. This poverty together with the influx of new immigrants in recent years, and the diversification of family forms all conspire to make the job of the ECE professional more challenging and demanding. These various trends in our society can become the opportunity for progress by seizing the initiative and working towards positive educational change in restructuring schools and redefining teacher roles and home-school-community relations. Obviously this requires a great deal of fine-tuning of the logos-praxis nexus.

The present chapter is directed toward this objective of enriching the field of ECE in this manner through raising and examining various issues that pertain to culture, play, and ECE. How does information concerning play of children across cultures help the theorist, the policymaker, the administrator; and the teacher? How does this inform DAP? What are some important themes and concepts that emerge? To assist us in this undertaking we took the liberty of asking several practitioners to read and comment upon excerpts of earlier drafts of select chapters in this text. Accordingly, their voices from our interviews with them will be heard in this chapter as we report some results of our teacher survey.

ISSUES

Many questions have been raised in the literature about culture and play, some of which possess more relevance for the field of ECE than others. As more Third World countries are turning to early childhood education and see child care programs as vital to their country's development, it is important to raise some of these questions for their benefit as well as our own given the growing and intensifying diversification occurring between our shores as well.

As Luria (1930/1978, p. 45) has noted, ". . . no psychological function can be understood except in terms of its development (i.e., the genetic approach) and in terms of its particular social conditions (i.e., the sociological approach)." Broad conceptual frameworks are widely acknowledged as necessary in order to begin to account for the full complexity of the human condition and development. For instance, some writers have advanced the theoretical models of cultural-ecological and developmental contextualism, respectively. According to these conceptual outlooks, cultural factors are critical to include in theoretical formulations about human development in context. The so-called "Vygotskian triangle" of person-object-culture relations, with culture serving as a modulating influence on nature-nurture interaction, is viewed as central in these kinds of dynamic, genetic theory constructions. These models serve to remind us of our culture-bound assumptions and limited and restricted perspectives and schemes in Western social and behavioral sciences. The narrow and subjective data base that exists, given the biased sampling of world cultures and its authorship in research writings, makes it very difficult if not well-nigh impossible to relate cultural beliefs to behaviors (i.e., "What is meant by behavior *x* in its cultural context?") and to do so productively in any kind of comparative sense.

A central if not dominating concern in cross-cultural psychology, for example, is the question of which personal (adult's or child's) traits, behaviors, abilities, dispositions, and so forth are universal and which are particular to the culture. This question of cultural-specific versus cultural-universal behavioral and developmental patterns, structures or organizations needs to be dealt with in connection with children's play, for most assuredly play has an important place in development and education and considerable commonalities as well as divergences have been noted in the play and culture literature (Schwartzman 1978).

Within ECE this realization is expounded upon, for example, in Spodek's (1986) three dimensional model of influences. These three dimensions of influence are the knowledge dimension, the developmental dimension, and the cultural context dimension. ECE as a field (e.g., "best practices" in the areas of assessment, curriculum, and instruction) is informed by all three dimensions. DAP had been mostly if not exclusively concerned with the developmental foundations of ECE programs, much to the dismay of others who have eloquently argued for equal emphasis on the remaining two sources for guiding ECE programming (Spodek 1986; Walsh 1991). Furthermore, there is strong sentiment from some quarters that the knowledge and the developmental dimensions are artifacts of the contextual dimension. Kessler (1991) has argued that the knowledge and the developmental dimensions are reflections of the particular cultural perspective and that the complex interrelations among the three dimensions are virtually impossible to untangle. Still, the three dimensional model is a useful heuristic device for ECE programming.

In this vein, then, what questions emerge as important to the discussion of play and culture and ECE from reading the pages of this volume? As noted, one might start with the time-honored distinction between culturally universal versus culturally specific phenomena and conceptualizations as applies to children's play. A couple of observations are offered.

First, are there underlying perceptual models for each culture or are there underlying universal models for the terms work and play? Fromberg's (1977) perceptual model cf the ECE curriculum is relevant in this regard. According to Fromberg (1977, 1992), distinctive perceptual models, mediated socially, emanate from the physical or perceptual world surrounding the child. As children experience various environments, such as the daycare facilities or the preschool or kindergarten classroom, they are presented with isomorphic structures of communication, schemes, scripts, or affect. Is there a repertoire of thematic material and physical activities that are significant and meaningful across cultures? Meanings of what is considered play and what is considered work would vary depending upon what Ogbu (1981) would call the different "models of culture" or the way things operate in a particular culture, the perceived social goals for that culture. Thus, Ogbu would argue against universal perceptual models and for more particularistic models of work and play, and this cultural relativity would be expressed during the early years and in ECE programs. For instance, Bloch and Adler (this volume) have demonstrated the different meanings, ways, and the amount of time children engage in various activities either segregated from, or joined with, adults in general. In contrast, perhaps Western-European and American adults joining with young children in play as opposed to work, and separating from them during work, is one of the best examples of ethnocentric notions of work and play in action. We need to become more fully aware of this for drawing out the implications for theory construction that deals honestly and comprehensively with cultural factors, play, and early childhood education. While Western culture might hold that play is a means of learning, in other cultures work is a means of learning. Both could be considered primary "businesses" of childhood.

Secondly, how do children in various cultures learn the social and task requirements of structured group activities versus individual rights and responsibilities? Are the origins of this orientation in intrafamilial relationships and parent-child interactions, or in ECE group experiences? To what extent is each involved and how do these two social systems interact? This question can be studied with microlevel analyses of the child's early experiences. The literature holds the assumption seemingly that success in life is based on acquiring middle-class values (Ogbu, 1981, p. 417). The cultural task for parents is to train children to have the competence considered important by the culture or the subculture of which they choose to be a part. The task for the teacher is to provide for this diversity and to debunk the myth of middle-class superiority. If one does not truly understand the differences underlying socialization values of other cultures, however, one can only give lip service to other cultures when one, for instance, attempts to incorporate them into education that is multicultural.

Few would object to the notion that the tendency for play is universal but the content and the cultural bonds are unique for individuals. Expressive functions of play reflect and comment upon particular cultures (Schwartzman 1978), yet the so-called generative functions of play, or as Sutton-Smith (1979) refers to as "first paradigm theory and research priorities," are becoming more universal, especially as cultures become homogenized with Western goals or ideals for education and development. Hence Spodek's (1982) recreational play (i.e., play as expression) may remain culturally unique, even while educational play or academic play is or becomes more uniform across different cultures as these cultures become more Westernized.

Are these issues that include questions, distinctions, and definitions relevant to the ECE practitioner in everyday practice? We wanted to evaluate the usefulness of this theoretical discussion (the relevance of this abstract discussion about play in diverse cultures for teachers) and so we turned to the voices of our practicing peers.

VOICES

A limited pilot study was conducted with seasoned teachers in the private daycare centers and preschools of the nearby University-affiliated community to determine what their reactions would be to the types of information contained in these chapters. Our purpose was to discover whether the contents of this book would have meaning and relevance to the everyday praxis of early childhood teachers.

We put together a questionnaire which consisted of six excerpts (table 10.1) taken from a number of the chapters. The teachers were asked to read each excerpt and respond. We asked four questions about each excerpt: (1) Was it understandable?, (2) Was it meaningful personally and professionally?, (3) Was it relevant to classroom instruction?, and (4) Was it useful for direct application to teaching? These questions were answered with a Likert-type scale with four points: negative, somewhat negative, affirmative, very affirmative. We followed up the questionnaire with in-depth one-hour interviews with eight respondents, asking for their comments about each one of the excerpts. Portions of those interviews are referred to later in this chapter.

TABLE 10.1
Excerpts from Chapters Used in Teacher Interviews

Japan: Video games

Do video games pose any salient developmental problems for children in Japan today? Many parents whose children play video games for a number of hours maintain that their children are unstable, perform poorly at school, and spend a great deal of money. Furthermore, ophthalmologists note that too much exposure to video games may have adverse effects on children's sight. Also, the long-term influences of video games may result in deficits in interaction between parents and children, problems in humans feeling separated from the real world, and the decrease of cooperation and empathy towards others. Because these are speculative concerns in Japan, they do require empirical substantiation.

India: Play in the Curriculum

Today, preschool and kindergarten programs are beginning to implement play as a major part of their curriculum. At this juncture, we would like to briefly describe one such program at Lady Irwin College at the University of Delhi. We should warn the reader that programs of this nature are still rare in India. The Saraswati Puri Nursery School (SPNS) at Lady Irwin College was established with the objective of providing practical experience to graduate and undergraduate students studying child development at the college and to provide a creative unpressured environment in which young children's social and cognitive growth could flourish. The program is guided by Piagetian principles of self-discovery-based learning coupled with native cultural practices. What distinguishes the program from other preschools in the city is its emphasis on nonformal education (i.e., the school's philosophy of education through play and other creative means such as art, craft, dramatization, and experimentation that exemplify the concept of learning through doing). A major proportion of the preschool programs in India teach children the regiments of the alphabets or how to count in order to prepare children for higher schooling. In the SPNS nursery, socioemotional, cognitive, and physical development are deemed to be equally significant aspects of development and are emphasized in the school's goals and policies. The program, although influenced by Western concepts of child development, weaves into its curriculum and traditional/local context using mainly indigenous and simple materials for art and play activities (e.g., matchboxes, broom sticks, leaves, clay, etc.)

(continued)

TABLE 10.1 (continued)

Marquesan: Group Play

    Marquesan children in this group play specialized roles to coordinate group activity. Noisy leaders introduce activities, direct group play and keep players on track. Quiet leaders invent new play, monitor the bossiness of noisy leaders, and care for peripheral toddlers. Initiate members follow the leaders and support each other as they go through the process of hazing. They also care for peripheral toddlers and generally hold the group together from the inside. Peripheral toddlers are interested observers. Their incompetence highlights the skills of the older children. Older children gain status by helping and teaching dependent toddlers.

    Children pass through peripheral, follower, and leader positions as they gain tenure in the group and as they acquire social skills. In each position, they learn crucial lessons about how to do the functions associated with that role and how to deal with others in the other positions. They learn how to be members of a group and about how to exercise autonomy within the tight group structure.

    Compared to Marquesan children, middle-class American children may suffer what Thomas (1979) calls a "cooperation deficit" (as cited in Ritchie & Ritchie 1979). They may also develop a rigid conception of the self as solely a goal-oriented agent. This rigid sense of self may become stressed when a child is frustrated in reaching his or her goals as is often the case in complex social situations. In these cases, American children may retreat to carefully negotiated social contacts or to solitary play.

Puerto Rico: Student Teachers and Parents

    The teacher trainees who visited the forty Puerto Rican families were of Puerto Rican heritage themselves. All expressed ethical dilemmas during their field experiences. First-year trainees expressed an initial concern about the delineation of parent roles and teacher roles. How involved should early childhood educators be in the personal lives of families? Should information be "imparted" or should "collaboration" be the norm? Is parent education of Hispanic or other minority families necessarily assuming a deficit stance when educators are the "experts" and parents are the "learners"?

Italy: Work or Play

    Work or play? There often appears to be no distinction in the minds of either the teachers or the children, as they collaborate on questions and avenues of interest. In each of the projects just described, the play of

(continued)

TABLE 10.1 (continued)

children is respected and expanded through opportunities to explore and interact with materials, objects, and each other. Teachers in Reggio Emilia consider the child's social and intellectual development as highly dependent on a collective social process that involves repeated encounters and exchanges with others. This theoretical perspective, which is somewhat consistent with Vygotsky's emphasis on the child's growing ability to understand the world through interactions with others (Bruner 1985; Wertsch 1985), emphasizes the importance of multiple points of view. Thus teachers capitalize on children's willingness to engage in discussions regarding their ideas, their perceptions, and their understanding of their experiences and the world around them. They also directly promote and facilitate such discussions. Teachers tape-record children's conversations during play as well as at group meetings, and then play back the tape to large or small groups of children, followed by such comments as "what do you think about that? Do you still feel the same way about it? Does anyone else have any thoughts on the subject?" Such dialogue might center around a discussion regarding the source of a shadow, the differences between boys and girls, or the meaning of death.

Taiwan: New Year's

Following the Chinese New Year Holidays is the Lantern Festival. During this festival, children prepare their own lanterns and when night falls go outside in groups lifting lanterns. Traditionally, the lantern design usually corresponds to the year's animal. There are twelve animals used by the Chinese to symbolize the different years. But, due to scientific and technological influences, commercial lanterns often employ TV or movie heroes for designs instead of the traditional Chinese symbols. With the advent of modern science, battery-lamps have replaced the candle in the lantern.

Another activity that Chinese children enjoy is kite flying. It is said that kites were used to send messages to assist armies thousands of years ago. In addition, the significance of the kite is illustrated by the saying, "let the kite fly away in tomb sweeping day." During "tomb sweeping" day, one may write down all of one's sorrow, pain, and sickness on the kites and let the kites fly away (*Han Sheng Magazine*, 1984). This symbolized the disappearance of all bad luck. Nowadays kites are increasingly being used as toys, and the designs on the kites reflect the versatility of Chinese designs—kites are shaped in forms of dragons, tigers, butterflies, one-hundred-leg worms, and so on.

In general, we found teachers reacted to the content of the excerpts based on their personal philosophies of education and experiences as teachers of children from other cultures. Most of the excerpts were understandable to the teachers, as more than half of the respondents indicated affirmative or very affirmative as their response. There was general agreement about the usefulness of the content to teaching as well. Excerpts dealing with pedagogy issues were rated higher than those dealing with social customs, with the exception of the excerpt dealing with Chinese customs. Probably due to the number of Chinese children in our community, that excerpt was rated high in all categories. Thus, we concluded that the contents of this book would have relevance to the practice and professional development of early childhood teachers and that the issues we were presenting were timely ones. Less endorsement was given by the respondents as to the meaningfulness and relevance of the excerpts, although this varied from excerpt to excerpt as shown in table 10.2

The Interviews

The interviews began by asking the experienced teachers, all of whom had college degrees and many years teaching experience and were well-integrated in the early childhood community, for their definitions of the terms play, work, multicultural educa-

TABLE 10.2
Results of Teacher Ratings of Chapter Excerpts
(N = 6 teachers)

	Under-standable	*Meaningful Personally*	*Relevant to Classroom*	*Useful for Teaching*
Japan: Video Games	16	15	12	13
India: Play in the Curriculum	22	21	21	20
Marquesan: Group Play	17	16	16	16
Puerto Rico: Student Teachers and Parents	18	16	16	16
Italy: Work or Play	20	18	18	16
Taiwan: New Year's	23	19	19	18

Note: Scores are weighted sum where 1 = Negative; 2 = Somewhat Negative; 3 = Affirmative; 4 = Very Affirmative. Highest possible score in each entry is 24 and lowest is 6.

tion and anti-bias curriculum. There followed a discussion of the selected excerpts as the interviewees elaborated upon their reactions to them, and gave their rationales for their ratings on the understandable, meaningful, relevant, and useful scales. Below are selective synopses of three of the interviews revealing the teachers' views on these matters.

Nina F. Since 1978 Nina F. has been a director and head teacher of a one classroom mixed-age childcare facility that serves ethnically diverse, mostly middle-class children and their families. Nina is very active in the child care community within her university-affiliated town and has been an officer in the local early childhood education organization.

She defined play as what children do to learn during the early years, doing it joyfully for the most part. Play becomes more worklike in her opinion when children are trying to figure things out. Nina reported that she does recognize the children's play at her childcare program as reflecting their home life and cultural background. She illustrated this point by relating how one five-year-old boy was really into sword play reflective of his East Indian background, in particular stories about Ranaan, a warrior god by tradition in his culture. This Indian child would elicit from peers theme-related play, such as Ninja Turtles. The play would sustain itself as children traveled into the art rooms and then outdoors to make quivers and arrows and bows before returning indoors to continue the Ranaan-Ninja Turtles thematic episode. This kind of play was possible because Nina F. allowed long periods for active play that produced a whole range of interactive behaviors among the children.

Nina F. defined multicultural education as children and families from many different countries or ethnic or minority backgrounds in the schools. In her words, "Multicultural education is making sure as a teacher that every child feels welcome and a part of the program, welcomed totally the way they are, and the way members of their family are. All families are good for us, your family is a good way to be." A challenge is to deal with cultural expectations and teacher expectations in a constructive way and to involve parents in the multicultural programs.

Responding to the excerpts, Nina said that she felt the book would be worthwhile and that she benefited from reading the passages from the six chapters. She elaborated that it is very interesting to see how things are done in other places, either in faraway lands or even down the street, and that she has found that early childhood programs can espouse similar principles but have very different classrooms. For instance, regarding the Saraswati Puri Nursery School in New Delhi, she said, "Yes, this information is very useful but I would want to learn more specifics about this program—see pictures of the classroom, how time is scheduled, sample activities, teacher interactions and the like. I've found that people can believe in the same principles but still have very different classrooms and practices."

Near the end of the interview, Nina F. summed up her reactions to the excerpts in this way: "Early childhood teachers cannot be walking encyclopedias and a little knowledge can be a dangerous thing. I have found that it is best to get information from the parents directly. Ask them, 'How could we celebrate or include your culture in our program? What is important to you?' If you find a song, ask the parent, 'What do you think about this?'" Nina emphasized the critical importance of communicating directly with parents, and if language is a barrier, via a friend who might serve as a translator. At first, she has found from her experience, it is necessary to be brave in order to overcome possible shyness or embarrassment. A great deal can be learned from informal conversations at school during arrivals or departures or at conferences, chatting and exchanging recipes and the like. Cultural taboos or customs relevant to the teacher's job can readily be picked up in this way. Nina closed by recommending that much more can be shared by having parents over for dinner, such as philosophical or political outlooks and religious views.

Colleen B. Colleen B. has been teaching in the same Montessori school for more than twenty years. During this period she has collected a large number of trade books dealing with children from other cultures to share with her students because she has always considered it very important to teach children to respect all cultures.

Her reactions to the excerpts were to say that, "I consider every paragraph of every excerpt to be important to my knowledge of other people." Colleen stresses with her children that our United States culture is different in different parts of the country and that this is just one more culture in the midst of a world with many, many cultures. Her student body has always contained children of various cultures and so she has tried to make them feel comfortable and at home.

She finds that over the years, distinctly cultural play has been homogenized by television viewing. She finds in recent times that most children play the same type of fantasy play—popular themes being Ninja Turtles, birthday party and Mommy-Daddy-baby scenarios. Children are very adaptive and she feels this is a universal quality of children. "They do not have walls built up; they adapt to one another."

When asked her opinions about children's work vs. children's play she answered, "It's both. They can consider it their work or they can consider it their play. Either way they want to be with a friend. They want to work collaboratively and they are learning that it's easier to do work with two or three people."

Colleen tries to be very sensitive to the cultural background of each child so much so that if the directive background of the child conflicts with the nondirective philosophy of her school, she has difficulty expecting the child to conform to the school's curriculum and is sensitive to the dissonance the child is experiencing. When two cultures clash, the culture of the home and the culture of the school in this case, she recommends that the similarities be emphasized and the dissimilarities be deemphasized. She holds the same should be true for two world cultures.

She thinks choice is very important to children and to the future of America. Parents need to be educated to make good choices of care for their children that will parallel the philosophy of child rearing they have used in the home. Children also need to learn how to choose activities that are meaningful to them. Schools need to exist to accommodate these varied perspectives. This pluralism in education is what will make America "work." People from different cultures and different perspectives need to collaborate together and cooperate with one another. "It shouldn't be a melting pot; it should be where you respect and encourage every individual difference." It is important to help children to realize problems can be approached from many different angles. Colleen feels sharing different cultural perspectives with children is one way of fostering this understanding.

She recommends all preschool personnel take a course in multicultural understanding at some point in their career. "Biases are very subtle and sometimes we are not even aware we have them," she states. Because preschool is a child's first experience with school, it is doubly important that teachers are prepared for cultural diversity.

Molly W. Molly W. is a teacher in a university day care center that enrolls many children of foreign parents studying in America. When asked if the foreign children were integrated along with the other children, she felt they were very integrated. She said she goes out of her way to make them feel a part of the center. She finds the children who speak English very supportive of the children who do not speak English. "That support is tremendous reinforcement for the child learning to speak."

Molly has a broad definition of play. It can be "sometimes just thinking about what animals and toys can do, just thinking in their heads, or it can be the actual manipulation of toys and objects. Work could be tasks, but tasks can be fun too. Or work can be deep absorption in an activity."

She finds play between children of different cultures very similar. She commented that children copy and imitate each other playing, so if a child initially doesn't know how to play with something because of a cultural inexperience, they learn by imitating.

She believes multicultural experiences can be enhanced by making use of the background of the children in terms of what they are used to. She encourages the children to bring unique toys from home, to share ethnic foods and tries to incorporate aspects of the cultures of her children into her curriculum. Molly has received anti-bias inservice training and attempts to be sensitive to stereotyping. She feels it is very important for the parents of these children to share their knowledge about their child with the school and to collaborate with them about the child's experiences.

In response to the excerpt that described "hazing" in a foreign context, she responded, "I've seen some kind of that thing done. I think it was done (in the excerpt) with the meaning that the children can't be too thin-skinned. They've got to be able to know if somebody is pulling their leg or joking with them. They have to develop a tough skin. In a way, they're right. But, there's got to be a way of doing it that isn't so hurtful to them. I've seen it done with young kids. They wouldn't call it hazing, they would call it just getting them acclimated to a world that isn't always nice, that isn't always for real. You're teaching children how to make sense out of a lot of different responses. Explain it to children so it becomes a learning situation and they begin to understand that some things people say you take seriously and some things you don't, and they will be able to know the difference."

Molly feels that the more talking children do with each other the better. To paraphrase: an aid to understanding is to hold discussions in which children have the opportunity to bounce their ideas off others, and to share new ideas. "I think you have to approach getting children interested in thinking and talking. Children may not bring up philosophical positions under ordinary circumstances, so you have to create these opportunities for them to share their questions and ideas. During these discussions, as a teacher, you cannot be looking for the 'right' answers. These must be times when children can learn to express any idea they have and be respected for their contribution."

CONCLUSIONS

Cultural studies and reflection are advantageous in general for revealing universal processes as well as variation, for showing that "we are all equal in our own way, we are all alike in our own way," to paraphrase sentiment expressed by the teachers interviewed in preparation for writing this chapter. Learning of and about other cultures not only assists us in building this knowledge base of other cultures, but also teaches us about our own culture as well. Like the fish in and then out of water, we often do not realize what our water means until we symbolically step outside our own culture, allowing ourselves to see differently, to be surprised our ideas don't work, to ponder new ways of looking at things, to be excited to make fresh starts.

The first tenet of education that is multicultural is "know thyself." It is critically important to be aware of personal biases to the extent possible and to strive to overcome them in order to foster education that is multicultural and anti-bias. Openness to experience, albeit vicarious, about play in diverse cultures allows one to evaluate the scope and limits of one's conceptions, the generalizability and the constraints on the phenomenon of interest. To implement DAP that is "contextualized" and "culture-sensitive" requires hard work to acquire the necessary knowledge base and functional dispositions to productively integrate this progressive perspective throughout one's curriculum and teaching. As Faust (1987, p. 91) has noted:

> Part of the teacher's role is to inform himself or herself about each child in his or her class, and in the multicultural classroom. This will include learning something of the dif-

ferent cultural backgrounds. The teacher who knows that in some cultures it is considered rude to maintain eye contact with a teacher, or that it is the norm to eat with one's fingers, can avoid making poorly informed judgements and confusing the child. However, there is a delicate balance between learning about and valuing the children's backgrounds, and assuming a rigid and stereotypical view of other cultures' child-rearing methods, for example. A sensitive and open-minded approach is essential here which both respects different cultural norms and recognizes diversity within groups.

The voices we heard listening to the teachers we interviewed made us believe that an internal transformation or personal conversion often is experienced by teachers in the process of implementing culturally appropriate practice. The direction this takes is movement away from a world view which embraces every culture and combination thereof but with the desire to homogenize children to one "middle-class, yuppie-approved" view of developmental appropriateness. We advocate instead a movement towards ECE programmatic visions of classroom culture and peer socialization that do not drown out different points of view but instead foster and enthusiastically invite freedom of expression and contributions that build a world view where we are all different but equal. As one teacher remarked, "Rather than looking for commonalties of experience perhaps we should be exploring our differences with children and their families. Respect comes when you know your friend is not exactly like you, but you still like her in spite of and because of those differences. We all have something to teach each other."

If the first tenet of education that is multicultural is "know thyself," a second tenet, then, would be a deeply felt and reasoned conviction that Culture A, Culture B, Culture C, etc. should be linked by "equal signs" and not "greater than" or "less than" signs. That is, a sense should be second nature to oneself that when it comes to cultures there is no room for superiority complexes or inferiority complexes.

Based upon the cultural-ecological framework (Ogbu 1981; Whiting 1980; Whiting & Edwards 1988), this volume has sought to spotlight the limitations of the monocultural perspective by revealing, across the very eclectic chapters of this collection, substantive variation in children's play and adult conceptions about play. Diverse geographic locations, methods of inquiry, and styles of exposition have been represented with all the contributors sharing a commitment to the contextualized and culture-sensitive perspective. Implicitly if not explicitly, each chapter raises questions about the universality versus cultural specifics of the phenomena of play, its antecedents, processes, correlates, and consequences. The value of a work like this is not primarily to capture cultural influence on play ("natural experiments") as much as to provide selective descriptions and some insight into what is meant by "play" within specific slices of a given cultural context.

This volume is cross-cultural although necessarily restrictive in its sampling across time and place. We hope that it adds to the readers' awareness of the rich panorama of children's play variation and adult involvements in children's play. Reinforced and extended in these pages, as well as known from previous research (e.g., Bloch & Pellegrini 1989; Whiting 1980), is the notion that cultural variations in household composition (i.e., nuclear versus extended families) and childrearing practices (i.e., maternal, paternal, sibling, extrafamilial caregivers) afford opportunities and set conditions for the nature of the social interaction that occurs—the play or the work, the certain kinds of play forms exhibited (e.g., solitary, social preference, games, etc.). A heuristic which adheres to cross-cultural developmental comparative study is the generation of specific social-scientific hypotheses or predictions about play forms, processes and functions within play contexts. Much work needs to be done to discern variable relations that pertain not only to household and childrearing variation, but also relates to across- and within-cultural differences in play as a function of dynamic variation along a number of dimensions: in preschool or childcare programs, parent education programs, the rise in parent educators, changing impacts of the media and of the toy industries, the use of playgrounds and other outdoor natural play spaces. These and other developments are taking place at an accelerating pace worldwide. Moreover, more in-depth research of the qualitative or ethnographic sort is required to flesh out or contextualize functional relations. For example, as the profession progresses, early childhood teachers worldwide can be called upon not only to implement developmentally appropriate programs in their specific locales, but also to embark upon collaborative action research to help construct understanding about how DAP gets operationalized or articulated within cultural contexts and of what consequences these different operations have for young children and their families. A more comprehensive and inclusive meaning of DAP would result, addressing the strident criticisms which have accused DAP as being essentially monocultural in its present published formulation. To the degree that some of this vision comes to pass, a volume such as this one will have proven well worth the considerable effort required for its materialization.

REFERENCES

Bloch, M. N. & Pellegrini, A. D. (1989). *The ecological context of children's play*. Norwood, NJ: Ablex.

Bredekamp, S. (1987). *Developmentally appropriate practice in early childhood programs serving children from birth through age 8*. Washington, D.C.: National Association for the Education of Young Children.

Bruner, J. (1985). Vygotsky: A historical and conceptual perspective. In J. V. Wertsch (Ed.), *Culture, communication, and cognition*. New York: Cambridge University Press.

Carta, J., Schwartz, I., Atwater, J., & McConnell, S. (1991). Developmentally appropriate practice: Appraising its usefulness for young children with disabilities. *Topics in Early Childhood Special Education, 11*(1), 1-20.

Christie, J. F. (Ed.) (1991). *Play and early literacy development*. Albany, NY: State University of New York Press.

Faust, H. (1987). The multicultural curriculum in early childhood education. In G. Blenkin and A. Kelly (Eds.), *Early childhood education: Developmental curriculum*. Liverpool: Chapman.

Fromberg, D. P. (1977). *Early childhood education: A perceptual model curriculum*. New York: Wiley.

Fromberg, D. (1992, April). *The significance of the knowledge base about play for early childhood teacher education*. Conference paper presented at American Educational Research Association, San Francisco.

Howes, C. (1992). *The collaborative construction of pretend: Social pretend play functions*. Albany, NY: State University of New York Press.

Jipson, J. (1991). Developmentally appropriate practice: Culture, curriculum, connections. *Early Education and Development, 2*(2), 120-136.

Johnson, J. E., Christie, J. F., Yawkey, T. D. (1987). *Play and early childhood development.* Evanston, IL: Scott Foresman.

Kessler, S. A. (1991). Alternative perspectives on early childhood education. *Early Childhood Research Quarterly, 6,* 183-197.

Kostelnik, M. (1992, May). MYTHS associated with developmentally appropriate programs. *Young Children, 47,* 17-23.

Luria, A. R. (1930/1978). A child's speech responses and the second environment (M. Vale, Trans). In M. Cole (Ed.), *The selected writings of A. R. Luria* (pp. 45-77). New York: M. E. Sharpe.

Ogbu, J. (1981). Origins of human competence: A cultural-ecological perspective. *Child Development, 52,* 413-429.

Ritchie, J. & Ritchie, J. (1979). *Growing up in Polynesia.* Sydney: George Allen & Unwin.

Schwartzman, H. (1978). *Transformation: The anthropology of children's play.* New York: Plenum Press.

Smilansky, S. & Shefatya, L. (1991). *Facilitating play: A medium for promoting cognitive, socio-emotional and academic development in young children.* Gaithersburg, MD: Psychosocial & Educational Publications.

Spodek, B. (1982). The kindergarten: A retrospective and contemporary view. In L. Katz (Ed.), *Current topics in early childhood education, 4,* 173-191. Norwood, NJ: Ablex.

Spodek, B. (1986). Development, values, and knowledge in the kindergarten curriculum. In B. Spodek (Ed.), *Early childhood education.* Englewood Cliffs, NJ: Prentice Hall.

Sutton-Smith, B. (Ed.). (1979). *Play and learning.* New York: Gardner Press.

Walsh, D. J. (1991). Extending the discourse on developmental appropriateness: A developmental perspective. *Early Education and Development, 2,* 109-119.

Wertsch, J. V. (Ed.). (1985). *Culture, communication, and cognition.* Cambridge: Cambridge University Press.

Whiting, B. B. (1980). Culture and social behavior. *Ethos, 2,* 95-116.

Whiting, B. B. & Edwards, C. P. (1988). *The company they keep: The effect of age, gender and culture on social behavior of children aged two to ten.* Cambridge, MA: Harvard University Press.

Index